W9-AUQ-544

SHOCKING REPRESENTATION

HISTORICAL
TRAUMA,
NATIONAL CINEMA, AND
THE MODERN HORROR
FILM

ADAM LOWENSTEIN

COLUMBIA UNIVERSITY PRESS / NEW YORK

Columbia University Press
Publishers Since 1893
New York   Chichester, West Sussex

Library of Congress Cataloging-in-Publication Data
A complete CIP record is available from the Library of Congress.
ISBN 978-0-231-13246-6 (cloth)
ISBN 978-0-231-13247-3 (paper)

∞

Columbia University Press books are printed on
permanent and durable acid-free paper.
Printed in the United States of America

Permission has been granted to reprint portions
of this book derived from earlier and shorter essay
versions, as follows:

"Allegorizing Hiroshima: Shindo Kaneto's *Onibaba* as
Trauma Text," in E. Ann Kaplan and Ban Wang, eds., *Trau-
ma and Cinema: Cross-Cultural Explorations*, 145–61. Hong
Kong: Hong Kong University Press, 2004.

"Cinema, Benjamin, and the Allegorical Representation
of September 11," *Critical Quarterly* 45.1–2 (Spring/Sum-
mer 2003): 73–84. Special issue on September 11, edited by
Colin MacCabe and Nancy Condee.

"'Under-the-Skin Horrors': Social Realism and Classlessness in *Peeping Tom* and the British New Wave," in Justine Ashby and Andrew Higson, eds., *British Cinema, Past
and Present*, 221–32. London: Routledge, 2000.

"Canadian Horror Made Flesh: Contextualizing David
Cronenberg," *Post Script* 18.2 (Winter/Spring 1999): 37–51.
Special issue on Canadian cinema, edited by Barry Keith
Grant.

"Films Without a Face: Shock Horror in the Cinema
of Georges Franju," *Cinema Journal* 37.4 (Summer 1998):
37-58.

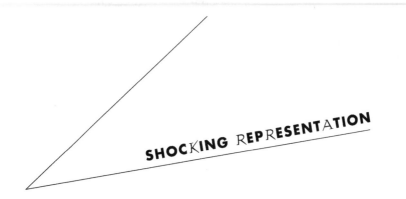

SHOCKING REPRESENTATION

FILM AND CULTURE   *JOHN BELTON, GENERAL EDITOR*

FILM AND CULTURE

A series of Columbia University Press
Edited by John Belton

For my family
and for Irina

CONTENTS

LIST OF ILLUSTRATIONS

ACKNOWLEDGMENTS

In certain ways, I feel like I have been writing this book forever. Not just in the concrete sense of the ten years that have passed since this project had its "official" beginnings as graduate-level research, but also in the more ineffable sense that the subject matter this book addresses has always been so personally important to me that it is hard to determine just how far back the project's "unofficial" beginnings really go. What I do know is that I cannot possibly thank all the mentors, colleagues, students, family members, and friends that have played vital roles in bringing this book to life. For those I neglect to mention here by name, please accept my apologies along with my deep gratitude for your contributions.

To begin at the "official" beginning, the members of my dissertation committee at the University of Chicago provided extraordinary stimulation and inspiration for my work that I continue to draw upon: Tom Gunning (my chair), Lauren Berlant, Miriam Hansen, James Lastra, and William Veeder. It has been a pleasure to maintain contact with all of these mentors as colleagues and friends in the years since I graduated from Chicago; I must single out Tom for his ongoing engagement with my work well above and beyond the call of duty. Other mentors at Chicago who contributed their expertise and enthusiasm include Susan Hayward, W. J. T. Mitchell, and Katie Trumpener. I was supported at Chicago through an Andrew Mellon Dissertation-Year Fellowship, along with a number of generous research and travel grants from the Committee on Cinema and Media Studies and the Department of English. I also had the good fortune of working with several teachers while I was still an undergraduate at the University of Virginia who encouraged me to believe I could pursue issues related to this book in an academic setting: Sara Blair, Alan DeGooyer, Arthur Kirsch, Bernard Mayes, Jahan Ramazani, and especially, Pat Gill.

As a professor at the University of Pittsburgh, I have been lucky to benefit from the input and support of a number of first-class colleagues and friends: Dave Bartholomae, Eric Clarke, Nancy Condee, Lucy Fischer, Jim Knapp, Carl Kurlander, Marcia Landy, Colin MacCabe, Vladimir Padunov, and Phil Watts. Keiko McDonald deserves special mention for her generosity in helping me to secure a research and travel grant from Pitt's Japan

Council, which enabled a trip to Tokyo that galvanized the writing of this book's third chapter. Keiko also opened a number of important doors in Japan for me: the Kawakita Memorial Film Institute (and the wonderfully helpful Yuka Sakano), the National Film Center at the Tokyo Museum of Modern Art, the International House of Japan, Donald Richie, and Shindo Kaneto. In addition, I have been supported at Pitt through a number of generous research and travel grants from the Office of the Dean, the Faculty of Arts and Sciences, the Graduate Program in Cultural Studies, and the Department of English.

The team at Columbia University Press has been a genuine pleasure to work with: editor Jennifer Crewe, assistant editor Juree Sondker, copyeditor Roy Thomas, designer Liz Cosgrove, indexer Anne Leach, the two anonymous manuscript readers (including the not-so-anonymous Thomas Doherty), and especially series editor John Belton, whose advice on getting this manuscript into shape was as sound as his advice to me years ago when I asked him where I should apply to graduate school. Other colleagues and friends who have graciously offered their support for my work along the way include: Richard Allen, Justine Ashby, Mick Broderick, Ian Christie, Carol Clover, David Desser, Aaron Gerow, Barry Keith Grant, Peter Harcourt, Andrew Higson, E. Ann Kaplan, Akira Lippit, James Naremore, James J. Orr, William Paul, Isabel Pinedo, Murray Pomerance, Matt Rockman, Adam Simon, Vivian Sobchack, Elliott Stein, and Ban Wang. Other institutions not previously mentioned that have enabled my research include the Bibliothèque du film (Paris), the British Film Institute (London), the National Archives of Canada (Ottawa), the Library of Congress (Washington, D.C.), the Joseph Regenstein Library (University of Chicago), the Hillman Library and Media Center (University of Pittsburgh), and New York University's Department of Cinema Studies.

Finally, this book would not exist without the many acts and thoughts of love and solidarity I've received from my father, Ed Lowenstein, my mother, Jane Lowenstein, and my brother, Noah Lowenstein. Without them, and without my partner-in-crime, Irina Reyn, I wouldn't be able to find the light in the darkness. I dedicate this book to my family and to Irina, with love.

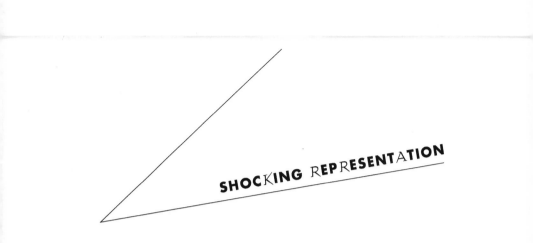

SHOCKING REPRESENTATION

INTRODUCTION

The Allegorical Moment

What does cinematic horror have to tell us about the horrors of history?

To speak of history's horrors, or historical trauma, is to recognize events as wounds. Auschwitz. Hiroshima. Vietnam. These are names associated with specific places and occurrences, but they are also wounds in the fabric of culture and history that bleed through conventional confines of time and space. To speak of *representing* historical trauma is to ask questions as central to today's cultural politics as they are resistant to definitive answers. What are the limits of representation? Do such limits exist? If so, what is the relation between art and these limits? If not, how do we navigate tensions between those who feel a certain traumatic event *cannot* be represented and those who feel the same event *must* be represented?

One major obstacle facing any response to such questions has been the tendency for theories of representation governing the study of trauma to constrict the intricate workings of the representations themselves. This book argues, in part, that films previously excluded from consideration as representations of historical trauma actually provide the means to recast key theoretical impasses in film studies as well as trauma studies. In the spirit of this argument, I want to move now from theory to representation:

The son leads his mother through the thick darkness of a cemetery, narrowly avoiding the headstones in their path. His gait is lurching and uneven—he is dying. Or, more accurately, he is dying again, having been killed once already in the jungles of Vietnam as a young American soldier. Now, as his living dead life force ebbs, his body returns to its rightfully decomposed state. Skin peels, wounds bleed, eyes yellow. His mother clings to him, refusing to believe that he is truly dead. As the wailing police sirens drift closer, he stumbles and begins crawling toward his intended destination. He has led his mother to a grave he has dug for himself, complete with a self-fashioned headstone bearing the jagged inscription, "ANDY BROOKS 1951–1972." He falls into the grave, desperately gathering the surrounding soil over himself, and gesturing for his mother to aid him with his burial. As the police arrive, the mother cries but finally capitulates, sprinkling dirt over her son's mangled body. His hand reaches forward in one last spasm—perhaps some mixture of pain and gratitude—and then he is still. While his mother kisses his hand, a car explodes in the distance. The blast briefly illuminates the graveyard in the eerie glow of a war-torn jungle, closing the space between this death in the cemetery and the death in Vietnam.

This is an evocation of the conclusion to *Deathdream* (also known as *Dead of Night*), a little-known horror film written by Alan Ormsby and directed by Bob Clark in 1972 (see fig. A1). It may seem puzzling or even disturbing to juxtapose a horror film with the weighty issues of Vietnam trauma, but it is here, in a film like *Deathdream*, that we catch a glimpse of what I will call an *allegorical moment*. I will explain my specific sense of allegory later in this introduction, but for now, let me define the allegorical moment as a shocking collision of film, spectator, and history where registers of bodily space and historical time are disrupted, confronted, and intertwined. These registers of space and time are distributed unevenly across the cinematic text, the film's audience, and the historical context, so that in this sequence from *Deathdream*, for example, shock emanates from the intermingling of a number of sources. The film's horrific images, sounds, and narrative combine with visceral spectator affect (terror, disgust, sympathy, sadness) to embody issues that characterize the historical trauma of the Vietnam War (gender, nation, generation, memory—see chapter 4 for a detailed investigation).[1]

The allegorical moment's complex process of embodiment, where film, spectator, and history compete and collaborate to produce forms of knowing not easily described by conventional delineations of bodily space and

FIGURE A.1 *Deathdream* (Bob Clark, 1972): Andy Brooks (Richard Backus), neither alive nor dead, begs his mother (Lynn Carlin) to bury him. (Courtesy of Matt Kennedy and Blue Underground, Inc.)

historical time, is distilled in *Deathdream* as the image of a living corpse. This paradoxical image of death in life, of neither life nor death, crystallizes the allegorical moment's challenge to the binary oppositions that govern the study of trauma and its representation: melancholia/mourning, acting-out/working-through, historically irresponsible/historically responsible, and realism/modernism. Trauma studies, for all its interdisciplinary breadth and conceptual ambition, still tends to reproduce these oppositions rather than maintain (as the allegorical moment insists) a productive tension between them. In fact, perhaps the best way to provide a snapshot of recent trauma studies theory is to revisit the classic formulations of Sigmund Freud that anchor these oppositions.[2]

In "Remembering, Repeating and Working-Through" (1914) and "Mourning and Melancholia" (1917), Freud draws clear distinctions between two different processes individuals may undergo when faced with the traumatic loss of a deeply valued object.[3] In the normal, healthy process of mourning, the ego works through the loss of the object by separating itself from the object, thereby remembering the loss as an event outside the self rather than an illness within the self. In the pathological, unhealthy state of melancholia, the ego refuses to let go of the lost object and instead acts out the loss compulsively, repeating (rather than remembering) the trauma by turning it inward and enacting the loss as self-torment. Although Freud himself offers hints about how mourning and melancholia, as well as acting-out and working-through, must be conceived as interdependent processes rather than stark oppositions, an unfortunate polarizing of terms often occurs when these concepts are transposed to the theoretical discussion of trauma's artistic representations. When the literary critic Dominick LaCapra valorizes high modernists such as Samuel Beckett for performing exemplary mourning work[4] or when the historian Hayden White calls for a modernist "middle voice" as trauma's proper mode of representation,[5] the implicit (and often explicit) object of critique are those representations that rely on "realist" rather than "modernist" modes, "narrative" rather than "nonnarrative" modes. But the allegorical moment in *Deathdream* conforms to neither the naïve verisimilitude of realism, nor to the self-conscious distantiation of modernism, just as its images seem to suggest both a mournful working-through of Vietnam trauma as well as its acting-out via melancholic repetition. Ultimately, the film throws into question the entire impulse to categorize representations of historical trauma according to the familiar binary oppositions. "Allegory" is derived from the Greek *allos* ("other") and -*agorein* ("to speak publicly"), and this allegorical moment in *Deathdream* "speaks otherwise" by inviting us to unite shocking cinematic representation with the need to shock the very concept of representation in regard to historical trauma.

The title of this book, then, uses the phrase "shocking representation" for several different purposes. To "shock representation" is to attempt to dislodge certain notions of representation from theories intent on prescribing film's relation to trauma, as well as trauma's relation to film. I wish to shock those critical trends within trauma studies that tend to diagnose representation as if it were a patient, where modernist representation is understood as encompassing healthy mourning and the integration of working-through, while realist representation is seen as encompassing unhealthy melancholia and denial in the form of acting-out. But it is also important to acknowledge why trauma studies has taken this modernist theoretical turn in the first place—it comes from the need for an ethics that respects victims/survivors of trauma and the depth of their experience. The wish is for representations of trauma to honor the awful pain and complexity of victim/survivor experience, so those experiences and memories can be protected from further harm. This desire to shield victims/survivors from the disempowering and destructive forces of, for example, Holocaust denial, is a noble and humane one. When this desire reaches its extremes, however, when traumatic experience becomes equated solely with the "unrepresentable," then this respect for victims/survivors transforms, paradoxically, into a silencing of both experience and representation.

Jean-François Lyotard has mounted an eloquent defense of the "unrepresentable" through his concept of the *differend*, where the irreconcilable nature of conflicting idioms, such as those belonging to Holocaust survivors and to Holocaust deniers, depends upon listening to the silence of one idiom in the face of its refusal to speak in the register of the other. It is important to note, however, that although Lyotard rightly values the difference between a survivor who cannot speak and one who *chooses* not to speak, he does not prescribe silence as the *only* means of respecting survivor experience. Instead, Lyotard suggests, "what is at stake in a literature, in a philosophy, in a politics perhaps, is to bear witness to differends by finding idioms for them."[6] The move to safeguard the idiom of survivors by treating their experience as "unrepresentable" evades the challenge of finding new idioms for that experience—it locks away survivor trauma inside an authentic moment in the past, free from the perilous present of cultural negotiation demanded by representation. What is preserved in such a move is the unquestionable authenticity of survivor experience; what is lost, I would contend, is the full possibility of that experience shaping our contemporary world.[7]

Representation, as that vital but precarious link between art and history, between experience and reflection, holds out the promise, however risky, that trauma can be communicated. But is this promise of communication even worth pursuing when its risks tap into representation's complex relation to history? Do the losses outweigh the benefits when representation communicates traumatic history in distorted, politically damaging ways? Berel Lang suggests that artistic representations of the Holocaust must be judged not only for their responsibility to historical fact but also for their ability to communicate with an audience. I would add that subordinating artistic representation's potential for communication to its responsibility to history, however reassuring in the face of irresponsible representations, defeats the possibility of making trauma matter to those beyond its immediate point of impact. In this sense, such subordination must be seen as a potential violation of what Lang calls the "moral weight" associated with

Holocaust representation, just as historically irresponsible representations may constitute related violations.[8]

For better or worse, the promise of representation stubbornly resists legislation. To diagnose representation as "healthy" or "unhealthy," to divide it into "realist" or "modernist" categories, or to judge it solely as "historically accurate" or "historically inaccurate" is to rob it of the power to negotiate meaning and feeling beyond such labels. Although Dominick LaCapra carefully reminds us that binaries such as these, emblematized for him by the acting-out of melancholia and the working-through of mourning, must be seen as "distinctions" rather than dichotomies and as "interacting processes," the possibility of respecting such distinctions often evaporates when confronted by the texts themselves. For example, LaCapra casually dismisses *Schindler's List* (Steven Spielberg, 1993) as a "redemptive narrative" aligned with false mourning while *Shoah* (Claude Lanzmann, 1985) becomes a "masterpiece," a "work of art" linked to the working-through of genuine mourning.[9]

Rather than simply repeat this pattern of polarized judgment, I want to argue along lines suggested by Miriam Bratu Hansen, who urges us to consider *Shoah* and *Schindler's List* as "competing representations and competing modes of representation."[10] The allegorical moment allows us to perceive these films not only in terms of the competing dimensions of "realist" and "modernist" cinema that Hansen refers to, but also in terms of their points of correspondence. Even more importantly, the allegorical moment opens a space where films that resemble neither *Shoah* nor *Schindler's List* may be considered as representations of historical trauma.

The films investigated in this book—Georges Franju's *Eyes Without a Face* (1960), Michael Powell's *Peeping Tom* (1960), Shindo Kaneto's *Onibaba* (1964), Wes Craven's *Last House on the Left* (1972), and David Cronenberg's *Shivers* (1975)—are themselves shocking representations. They are shocking in the sense that they are examples of the modern horror film, a genre often dedicated to terrifying and/or disgusting its audience with displays of graphic carnage. But they are also confrontational in the sense that they border on the territory of a cinema conventionally perceived to exist at the furthest remove from the horror film: the art cinema.[11] In fact, this book insists on a shared intimacy between these horror films and art films such as *The 400 Blows* (François Truffaut, 1959), *Room at the Top* (Jack Clayton, 1959), *Night and Fog in Japan* (Oshima Nagisa, 1960), *The Virgin Spring* (Ingmar Bergman, 1960), and *Crash* (David Cronenberg, 1996). By choosing this admittedly specialized subset of modern horror films to trace the allegorical moment and by attaching them to the realist/modernist bind of trauma studies, I have sought to question two major theoretical binds from film studies: genre film/art film and national cinema/popular cinema.

GENRE FILM/ART FILM

Within film studies, the "art film" and "genre film" are still typically understood as diametrically opposed.[12] However, examining historical trauma in the context of this distinction produces some surprising conjunctures. If we agree with David Bordwell's decision to date the art film's beginnings as a "distinct mode" to 1945,[13] then both the art film and the modern horror film genre emerge as post–World War II phenomena. The art film's persistent reliance on the war as subject matter, as the motivation for a variety of "neorealisms" and melodramatic "anti-neorealisms" running from *Open City* (Roberto Rossellini, 1945) to *Hiroshima, mon amour* (Alain Resnais, 1959) to *The Damned* (Luchino Visconti, 1969) to *The Marriage of Maria Braun* (Rainer Werner Fassbinder, 1979) to *Shoah* and beyond, is well-known.[14] Equally well-known is the postwar transition of the horror film from its classic to modern phases, when all-too-human threats replace gothic, otherworldly monsters, and graphic violence replaces suggested mayhem. Could this transition itself be construed in part as a response to, and an engagement with, the traumatic impact of the war? Does the modern horror film, like the art film, draw on the war for the fiber of many of its representations?

The film most often credited with ushering in modern horror is, of course, Alfred Hitchcock's *Psycho* (1960). Returning to Robin Wood's landmark *Hitchcock's Films* (1965) reveals a fascinating crossroads where art, genre, and historical trauma intersect, all under the sign of *Psycho*. Wood begins his book by asking, "Why should we take Hitchcock seriously? It is a pity the question has to be raised: if the cinema were truly regarded as an autonomous art . . . it would be unnecessary. As things are, it seems impossible to start a book on Hitchcock without confronting it."[15] Today, with *Psycho* enshrined in the American Film Institute's pantheon of the "100 greatest American movies of all time" and more writing devoted to Hitchcock "than any other film director, and more about *Psycho* than any of his . . . other films,"[16] Wood's question may seem somewhat disconcerting. Yet the chasm between genre and art that informs Wood's call for a "serious" consideration of Hitchcock extends to conceptions of Hollywood commercial cinema versus European art cinema that are still very much with us. Wood claims that Hitchcock's mainstream popularity and his association with the "suspense-thriller" genre contributes to a "widespread assumption that, however 'clever,' 'technically brilliant,' 'amusing,' 'gripping,' etc., [Hitchcock's films] may be, they can't be taken seriously as we take, say, the films of Bergman or Antonioni seriously." Instead, Wood argues for a recognition of *Psycho* as art, labeling the film "one of the key works of our age" and noting its thematic resemblances to *Macbeth* and *Heart of Darkness*. He also points out that *Psycho* is "founded on" the "twin horrors" of the Nazi concentration camps: "the utter helplessness and innocence of the victims, and the fact that human beings, whose potentialities all of us in some measure share, were their tormentors and butchers."[17]

In his desire to establish the artistic worth of *Psycho*, Wood produces what Leo Bersani describes (in a different context) as an "aesthetic morality" characteristic of our modern "culture of redemption." According to Bersani, "a crucial assumption in the culture of redemption is that a certain type of repetition of experience repairs inherently damaged or valueless experience. Experience may be overwhelming, practically impossible to absorb, but it is assumed . . . that the work of art has the authority to master the presumed raw material of experience in a manner that uniquely gives value to, perhaps even redeems, that material."[18] In Wood's reading, *Psycho*'s horror is redeemed as art through its ability to lend meaning to the unfathomable horror of the Holocaust; *Psycho*'s "exceptionally mature and secure emotional viewpoint . . . enables the film to contemplate the ultimate horrors without hysteria, with a poised, almost serene detachment."[19] But as Bersani argues, "such apparently acceptable views of art's beneficently reconstructive function in culture depend on a devaluation of historical experience and of art. The catastrophes of history matter much less if they are somehow compensated for in art, and art itself gets reduced to a kind of superior patching function, is enslaved to those very materials to which it presumably imparts value."[20]

My own account of the allegorical moment attempts to shift cinema's relation to history from compensation to confrontation—to depart from Wood's generalized, ahistorical invocation of *Psycho*'s redemptive relation to the Holocaust in favor of culturally specific, historically contextualized cases where the intersections of cinema and trauma can be investigated more closely.[21] In these cases, the films do not redeem traumatic experience through art; instead, they call into question this very desire for redemption. At the same time, they interrogate the need to diagnose representations of trauma as "healthy" or "unhealthy." Rather than offering reassuring displays of artistic "meaning" validated as "productive" in the face of historical trauma, they demand that we acknowledge how these impulses to make productive meaning from trauma often coincide with wishes to divorce ourselves from any real implication within it. In short, these films invite us to recognize our connection to historical trauma across the axes of text, context, and spectatorship. They do so through the agency of an allegorical moment, situated at the unpredictable and often painful juncture where past and present collide. Each case reveals a different set of social and political variables that contribute to a jagged composite portrait of trauma's relation to cinematic representation, rather than a smooth, broadly thematic version of this relation that does not reckon with the intractable substance of history and culture.

These cases also function together to remap traditional accounts of genre history that neatly chart the modern horror film's "evolution" after its genesis in *Psycho*.[22] Such accounts tend to trace a familiar progression from *Psycho* through *Night of the Living Dead* (George A. Romero's 1968 variation on Hitchcock's 1963 *The Birds*), the slasher films of the 1970s and 1980s, and finally the neo-slasher serial killer films of the 1990s and the "postmodern" slasher parodies popularized by *Scream* (Wes Craven, 1996)—including, of course, Gus Van Sant's 1998 remake of *Psycho*. This kind of progression sustains the troubling critical trend Rick Altman summarizes as treating genres "as if they spring full-blown from the head of Zeus,"[23] where the modern horror film emerges not only as a uniquely American phenomenon, but as a matter of simply adding increased doses of gore to themes and formulae apparently invented by Hitchcock. Recent work on film genre has underlined the need to combat such linear, static, or even circular models of genre "evolution,"[24] and to distinguish between (but also to acknowledge the interrelatedness of) the commercial, producer-to-viewer discourses of "genre production and marketing" and analytical, critic-to-reader discourses of "genre criticism."[25] My study of the allegorical moment within the modern horror film is an act of genre criticism; I am not defining these films as a genre cycle initiated by film producers and recognized as such by contemporary audiences. In fact, many critics may argue that the films analyzed in this volume are not horror films at all. The question I pose is not so much "Can this film be categorized as horror?" as "How does this film access discourses of horror to confront the representation of historical trauma tied to the film's national and cultural context?"

This is not to say, however, that my account of the allegorical moment does not aim to challenge standard views of both the modern horror film and the workings of genre itself. By emphasizing the modern horror film's intersections with non-American art cinemas and by placing historical trauma alongside generic codes, I am contesting Hollywood-centered models of hermetic genre development that conceive of the art film and the genre film as antithetical sites rather than forms engaged in interactive exchange. Hitchcock's famous disciplining of audiences by refusing them admission to *Psycho* after the film began need not mirror an analogous constraint on the writing of film history, where *Psycho*'s critical positioning as *the* representative modern horror film often goes uncontested.[26] In other words, we are still stranded in the shower at the Bates Motel—blind to the various national and cultural contexts that must complicate our understanding of the modern horror film as a genre very much engaged with, rather than estranged from, traumatic history. This book offers the allegorical moment as a means of understanding these contexts, suggesting instead that the modern horror film may well be the genre of our time that registers most brutally the legacies of historical trauma.

NATIONAL CINEMA / POPULAR CINEMA

Commonplace references to modern culture as a "post-traumatic culture"[27] or a "wound culture" structured by "public fascination with torn and opened bodies and torn and opened persons"[28] indicate trauma's privileged position as an index not only to affect, but to identity itself. Indeed, mantras for our time could well include "I am traumatized, therefore I am," along with its corollary, "You are traumatized, therefore you are." With historical trauma, this index of personal identity extends to the realm of national identity. It is unthinkable to address the idea (or perhaps the desire for the idea) of contemporary "France" without the Occupation, of contemporary "Britain" without the Blitz, of contemporary "Japan" without Hiroshima, and of contemporary "America" without Vietnam. This book examines each of these cases in order to challenge assumptions concerning how historical trauma becomes mapped onto national identity, particularly in relation to the concept of national cinema.[29]

As Alan Williams has noted, following Rick Altman, national cinemas are not at all self-evident quantities. Instead, they must be regarded as "sites of conflict among different interest groups."[30] One such site of particular importance for this book is the long-standing critical definition of national cinema as synonymous with a nation's art cinema. Fortunately, much valuable recent work in film history has been devoted to recovering the often neglected "popular" cinemas that have been overshadowed by "national" cinema frameworks.[31] Nonetheless, these popular cinemas are usually excavated to enlarge the scope of the national cinema in question, rather than to interrogate the concept of "national cinema" itself. This is not simply a problem remedied by expanding the national canon to include "popular" films as well as "art" films; there is a structural problem in the very concept of "national cinema" that mirrors dominant narratives of national history. Certain "national" traditions, whether based in popular films or art films, become the lens through which a nation's cinema is understood to "evolve," just as the nation's history "evolves" in accordance with dominant national narratives. How might we disrupt this trajectory, with its reliance on illusory national "essences"? How might we cast national history, the history of a particular national cinema, and the relation between the two into a constellation that denaturalizes their interconnection, rather than rationalizes it? In other words, how can we redefine national cinema as a contested *process* of debate and dialogue, rather than a set of "given" abstractions and "self-evident" classifications?

The films studied in this volume are especially crucial to consider in light of these questions, for they straddle the divide between genre film and art film that most models of non-U.S. national cinema are built upon and regulated through. From 1945 up until the 1980s, a nation's art cinema was often (but not always) earmarked for export and thus doubled as the country's "national cinema" in terms of international visibility, while its genre cinema often (but not always) remained a matter of domestic distribution. Of course, as Geoffrey Nowell-Smith points out, "many of the films marketed in Britain and America under the 'art cinema' label, and imagined to be somehow different from 'commercial' [or "genre"] films, were in fact . . . mainstream products in their country of origin."[32] But few of these "popular" art films manage to interrogate the equation (again, framed with regard to international visibility) of art cinema = nongenre cinema = national cinema; in this sense, the films analyzed in this book constitute significant exceptions. These films illuminate the collusion between desires for "national cinema" and for "national identity." How can film history attend to such illuminations?

When David Bordwell asserts that "the fullest flower of the art-cinema paradigm occur[s] at the moment when the combination of novelty and nationalism" converges in an ideal marketing package, such as a film representing a distinct national movement or "New Wave,"[33] he reminds us how commercial discourse can set the terms that film history comes to rely upon. The concept of a "New Wave," a group of films whose affinities are perceived as articulating a new aesthetic that challenges (or at least distinguishes itself from) a nation's established cinematic traditions, is understandably indispensable to film marketing and film journalism, but what happens when film history uncritically adopts the very same designation? A certain brand of film history is written, one that tends to elevate a particular kind of aesthetics and politics to the privileged status often connoted by the term *New Wave*, while other contemporary films are left by the wayside. This book argues that when certain films resistant to national/popular labels speak about historical trauma, with its intimate connection to national identity, the conventional categorizations of "New Wave," "national cinema," and ultimately, "national identity" itself, are challenged. The films examined in this book have strong ties to the New Wave (or "Renaissance") movements of France, Britain, Japan, and the United States as well as the horror film, granting them a speaking position with regard to the national/popular question that mirrors their position vis-à-vis realism/modernism. They are poised to refigure not only the relation of the terms *national/popular* and *realism/modernism* to each other but also the impulse to legislate representation through these same terms. The politics of the allegorical moment involve questioning how history (as well as film history) is narrated, and, more specifically, how cinematic representation works to communicate historical trauma. The allegorical moment exists as a mode of confrontation, where representation's location between past and present, as well as between film, spectator, and history, demands to be recalibrated.

BLASTING OPEN THE CONTINUUM OF HISTORY

The specific sense of "allegory" and "shock" mobilized in this book must be understood as deeply indebted to the German-Jewish philosopher Walter Benjamin and the particular inflections he grants to these terms.[34] Benjamin, himself a tragic casualty of forces that signaled World War II, inspires the theoretical frame of this project; although his concepts are developed further through applications in each of the book's chapters, I will conclude this introduction with a guide to the major ideas that organize *Shocking Representation*'s engagement with trauma and history.

In *The Origin of German Tragic Drama* (1928), Benjamin posits the human skull, or "death's head," as the allegorical sign animating the seventeenth-century German *Trauerspiel*, or "mourning play."[35] As opposed to the eighteenth-century "symbol" of German romanticism, which emphasizes the "perfected beautiful individual" (OD:161), "classical proportion" (OD:166), and "humanity" (OD:166), allegory's death's head captures "everything about history that, from the very beginning, has been untimely, sorrowful, unsuccessful" (OD:166). Baroque allegory represents history as a "petrified, primordial landscape" (OD:166) of "irresistible decay" (OD:178) rather than the romantic symbol's intimation of history as idealized beauty and "the process of an eternal life" (*OD*:178). Allegory insists on literalizing cruelty, anguish, and horror in forms such as beheadings, dismemberments, and cannibalism, to the point where Benjamin claims, "In the *Trauerspiel* of the seventeenth century the corpse becomes quite simply the pre-eminent emblematic property" (*OD*:218).

How can allegorical "meaning" reside in the corpse, the body *emptied* of all meaning? Consider this passage that Benjamin quotes from a 1682 mourning play by Johann Christian Hallmann: "For if we consider the innumerable corpses with which, partly, the ravages of the plague and, partly, weapons of war, have filled not only our Germany, but almost the whole of Europe, then we must admit that our roses have been transformed into thorns, our lilies into nettles, our paradises into cemeteries, indeed our whole being into an image of death" (*OD*:231). Benjamin is drawn to this passage for its treatment of contrast and metamorphosis. For him, this type of moment in the *Trauerspiel* is "tirelessly transforming, interpreting, and deepening"—"it rings the changes on its images" in such a manner that "even the contrast of being and appearance does not accurately describe this technique of metaphors and apotheoses" (*OD*:231). In short, these allegorical images present "meaning" not as a fixed quantity, but precisely as an *image*, as an instant of occurring transformation. Benjamin's images exist in the allegorical moment *between* being and appearance, *between* subject and object, *between* life and death. This allegorical (and dialectical) betweenness of the image is indicated by the "meaningful" corpse and crystallized by the death's head—what Benjamin refers to as "the heart of the allegorical way of seeing" (*OD*:166). The realm of the image, with its connotations of ruin, fragmentation, and death, is thus also, for Benjamin, the realm of history's representation.

Indeed, Benjamin's distinctions between baroque allegory and the romantic symbol are echoed in his later essay "Theses on the Philosophy of History" (1940), where he distinguishes between historical materialism and historicism as methods of inquiry into the past.[36] Historicism, like the romantic symbol, becomes aligned with depicting history as "eternal" (TH:262), "universal" (TH:262), and as "progress" (TH:261), where the historicist merely establishes "a causal connection between various moments in history" (TH:263). Historical materialism, on the other hand, "blast[s] open the continuum of history" (TH:262) by forsaking historicism's "homogenous, empty time" in favor of what Benjamin calls "*Jetztzeit*," or "time filled by the presence of the now" (TH:261). *Jetztzeit* is a risky, momentary collision between past and present, when one can "seize hold of a memory as it flashes up at a moment of danger" (TH:255). The moment of *Jetztzeit*, then, is an allegorical moment, an instant in which an image of the past sparks a flash of unexpected recognition in the present. Not surprisingly, Benjamin's account of *Jetztzeit* in "Theses on the Philosophy of History" is strikingly anticipated in this description of baroque allegorical poetics from *The Origin of German Tragic Drama*: "The mystical instant [*Nu*] becomes the 'now' [*Jetzt*] of contemporary actuality; the symbolic becomes distorted into the allegorical. The eternal is separated from the events of the story of salvation, and what is left is a living image open to all kinds of revision by the interpretative artist" (*OD*:183).

However, what Benjamin underlines in his later essay is that the allegorical moment of *Jetztzeit* is not only disruptive, unpredictable, and open to revision, but also potentially dangerous—it is vulnerable to appropriation by those who wish to manipulate history to oppressive ends (TH:255). It must also resist the kind of rationalist narrativizing that would reinstate the moment of *Jetztzeit* within historicism's universalist chronicles of history. Benjamin seems to sense that even historical materialism itself, with its Marxist master narratives concerning the movement of history, might neutralize the shock of this moment. To this end, he insists on a mystical, theological dimension to *Jetztzeit*—it is a temporality characterized by a "Messianic cessation of happening, or, put differently, a revolutionary chance in the fight for the oppressed past" (TH:263). The Messianic ability to arrest time, to reorganize relations between past and present, charges each moment with a potential future inflected by the politics of historical materialism, where the oppressed past no longer languishes unrecognized. This enigmatic juxtaposition of Messianic theology with Marxist radicalism checks the totalizing impulses of both modes of thought and preserves the shock of *Jetztzeit*. For Benjamin, it is the responsibility of the historian, above all else, to generate this shock as a means of blasting open the continuum of history.

But just how does this blasting open occur? If the goal is defamiliarization, then the methods must necessarily vary widely. As Benjamin points out in *The Origin of German Tragic Drama*, "If it is to hold its own against the tendency toward absorption, then the allegorical must constantly unfold in new and surprising ways" (*OD*:183). One method is to imagine the present through the past in such a manner that flashes of unexpected recognition pass between the two temporalities. Benjamin cites the French Revolution's ability to imagine itself as ancient Rome in this regard (TH:261). Another method entails remembering that "nothing that has ever happened should be regarded as lost for history" (TH:254). Benjamin locates history not only in major events like the French Revolution, but in the cultural ephemera of fashion and entertainment. He begins "Theses on the Philosophy of History" by illustrating his two central theoretical terms—theology and historical materialism—through the grotesque, amusement park imagery of a chess-playing Turkish puppet (historical materialism) controlled by an unseen, hunchbacked puppeteer (theology) (TH:253). This invocation of the fairground attraction (a realm indivisible from cinema)[37] not only highlights the significance of mass culture for history, but draws attention to how Benjamin's very writing style, with its epigraphic fragments and metaphorical descriptions, could be read as attempts to enact the defamiliarizations capable of blasting open the continuum of history. In short, the death's head, that elusive sign of the allegorical representation of history, may be found where we least expect it—as the past erupts in the present, in the flicker of a cinematic image, in a disorienting turn of phrase. *Shocking Representation* endeavors to locate and to generate the allegorical moment in all of these forms.

In *The Arcades Project* (1927–1940), Benjamin states, "It's not that what is past casts its light on what is present, or what is present its light on what is past; rather, image is that wherein what has been comes together in a flash with the now to form a constellation."[38] Such an image, for Benjamin, is a "dialectical image";[39] it represents history not by re-creating a "true" past, but by uniting past and present in a volatile, momentary flash. This flash of the dialectical image encompasses the allegorical image of the death's head, but it also reappears in "Theses on the Philosophy of History." There Benjamin writes, "The past can be seized only as an image which flashes up at the instant when it can be recognized and is never seen again . . . for every image of the past that is not recognized by the present as one of its own concerns threatens to disappear irretrievably" (TH:255).

Benjamin's notion of historical representation as allegory, as a dialectical image of death where the past becomes *recognizable* to the present only through "the violence of the dialectic movement within these allegorical depths" (OD:166), forces us beyond the constricting theoretical frames placed on representation by trauma studies. Allegory cannot be fully psychologized or interiorized; it also insists on the exteriority of the corpse. Allegory resists fantasies of strictly teleological history in favor of fleeting instants where "meaning" is forged between past and present, in "the depths that separate visual being from meaning" (OD:165). And finally, allegory disrupts the realism/modernism dichotomy by partaking of the real without adopting "naturalized" realism, and by partaking of the abstract without mandating a modernist aesthetic of absence and self-reflexivity. In short, allegory honors representation's promise that trauma can be communicated—its commitment to the image of death is simultaneously a commitment, however conflicted and provisional, to recognition, to the past's value for the present.

Allegory's alignment with the image of death is also an alignment with the cinema. Despite the shift in historical period from the seventeenth to the twentieth century, such a connection seems well-justified; Benjamin's conception of *The Origin of German Tragic Drama* as an engagement with art in his own time[40] touches on his prominent concerns with the cinema as an emblematic expression of, and reaction to, mid-twentieth-century modernity.[41] In fact, *The Arcades Project*, perhaps Benjamin's most ambitious meditation on modernity, is littered with references to *The Origin of German Tragic Drama*.[42] Benjamin's notion of "shock," which I pursue in greater detail in chapter 1, is central to his vision of modernity. Shock testifies to the overwhelmed and impoverished state of modern experience, where sensory overstimulation demands shocks in order to register reaction, but shock is also a potential catalyst for the reawakening of experience to history. Cinema occupies a significant space in Benjamin's landscape of modernity—it embodies both the threat and the promise of shock. When I use the term *shock* in the title of this book, I wish to activate this double-edged sense of risk. For setting out to shock the notion of representation entails dangers as well as potential benefits.

Shocking Representation culminates with a chapter devoted to David Cronenberg, a director whose oeuvre hinges on evoking visceral horror, disrupting genre/art categories, and carving out an enigmatic place within Canadian national cinema that consists of equal parts "national model" and "national anomaly." Cronenberg provides the occasion to consolidate and deepen the book's main theoretical arguments by revealing the roots of the allegorical moment's relations to trauma and identity. If Benjamin posits allegory as a mode where the corpse becomes the "pre-eminent emblematic property," then Cronenberg reimagines the corporeal itself, depicting the body not as a site for selfhood but for meaning as a state of violent transformation. Cronenberg's own avowed intention "to show the unshowable, to speak the unspeakable"[43] returns us to allegory's capacity to "speak otherwise" and prepares us for the work of blasting open the continuum of history—the work, in other words, of shocking representation.

HISTORY WITHOUT A FACE

Surrealism, Modernity, and the Holocaust
in the Cinema of Georges Franju

> And wiping off the tears of blood that furrowed his cheeks, he turned
> away from the girl to hide from her the death of the Jewish people,
> which was written clearly, he knew, in the flesh of his face.
>
> —André Schwarz-Bart[1]

> Franju does not tremble on the brink. He dives in. He leads us impla-
> cably on to the very limits of what our nerves can stand.
>
> —Jean Cocteau[2]

> The trouble with [director Henri-Georges] Clouzot is that he tries to
> knock the audience's head off. That's wrong; you should twist it off.
>
> —Georges Franju[3]

When Georges Franju died in 1987, he felt bitterly dissatisfied with the
spotty critical reception of his film career. Perhaps some of this neglect
can be attributed to his allegedly volatile personality—at least one critic has
described his reputation as "the Céline of conversationalists, a man of 'tor-
rential vehemence' spitting out excremental expletives like a tracer-stream
of olive pits."[4] But Franju's shadowy presence in film history probably has
more to do with a remarkably multifaceted career that resists convenient
categorization into any of its individual components: cofounder (with Henri
Langlois) of the Cinémathèque Française (1937), secretary-general of the
Institut de Cinématographie Scientifique (1944–1954), documentarist, fiction filmmaker, Left Bank director, proto-New Wavist, and Surrealist heir.
This chapter seeks to add yet another label to this unwieldy list: pioneer of
the modern horror film as a mode of engagement with traumatic history.

By examining the development of an allegorical, horror-inflected aesthetic in Franju's two most significant films, *Le Sang des bêtes* (*Blood of the*

Beasts, 1949) and *Les Yeux sans visage* (*Eyes Without a Face*, 1960),[5] I hope
not only to shed light on a career that has not received the recognition it
deserves, but to situate Franju alongside questions of modernity and national cinema in contradistinction from the contemporaneous French New
Wave. I will argue that it is through a shocking, allegorical encounter with
historical trauma that a synthesis of Franju's disparate influences occurs,
and that his crucial contribution to the modern horror film begins to take
shape. In order to trace the formation of Franju's aesthetic, we must first
turn to Surrealism.

SURREALISM, MODERNITY, AND *BLOOD OF THE BEASTS*

Franju's professional awakening to cinema occurred while under the spell
of Surrealism, and the movement's inspiration marks his entire career.
Among the films Henri Langlois introduced him to when they met in 1934
were Luis Buñuel's two Surrealist cinema milestones *Un Chien andalou* (*An
Andalusian Dog*, 1929) and *L'Age d'or* (*The Golden Age*, 1930), and the very
first Langlois/Franju *ciné-club* program was fittingly entitled "Le Cinéma
Fantastique."[6] Franju's work as a film archivist nurtured his deep admiration for certain early filmmakers, notably Surrealist favorites Louis Feuillade and Georges Méliès. Franju knew Méliès personally and appointed
him first curator of the Cinémathèque Française in 1937. He paid tribute
to him in the documentary *Le Grand Méliès* (1952), and did the same for
Feuillade in the feature *Judex* (1963). At one point, Franju even planned to
give a lecture with André Breton himself "on those fragments of bad films
which correspond to Surrealist notions."[7]

But what kind of Surrealism actually made its way into Franju's film
practice? Franju's Surrealism has little to do with the popular image of
Surrealism as an art movement characterized by romantic investments in
psychic automatism, dreams, and liberating love. As early as 1929, Walter
Benjamin was calling for the "dissection" of this "romantic dummy" version of Surrealism in order to expose what is "usable inside": "the cult of
evil as political device."[8]

Benjamin's metaphor of dissection seems especially well-chosen, because the iconoclastic forces within Surrealism which he identifies with
a "cult of evil" trace their origins to the very real ruptured bodies of World
War I. Many of the Surrealists served in the Great War, and they all lived
in a postwar environment haunted by the presence of wounded survivors
(numbering up to 1,100,000 in France alone).[9] Surrealist art's bizarre,
tormented refigurations of the human body should not stand merely as

abstract explorations of the unconscious; they also respond to the social presence of horribly maimed veterans.[10] The Surrealists registered the bitter end of illusions of modernity as a meaningful evolution of technology—the innovations in gas, air, and artillery warfare only resulted in unprecedented mass destruction and bodily disintegration. Faith in assumptions of modernity's progress were replaced with confusion, irony, or pessimism.[11] Benjamin reflects this dramatic change in worldview when he praises Surrealism's "pessimism all along the line," where "unlimited trust" can only be placed (sarcastically) in "I. G. Farben and the peaceful perfection of the air force."[12] For Benjamin, Surrealism's political value as a "cult of evil" lies in its ability to "disinfect and isolate against all moralizing dilettantism" (characteristic of left-wing bourgeois optimism and "sentiment") through the "profane illumination" of dialectical materialism.[13] In other words, Surrealism might be better understood as a violent, embodied assault on the social structures propping up modernity, rather than a romantic retreat within the self.

Benjamin's support of Surrealism hinges on its potential for a "profane illumination" of modernity, but he also criticizes the movement for its failure to realize this potential. He regards Surrealism's attraction to a romantic aesthetic of "surprise" an abandonment of any capacity for radical negativity:

> The aesthetic of the painter, the poet, *en état de surprise*, of art as the reaction of one surprised, is enmeshed in a number of pernicious romantic prejudices. . . . For histrionic or fanatical stress on the mysterious side of the mysterious takes us no further; we penetrate the mystery only to the degree that we recognize it in the everyday world, by virtue of a dialectical optics that perceives the everyday as impenetrable, the impenetrable as everyday.[14]

Benjamin locates the origin of the flawed Surrealist aesthetic of surprise in Apollinaire, and sets it against a more profane aesthetic of "hatred" running through Rimbaud and Poe.[15] Benjamin's commentary seems prescient of a decisive break within Surrealism that would occur one year later when Breton denounces Georges Bataille as "wallow[ing] in impurities" and "wish[ing] only to consider in the world that which is vilest, most discouraging, and most corrupted."[16] If we imagine this split in Benjamin's terms of surprise and hatred, then Breton would fall on the side of the former, and Bataille on the latter.[17] *Blood of the Beasts* testifies to Franju's investment in an "impure," Bataillean Surrealism, and thus also to a Benjaminian dialectical optics.

Bataille, like Franju, admired *Un Chien andalou*. Bataille's reaction to the film might well serve as a blueprint for the creative impulse behind *Blood of the Beasts*: "How then can one not see to what extent horror becomes fascinating, and how it alone is brutal enough to break everything that stifles?"[18] The horror of Franju's film is truly brutal, as it chronicles the activities of Paris slaughterhouses (located chiefly in the suburb of La Villette) in unflinching, transfixed clinical detail. Franju's brutality seems characterized by a rage aimed at "breaking all that stifles," of engendering a fierce new way of seeing for his audience. Franju's frustration with the weakness of the human eye echoes Bataille's: "It's the bad combination, it's the wrong synthesis, constantly made by the eye as it looks around, that stops us seeing everything as strange."[19]

Franju's mission of restoring the strange or other as primary in perception mirrors the strategy behind Bataille's journal *Documents* (1929–30), which utilizes the techniques of juxtaposition and collage to decenter cultural standards of high and low, primitive and modern, known and unknown. The sixth issue of *Documents* (November 1929) sets critical dictionary definitions against enlarged microscopic views of crustaceans, and stills of dance numbers from *Fox Follies*.[20] Also included are Eli Lotar's slaughterhouse photographs from La Villette, with their emphasis on dismembered limbs, blood-soaked floors, and workers busy at their craft. Lotar's photographs seem eerily like outtakes from the film Franju would make twenty years later. In fact, the adjoining microscopic photographs are by the physician and Surrealist filmmaker Jean Painlevé, who would work with Franju at the Institut de Cinématographie Scientifique and contribute the commentary to *Blood of the Beasts*.[21] Bataille's own dictionary definition of "Abattoir" (also included in this issue) criticizes those who refuse to acknowledge the sense of the sacred in slaughterhouses, those "fine folk who have reached the point of not being able to stand their own unseemliness" and have ensured that "the slaughterhouse is cursed and quarantined like a boat with cholera aboard."[22]

A haunting image from *Blood of the Beasts* brings to life Bataille's metaphor of the abattoir as a cursed ship.[23] Near the documentary's conclusion, as we make the transition between the slaughterhouse and the outlying districts of Paris that open the film, an extreme long shot lingers on a barge passing through a landscape of barren shore and gray sky. As the ship floats by slowly from left to right, we see a lone man at the bow, a clothesline with sheets rustling in the wind across the vessel's bridge, and finally the aft with its heavy machinery that resembles artillery. This shot fades out, and the subsequent shot reveals a view of the canal that borders the abattoir and the bridge where we've seen the cattle and sheep cross on their way to slaughter. The second shot discloses what the first shot remarkably conceals—that the barge is traveling on water at all. Franju composes the frame in such a manner that the barge, like a ghost ship, seems to trace an unnatural path between land and sky, with no water visible. The director notes that this unsettling spectacle was very deliberately constructed:

> I waited several days, came back over a period of several weeks to get a barge going through a wasteland. . . . It's therefore a very artificial way of seeing. . . . But I maintain that a barge which cuts a wasteland in half without being able to see the water is much more . . . of a barge than a barge.[24]

When this "artificial way of seeing" is paired with the specific context of the second shot, Franju's disorientation of the viewer takes on deeper meaning. He visually links this ghost ship not only with the abattoir, but with the bridge that connects the slaughterhouse and the market, and thus also with the passing sheep which have been described by the narrator as "condemned men" who "will not hear the gates of their prison close, nor the Paris-Villette train which pierces the pastoral night to gather the victims for tomorrow." The voice-over narration also states that the sheep are "led by the 'traitor' among them, who knows the way and whose life will be spared."

In this sense, I argue that the "barge is more than a barge" because it undermines its own everyday appearance and forces a reckoning with the disturbing historical events that haunt it: the long shadows of World War II, specifically the German Occupation and the Holocaust. Franju's "artificial way of seeing" stunningly reminds us that the barge is impregnated with the strange and painful, with the substance of death, war, deportation, concentration camps, and "traitorous" collaborationist guilt. If Franju brings Bataille's ship into shore, then its cargo is not finally cholera, but vision—a radically altered vision that restores unseemliness to a society ordered by the anesthetizing of historical trauma.

Siegfried Kracauer touches briefly but powerfully on the allegorical and historical dimensions of Franju's vision in *Theory of Film: The Redemption of Physical Reality* (1960). The sole passage in the book's published version that speaks explicitly about the Holocaust juxtaposes the "rows of calves' heads" in *Blood of the Beasts* with "the litter of tortured human bodies" in films about Nazi concentration camps. Kracauer links these images because they both "beckon the spectator to take them in and thus incorporate into his memory the real face of things too dreadful to be beheld in reality."[25] Kracauer includes this observation in a subsection entitled "The Head of the Medusa," where he remarks that Perseus's greatest feat was not the actual beheading of Medusa, but his courageous look at her reflection in his shield. In Kracauer's reflective surface, Franju's "way of seeing" acquires the power of a present-day reckoning with traumatic history. As Kracauer's formulation suggests, *Blood of the Beasts* insists on disclosing connections between everyday life and the horrors of history. But Kracauer does not fully address the effects of displacement in this dynamic, or the temporal rift between past history and contemporary existence. For this we must return to Benjamin's notions of allegory and dialectical optics, where the past and present collide.[26]

Benjamin's dialectical optics describe a profane Surrealist mode of perception that "perceives the everyday as impenetrable, the impenetrable as everyday." One way in which Surrealism unmasks this dialectical face of reality, according to Benjamin, is by dwelling on "the revolutionary energies that appear in the 'outmoded.'"[27] Benjamin's catalog of the outmoded captures Surrealism's well-known affection for enigmatic objects seemingly unhinged in time: "the first iron constructions, the first factory buildings, the earliest photos, . . . grand pianos, the dresses of five years ago, fashionable restaurants when the vogue has begun to ebb from them." These outmoded objects allow "the substitution of a political" for a narrowly historicist "view of the past."[28] How might we imagine the effects of such a substitution? The outmoded transforms cultural decay into political significance by "challeng[ing] this [bourgeois] culture with its own forfeited dreams, test[ing] it against its own compromised values of political emancipation, technological progress, cultural access, and the like."[29] A Surrealist concentration on the outmoded aims to disturb capitalist culture's mythic assumptions of a rationalized, evolving history (and modernity) by provoking the interpenetration of past and present. But as Benjamin intimates, the recovery of this interpenetration *depends* on the catalyzing force of horror (Surrealism at its most profane), and on a shocking recognition of history's horrors within the fabric of the everyday.

Blood of the Beasts opens with a dreamlike display of the outmoded. The film does not take us immediately to the abattoir, but to the outskirts of Paris. Here we observe a kaleidoscope of wildly contrasting Surrealist images that underline the impossibility of a soothingly familiar world to comfort us before we descend into the nightmare of the slaughterhouse. Cars, busy city streets, and towering buildings give way to skeletal trees and junkyard oddities like old phonographs, broken mannequins, bedsprings, and an umbrella. Plastic sheets sway in the wind, a man sits alone outside at an antique table, children hold hands in a circle, a lamp hangs in the air as if suspended from a tree. The narrator tells us, "These are the gardens of the poor, whose blossoms are the debris of the rich."

This opening sequence establishes a setting for Benjamin's theory of modern industrial culture as a "dream world" due for an "awakening" that will be "synonymous with historical knowledge."[30] Benjamin, like the Surrealists, believed the rapidly metamorphosing urban-industrial landscape simulates a mythic, enchanted dream state of consciousness. Bretonian Surrealists like Louis Aragon (although he too would eventually sever ties with Breton) celebrated mass culture's objects, and even cities themselves, as dream images. Benjamin, by contrast, feared the Surrealist tendency to become "stuck in the realm of dreams."[31] Though enamored with Aragon's writing, Benjamin wished to *transform* these dream images into dialectical images by exposing their historical content.

Franju seems to share Benjamin's frustration with the limits of Bretonian Surrealism. *Blood of the Beasts* self-consciously presents the "classic" Surrealist outmoded only as a point of departure, and not without a satirical edge. The opening sequence concludes with a wipe in the shape of an ornate fan (connoting courtly love) and a couple kissing amidst the ruins to Joseph Kosma's romantic orchestral score. This exaggerated enactment of Breton's dictum of "convulsive beauty" and transcendent love recedes into unreality (along with the music) as Franju cuts to the stark image of a train moving beneath clawlike electrical posts. The ghostly train functions as an emblem of industrial modernity (including the industrial killing of the Holocaust), as well as the transition between prologue and diegesis, city and slaughterhouse. The train reappears at the end of the film, but then it moves steadily *toward* us and away from the slaughterhouse, rather than vice versa. The orchestral score also returns during this conclusion, but the closure it intimates by recalling the Bretonian prologue is impossible given all the horror that has transpired in the interim—rather than revisiting the site of the Surrealist outmoded, the film fades to black. The dreamlike collage of outmoded objects that begins the film becomes dialectical only when it converges with an awakened awareness of modernity and horror's blood brotherhood. Franju achieves this awakening by persistently linking horror to history, and particularly to industrial modernity's rationalizations of productivity and progress.

The ties between labor and horror are especially pronounced in *Blood of the Beasts* during the sequence depicting axe-man Henri Fourmel splitting an ox during the twelve chimes of noon. Franju cuts between Fourmel's steady work on the hanging carcass and shots of the world outside, with its buildings, roadways, and city square. The ringing of the chimes on the sound track unites the series of shots and indicates the interpenetration of these various social structures. Fourmel's grisly labor taints the traffic in the city square, just as the everyday business in the city square asserts the "normality" of Fourmel's work. Nothing remains safely isolated in its own conventional category; even the static shots of buildings emphasize eerie shadows and stillness to suggest a chaotic force just below the "solid" surface.

The estrangement from modern industrial production occurs again in the sequence where a Charles Trenet love song ("La Mer") accompanies a montage of slaughterhouse imagery. The workers may whistle or sing while they do their jobs, but Franju pushes this bit of documentary detail to its limits—the discrete elements of the song and the work blur together, each infecting the other's presence to the point where the initial "reality" of the workplace seems irrevocably altered. Trenet's nondiegetic voice (supported by harmonizing offscreen whistling, as well as the baying of sheep) is supplemented with strikingly literalized images: a pool of blood for "Dancing white-caps of the sea, foaming in the limpid bays"; a man hosing down the filthy courtyard for "Reflections changing in the rain, overhead the summer day"; sheep caged in a pen for "Fleecy clouds like white sheep feign"; and a pot filled with reeds used for the braining of animals for "Whose gardens are the tall, moist reeds, whose music is the lone gull's cry." In the charged tension between sentimental lyrics and horrific visual translation, between documentary realism and constructed spectacle, we experience something of Benjamin's awakening from modernity's dream world.

Franju extends the aesthetic of awakening to our position as spectators of documentary film as well. We cannot simply disengage ourselves from the horror of *Blood of the Beasts* through a resignation to the onslaught of an unmediated "documentary reality" because Franju highlights the constructedness of documentary realism throughout the film. In addition to the self-conscious manipulations of sound described in the chimes of noon and "La Mer" sequences, he inserts jarring wipes in the shape of a fan or a book cover, dissolves between a dead horse and a painting of one, and switches abruptly to a piano interlude on the sound track while focusing on a portrait of two women at a piano. Franju despises the illusory objectivity of *cinéma vérité*, so he opts instead to foreground the artificiality of documentary: "There isn't any *cinéma vérité*. It's necessarily a lie, from the moment the director intervenes—or it isn't cinema at all. . . . You must re-create reality because reality runs away; reality denies reality. You must first interpret it, or re-create it."[32]

Franju's vision in *Blood of the Beasts* is profoundly Benjaminian in its dialectical goal of imbricating perceptions of the familiar with those of the unfamiliar, even in the process of audience reception of documentary "reality." His film returns to the climate of Surrealism in the late 1920s and 1930s, an era James Clifford describes by pointing to a "secret sharing" between Surrealism and ethnography, a moment when one's own culture can be investigated as "a contested reality." Clifford traces the intertwined development of ethnography and Surrealism in 1920s France (*Documents* testifies to this conjuncture) and sees the Surrealist attitude as "comparable to that of the fieldworker who strives to make the unfamiliar comprehensible" but instead "tended to work in the reverse sense, making the familiar strange."[33] Franju turns a certain ethnographic sensibility inward in order to defamiliarize modernity and restore a sense of horror and disorder, but he does not allow the scientific discourse that underlies this project to go uninterrogated.

The voice-over commentary of *Blood of the Beasts* (scripted by Jean Painlevé) stands out as much as the visuals but for the opposite reason: bloodless clinical description versus blood-soaked imagery. Franju borrows the objective tone of the science film, but undermines the typical unitary authority of the science film narrator by alternating the older male and younger female voices of Georges Hubert and Nicole Ladmiral. Yet this is only one method the film employs to interrogate science as a component of modernity. The influence of ethnographic Surrealism mixes with Franju's and Painlevé's involvement at the Institut de Cinématographie Scientifique to create a unique mutation of the science film, where rationalist scientific discourse itself undergoes an uncanny defamiliarization.[34]

The science film is invoked directly as *Blood of the Beasts* arrives at the abattoir. Slaughtering devices arrayed on a table are introduced instrument by instrument, as an anonymous hand lifts each device in time with the narrator's description ("the reed . . . the pole-axe . . . and the Behr-gun, which stuns the animal by percussion"). The table shot dissolves to a white horse being led by a man into a stall. In quick succession, the horse collapses after a blow to the skull from the Behr-gun, its front legs jerk spastically, its mouth and neck are sliced open, steaming blood pours onto the ground, and its body is dragged off by a single hind leg. (See fig. 1.1.) At this point, the narrator calmly states, "The bleeding process ends with the horse being hoisted by cable. It is immediately lowered for skinning. Air, pumped under the hide, loosens the skin."

The contrast between the clinical account of the mechanics of slaughter and the visceral horror of the visuals (often enhanced by close-ups,

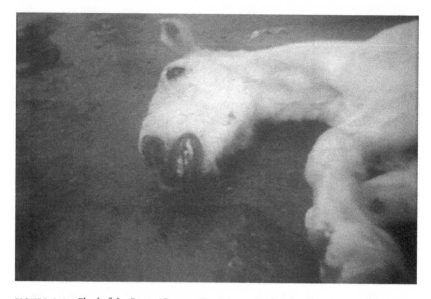

FIGURE 1.1 *Blood of the Beasts* (Georges Franju, 1949): Slaughterhouse Surrealism as historical awakening (frame enlargement).

extended shot duration, and a minutely detailed diegetic sound track) is so pronounced that the scientific discourse ultimately collapses on itself like the corpse it attempts to process. By juxtaposing the shocking carnage with matter-of-fact commentary, the scientific discourse implodes under pressure from the sheer visual display of all it denies. Franju restores strangeness and violence to the distant, rationalist tone of the science film, and reintroduces all the painful affect that this discourse of modernity represses. Again, Franju aggressively insists on a dialectical optics in this profane presentation of violence. As the director explains, "Violence is not an end, it's a weapon which sensitizes the spectator and which lets him see what's lyric or poetic beyond or above the violence, or what's tender in the reality. Violence, for me, is a means, like blasphemy for Buñuel."[35]

Franju's description of violence as a means of sensitization intersects significantly with Benjamin's notion of "shock."[36] Benjamin perceived modernity as an "inhospitable, blinding age of big-scale industrialism" where assaultive sensory stimuli (shocks) cause the human subject to erect a consciousness shield as a defense against overstimulation.[37] But the shield divorces sense impressions from one's integrated realm of sense-memories or "experience [*Erfahrung*]"; instead, these impressions remain locked at the particular, unreflective level of "a certain hour in one's life [*Erlebnis*]."[38]

The shocks of industrial modernity thus contribute to sensory alienation and the decay of experience. Yet for Benjamin, "film is the art form that is in keeping with the increased threat to [modern] life" represented by shock. He claims that "man's need to expose himself to shock effects is his *adjustment* to the dangers threatening him."[39] So film's "staged shocks" (or "countershocks") become the vehicle for redeeming experience debased by modern shock in the first place.[40] Shock for Benjamin, like violence for Franju, works ultimately to reclaim what is "tender in the reality" of modernity. The pain of Franju's allegorical horror is the agony of awakening—to the body, and to history.

THE POLITICS OF AWAKENING AT THE DAWN OF THE NEW WAVE

What exactly does it mean to awaken to history in the context of postwar France, particularly during the years spanning the release of *Blood of the Beasts* in 1949 and *Eyes Without a Face* in 1960? The historian Henry Rousso has identified much of this period as a particularly crucial era in the development of a French "Vichy syndrome," a "diverse set of symptoms whereby the trauma of the Occupation [1940–1944], and particularly that trauma resulting from internal divisions within France, reveals itself in political, social, and cultural life." Rousso characterizes the years 1954–1971 as a time when the myth of "resistancialism" dominates French culture, although the seeds of resistancialism were sown at least as early as August 25, 1944.[41] On that date, General Charles de Gaulle marked the liberation of Paris from the Nazis and from the Vichy regime by exclaiming, "Paris! Paris humiliated! Paris broken! Paris martyrized! But Paris liberated! Liberated by itself, by its own people with the help of the armies of France, with the support and aid of France as a whole, of fighting France, of the only France, of the true France, of eternal France."[42] What de Gaulle begins to build in these legendary sentences is an ideology of resistancialism, which Rousso defines in terms of "a process that sought to minimize the importance of the Vichy regime and its impact on French society, *including its most negative aspects*"; "the construction of an object of memory, the 'Resistance,' whose significance transcended by far the sum of its active parts"; and "the identification of this 'Resistance' with the nation as a whole."[43] My earlier account of *Blood of the Beasts* as an allegorical illumination of the ghosts of the Occupation and the Holocaust should be read as an interrogation of resistancialism, as a reckoning with all that resistancialism wishes to deny—collaboration, deportation, annihilation.[44] But in the end, this is only one layer of the national and historical awakening encouraged by

Franju's cinema. For the others, we must continue to examine the French postwar cultural context.

Literary critic Philip Watts calls attention to another aspect of the Vichy syndrome that is particularly significant for the writers and intellectuals of postwar France: the legacy left behind by the purge, those trials of suspected collaborators following the Liberation. Although the purge ends officially in 1953, and by 1964 there is not a single collaborator serving time in prison,[45] Watts argues that the purge remains, in a very powerful sense, ongoing. One way that the purge lives on, according to Watts, is through debates raised by the trials that have yet to be resolved, debates involving the relation of literature to politics and to issues of social responsibility. During the purge, prominent French intellectuals (in addition to politicians and others) stood trial as collaborators based heavily on the writing they produced during the Occupation. The failure of the purge to engage sufficiently the question of whether art can be judged as either political or apolitical makes the purge of intellectuals seem, at least from today's perspective, "excessively violent, arbitrary, highly politicized, and on the whole, ineffective." Yet the trials of the purge "crystallized the opposition between committed literature and 'art for art's sake'" in such an influential manner that "the accusations, judgments, and verdicts of the purge inflected the entire intellectual production of the postwar years and left their trace on every genre and almost every writer of the time."[46] One artistic genre of vital importance to French culture in the postwar period lies beyond the purview of Watts's study, but still bears the scars of the purge: cinema.[47]

In fact, I wish to argue that the most (in)famous French document concerning the cinema during these years, François Truffaut's "A Certain Tendency of the French Cinema" (1954), must be understood, along with the influential output of the journal *Cahiers du cinéma* (where Truffaut's essay appeared) and the accompanying early films of the French New Wave, as phenomena very much haunted by the purge. Indeed, when *Cahiers* editor Jacques Doniol-Valcroze looks back on the impact of Truffaut's controversial article from the vantage point of 1959, he observes that

> the publication of ["A Certain Tendency of the French Cinema"] marks the real point of departure for what, rightly or wrongly, *Cahiers du cinéma* represents today. A leap had been made, a trial begun with which we were all in solidarity, something bound us together. From then on, it was known that we were *for* Renoir, Rossellini, Hitchcock, Cocteau, Bresson . . . and against X, Y and Z.[48]

Doniol-Valcroze's language of "trial," "solidarity," and "for/against" not only echoes the purge, but finds its reflection in the discourse of the *Cahiers* editorial collective, that now-legendary roster of critics-turned-New Wave directors that includes Truffaut, Jean-Luc Godard, Jacques Rivette, Eric Rohmer, and Claude Chabrol.[49] For example, Godard, writing in 1959 on the occasion of Truffaut's feature film debut *Les Quatre cents coups* (*The 400 Blows*, 1959) being selected to represent France at the Cannes Film Festival (where Truffaut would win the Best Director prize) speaks of the New Wave's triumph as the "true face of the French cinema" over the "false technique" of certain older French directors associated with a stagnant, anti-cinematic style. "Today, victory is ours . . . although we have won a battle, the war is not yet over."[50] The "war" Godard refers to certainly recalls the purge implicitly, but its battle lines of "true" French cinema against "false" French cinema are drawn directly from Truffaut's influential salvo from five years earlier.

"A Certain Tendency of the French Cinema" clears a path for the "true" films of the New Wave by defining all that is "false" in French cinema under the rubric of a "Tradition of Quality."[51] Truffaut describes the Tradition of Quality as films dominated so completely by their screenwriters (specifically Jean Aurenche and Pierre Bost) and their commitment to a false "psychological realism" that the potential contribution of the director or the novel upon which the film is based is rendered meaningless. The resulting films display "little enough invention for a great deal of betrayal" (CT:228) and are guilty of "treason" against the novels that inspired them (CT:229) ("*unfaithful* to the spirit as well as the letter" [CT:228; emphasis in original]). Truffaut's attack enacts the rhetoric of the purge not only in its vitriol, but by accusing the Tradition of Quality of acts that amount to national indignity.

Individuals charged with "national indignity" during the purge were judged guilty of acts of collaboration during the Occupation that "betrayed a certain idea of France," including democracy, tolerance, virility, frugality, and intellectual responsibility.[52] Although those deemed guilty of "national indignity" escaped the death penalty meted out to other collaborators, their sentence could include (in addition to jail time) "national degradation"—the loss of French citizenship.[53] The charge of "national indignity" illuminates the true stakes of the purge: this was a struggle to purify "Eternal France" of the contamination of a diseased France, to remove the "false" France and restore the "true" France, to assert a certain notion of national identity. In this sense, Truffaut's assault on the Tradition of Quality must be seen as continuous with the purge's project of national redefinition and thus as a call for a purified French national cinema. Indeed, Truffaut begins his article by referring to the Tradition of Quality as those dozen high-profile, big-budget French films released each year that earn "the admiration of the foreign press" and that "defend the French flag . . . at Cannes and at Venice where, since 1946, they regularly carry off medals, golden lions and *grands prix*" (CT:225).

For Truffaut, the Tradition of Quality is an impure national cinema characterized by "scenarists' films" (CT:225) that must be purged in order to make way for a pure national cinema, an "*auteur*'s cinema" created by true "men of the cinema" (CT:234) capable of writing and directing films that testify to a particular "world-view" (CT:233). Truffaut presents this desired worldview in terms of purity and faithfulness, where a pure French cinema faithful to the real France must resist the impurities of the Tradition of Quality—its formulaic anticlerical, antimilitarist, and antibourgeois tendencies, along with its proclivities toward, on the one hand, the "uniformity" (CT:231) of "scholarly framing, complicated lighting-effects, [and] 'polished' photography" (CT:230) and, on the other, the "filthiness" (CT:231) of profanity, blasphemy, violence, death, and depictions of homosexuality (CT:234). Again, Truffaut's charges against the Tradition of Quality correspond to important aspects of the "national indignity" definition, notably its violations of intellectual responsibility (the unfaithfulness to the source novels), frugality (the insistence on bloated, expensive production values), and virility (the gay content). Similarly, his statement that "I do not believe in the peaceful co-existence of the 'Tradition of Quality' and an '*auteur*'s cinema'" (CT:234) echoes the purge's undoing of democracy and tolerance, even as it claimed to safeguard these very values.

I call attention to Truffaut's revisiting of the purge in order to foreground the complicated origins but often problematic politics of "A Certain Tendency of the French Cinema" and, by extension, of *Cahiers du cinéma* and the early films of the New Wave. By embracing the rhetoric of the purge (and particularly by endorsing a notion of "pure" national cinema) while simultaneously imagining itself as somehow beyond politics, the New Wave opens itself to the politics of reaction. The left-wing French film journal *Positif*, *Cahiers'* most significant rival at the time, understood this danger. Robert Benayoun, writing in *Positif* in 1962, refers to the New Wave in these terms:

> I always mistrust those who display complete indifference to anything in the sphere of ideology. An inquiry in *Cahiers du cinéma* imagined that the difference between right-wing and left-wing criticism could

be removed; it would be done by "the removal of ethics to the advantage of aesthetics." . . . This is the kind of furtive hide-and-seek that eventually reveals the most treacherous characteristics of right-wing thinking. There are not many intellectuals nowadays who avouch reactionary ideology. But the subtle talkers who are deaf to their own words, the over-zealous champions of form as opposed to content . . . all unfailingly reveal a nostalgia for arbitrary power.[54]

Benayoun's critique of the New Wave is itself clearly embedded in purge rhetoric, so the concluding alignment of the New Wave with an active nostalgia for fascism rings of forced hyperbole. Nevertheless, it is during these early years of the New Wave that Truffaut can say, referring to the political beliefs of the viciously anti-Semitic critic Robert Brasillach (executed for collaboration) and the fascist author Pierre Drieu la Rochelle (who committed suicide following the Liberation), "The political ideas of Brasillach were the same as Drieu la Rochelle's; ideas which result in their authors being sentenced to death are necessarily estimable."[55]

Given the bitter aftertaste left by the arbitrary, politicized excesses of the purge itself, Truffaut's stance may be comprehensible as a well-intentioned but naïve "anti-politics" within the postwar climate characterized by the Vichy syndrome.[56] Yet the propensity for these "anti-politics" to tread reactionary territory means that they must be critiqued, not rationalized. Film historiography has mounted the beginnings of such a critique, but the impulse to qualify the New Wave's relation to conservative politics remains powerful. John Hess provides a valuable early assessment of the New Wave's "la politique des auteurs" as "justification, couched in aesthetic terms, of a culturally conservative, politically reactionary attempt to remove film from the realm of social and political concern."[57] Some of the most important recent scholarship on French cinema incorporates Hess's critical tone to a certain degree, but then finds redemptive aspects of the New Wave that soften any sustained critique. For example, Alan Williams's Republic of Images quotes Hess approvingly on his interpretation of the conservative early writings of Cahiers, but then claims his account "does rather serious violence" to the fact that the New Wave writers often championed progressive films within the journal, including those of Jean Cocteau and Max Ophuls.[58] Susan Hayward's French National Cinema stakes out the key political differences between Cahiers and Positif and usefully deflates the legendary status of the New Wave as a "misnomer made myth," but goes on to defend the New Wave as an aesthetic and technological (if not political) "counter-cinema" that paved the way for a repoliticization of French cinema in the late 1960s and 1970s.[59] Finally, Dudley Andrew's entry on Truffaut's "A Certain Tendency of the French Cinema" in *A New History of French Literature* admits that Truffaut's article "exposed the *Cahiers* revolution as one of reaction, perhaps even a revolution of the cultural right," but maintains that "regardless of the ideology of the *Cahiers* critics and filmmakers, their notions of cinematic art and of the modern world were exactly the ideas that were needed in the mid-1950s. . . . They can be said to have made possible a modern cinema no matter what sorts of films the new wave would ultimately produce."[60]

As a result of such accounts, the French New Wave continues to occupy a nearly unrivaled place of pride and affection in film history. This deep admiration for the New Wave films, however understandable and well-justified, has hindered a critical examination of their political role within French culture in the 1950s and early 1960s. This is the cultural and political context the routinely marginalized figure of Franju exists within and, as I will argue further below, interrogates; his films question the investment in "pure" and "impure" values so central to the phenomenon of the New Wave. One major reason for Franju's marginality is the same reason he is poised to perform these acts of interrogation: he has ties to both the New Wave and a concurrent, more politically engaged school of French filmmakers, the Left Bank, while never really belonging to either of these two groups.

Franju was born in 1912, making him almost twenty years older than Godard and Truffaut. The filmmakers of the Left Bank, such as Agnès Varda, Chris Marker, Alain Robbe-Grillet, Marguerite Duras, and Alain Resnais, are closer to Franju's age and share with him (perhaps with the partial exception of Varda) "an obsessional interest not only in warfare, but more generally in violence and torture, and in the lasting effects of various sorts of physical and psychological trauma."[61] Other similarities Franju shares with several members of the Left Bank include a training in documentaries before turning to features, a gravitation toward *Positif* (a haven for like-minded representatives of the French left, including Marxists and Surrealists), and a willingness to collaborate on each other's projects (Franju directed *Les Rideaux blancs* [*The White Curtains*, 1965] from a script by Duras). However, Franju's ties to the New Wave are also significant. Truffaut mentions Franju in the same breath with himself and Chabrol as men inspired to make their first features after seeing the example of Rivette's *Le Coup du berger* (*Fool's Mate*, 1956). Indeed, Truffaut interviewed Franju for *Cahiers*, and admired the director's often imitated talent: "I love the flashes of madness in Franju, and I detest the brain waves that are 'worthy of Franju.'"[62] Truffaut's admiration extended to making frequent visits to the set of *Eyes Without a Face* during the production of *The 400 Blows*—a film which Franju, in turn, told Truffaut he was "delighted with."[63] Franju's first feature, *La Tête contre les murs* (*Head Against the Wall*, 1959) displays a number of elements in keeping with the early New Wave films, including a young antihero, everyday depictions of the youth scene, and older male authority figures as victimizers. This story of a young man's forced institutionalization by his tyrannical father was one of the top ten films of 1959 according to Truffaut, Godard, Chabrol, Rivette, and other *Cahiers* critics.[64] Godard, in particular, devoted considerable praise to Franju's mission in the film: "He seeks the madness behind reality because it is for him the only way to rediscover the true face of reality behind this madness. . . . Let us say that Franju demonstrates the necessity of Surrealism if one considers it as a pilgrimage to the sources. And *La Tête contre les murs* proves that he is right."[65]

But just one year later, following the release of *Eyes Without a Face*, the *Cahiers* critics no longer seemed so sure that Franju was right. Although *Eyes Without a Face* appeared on a number of the *Cahiers* critics' top ten lists for 1960, the film does not rank with either Godard or Truffaut.[66] Franju, for his part, may have anticipated (or precipitated) some of this reaction by commenting in his 1959 interview with Truffaut, " 'The New Wave'? There's a film to make about that. I've already got the title: 'Low Tide.' "[67] But by 1962, even *Positif*, that pillar of support for the Left Bank, also describes Franju with a certain disdain: "There's something very saddening in Franju's career, and his steadily widening distance from all the hopes we placed in him, his self-burial in conventional productions, in five-finger exercises of style, and in Selected Classics."[68] So if Franju, in the final analysis, belongs fully to neither the New Wave nor the Left Bank fold, why is it important to describe the political significance of his work in relation to these two groups? If we aim to demythologize the New Wave so its cultural politics are illuminated, then one important task entails recognizing how *Cahiers* often minimizes (or effaces) the considerable political differences between the New Wave and the Left Bank in order to present the inaccurate vision of a whole, new, "pure" French cinema sanitized of politics. Some Left Bank films, most notably Resnais/Duras's landmark *Hiroshima, mon amour* (1959), lend themselves to this vision; several of Franju's films, as neither New Wave nor Left Bank cinema, resist and question it.

For example, witness how a 1959 roundtable discussion at *Cahiers* praising *Hiroshima, mon amour* transforms Resnais's feature from a political Left Bank film overtly engaged with the trauma of World War II (and with the Occupation and the purge in particular) into a film consonant with the

New Wave's apolitical tendencies. The *Cahiers* critics repeatedly minimize the film's war-related subject matter, opting instead to describe *Hiroshima* as a film that presents the atomic bomb primarily in figurative terms, unattached to any worldly events or even to time itself. For Rivette, "*Hiroshima* is a parenthesis in time . . . the passage of time is effaced because it is a parenthesis within duration."[69] And in a certain sense, Rivette is right about the film's desire to exist outside of time and history—*Hiroshima*'s emphasis on the abstract structure of memory (rather than its social and political referents) results in a film that, however sophisticated, often eludes or defeats political analysis.[70] In fact, when Godard asks whether *Hiroshima* is "a left-wing film or a right-wing film," the roundtable participants are easily able to relocate the film beyond such explicitly political terms.[71] Jean Domarchi responds to Godard by insisting that

> Resnais has gone back to the romantic theme of the conflict between the individual and society, so dear to Goethe and his imitators, as it was to the nineteenth-century English novelists. But in their works it was the conflict between a man and palpable social forms that was clearly defined, while in Resnais there is none of that. The conflict is represented in a completely abstract way; it is between man and the universe. One can then react in an extremely *tender* way towards this state of affairs. I mean that it is no longer necessary to be indignant, to protest or even to explain.[72]

Rivette replies similarly, claiming that "Resnais is able to see the modern world as it is . . . since this is the world in which we live and love, then for Resnais it is this world that is good, just and true."[73] By this point, the conversation has completely evacuated *Hiroshima* of its Left Bank political content and incorporated the film into a romantic, utopian New Wave worldview of the "good, just and true." When the Left Bank is subsumed under the New Wave in this manner, it is the very distinction between political and apolitical that threatens to vanish from sight.[74]

Of course, it is impossible not to hear the echo of André Bazin in the pronouncements of Domarchi and Rivette. Bazin's powerful critical influence over his colleagues at *Cahiers* is well-known, and his shadow must have loomed especially large during the discussion of *Hiroshima*. After all, Bazin had died only recently (on November 11, 1958) and Truffaut, although not present for the discussion, had dedicated *The 400 Blows* to his memory during that same year. This is not to say that Bazin's rich and complex body of critical work can or should be reduced to the label of "apolitical," even with regard to the specific terms of his legacy for the New

Wave critics/directors; on the contrary, it is Bazin who, during a similar *Cahiers* roundtable on French cinema in 1957, responds to Rohmer's incredible assertion that "nothing new has altered the French way of life since . . . 1930, except what reaches us from America"[75] by reminding his colleagues of "wars in Indochina or in Algeria." Still, it is also Bazin who comments during this same discussion that "for each individual [filmmaker] the key [to representing the social world] will be political or moral, while it should in fact be beyond politics and morality."[76] Bazin does not deny the significance of politics for cinema, but he does express a desire for cinema to move beyond politics. This desire for transcending the political can also be detected in some of Bazin's earlier, seminal essays on film, including "The Ontology of the Photographic Image" (1945):

> The aesthetic qualities of photography are to be sought in its power to lay bare the realities. It is not for me to separate off, in the complex fabric of the objective world, here a reflection on a damp sidewalk, there the gesture of a child. Only the impassive lens, stripping its object of all those ways of seeing it, those piled-up preconceptions, that spiritual dust and grime with which my eyes have covered it, is able to present it in all its virginal purity to my attention and consequently to my love.[77]

In this passage from Bazin we find so much that will be adapted (albeit in an often simplified form) as the ideological position of the early New Wave. Recall, for example, Truffaut's investment in formulations of French national cinema as pure and impure, or Rivette's interpretation of Resnais's modern world as "good, just and true," or even the tendency of early New Wave films such as Godard's *À Bout de souffle* (*Breathless*, 1960) and Truffaut's *The 400 Blows* (where Bazin's "gesture of a child" is fully realized) to fetishize the everyday as the "reality" that must be "laid bare," rather than the reality of political events. It is to this tendency that *Positif*'s Robert Benayoun refers when he claims the New Wave demonstrates "the ability to *see* everything without *looking* at anything."[78]

Franju, on the other hand, demands a mode of perception based on the interdependence of "seeing" and "looking." In this sense, Franju's vision once again proves itself closer to the film theory of Kracauer than that of Bazin and the New Wave. When Kracauer describes "the turn to photography" in a 1927 essay as "the *go-for-broke game* of history," where photographs intertwine the risks of eradicating historical consciousness along with the benefits of emancipating historical consciousness, he develops a different schema than the one constructed later by Bazin in "The Ontology of the Photographic Image."[79] Bazin values the photograph for its ability to remythologize the external world, to restore its state of "virginal purity" after being soiled by the experience of the perceiver—the contaminating experience, in other words, of history. For Kracauer, photographs contain the potential to demythologize the external world and force a shocking recognition of this world as shaped by the currents of history. Although Kracauer will later bestow the rather Bazinian (and somewhat misleading) subtitle "the redemption of physical reality" on his own book *Theory of Film*, the two theorists ultimately present very different versions of redeeming the real. Bazin's redemption reclaims the pure and the virginal in the name of love, while Kracauer's redemption captures the reflection of Medusa in Perseus's shield—the real face of things too dreadful to be beheld in reality."[80] Kracauer, like Franju, believes in cinema as a means of reckoning with the horrible, the ugly, the painful, and the impure. This is, inevitably, the real of history, politics, and traumatic events, while Bazin's real is just as inevitably contingent on suspending precisely these elements so that purity might be regained.

By aligning Franju with a political, historical "impurity" connected to Kracauer's film theory, Benjamin's dialectical optics, and Bataille's Surrealism, I mean to underline his differences from the ahistorical aspects of Bazin's film theory, the most romantic components of Breton's Surrealism, and the passion for "purity" espoused by Truffaut and the New Wave in the cause of remaking French national cinema. I have traced the cultural and political implications of these differences through a number of issues constitutive of the Vichy syndrome, but the significance of these differences extend to other cultural discourses central to France's identity in the 1950s and early 1960s—namely, capitalist modernization and the decolonization of Algeria. To continue examining how Franju addresses these discourses in a manner resistant to the New Wave, we must study *Eyes Without a Face*.

EYES WITHOUT A FACE AND THE 400 BLOWS: OF MODERNIZATION AND THE ALGERIAN WAR

Eyes Without a Face tells the lurid tale of Dr. Genessier (Pierre Brasseur), a plastic surgeon driven to remove facial tissue from young female victims in order to restore the disfigured face of his daughter, Christiane (Edith Scob); Genessier himself ruined Christian's face in a car accident. The grafting attempts continually fail, the corpses multiply, and Christiane's resentment builds until she unleashes her murderous rage on her father and his assistant/mistress, Louise (Alida Valli). The film begins with a haunting title sequence, where Maurice Jarre's lurching score, suggestive of a dark carnival, accompanies tracking shots taken from a car at night. But we do not see the road, only the eerie outlines of trees overhead, illuminated momentarily. After the titles end, we join a woman who is driving at night. She appears nervous and apprehensive. A shot from the car's backseat, facing forward toward the driver, implies the woman may not be alone in the car. And indeed, she soon adjusts her rearview mirror to reveal a mysterious figure in the backseat. The figure, completely covered by a hat and jacket, veers precariously with the car's motion as if asleep. After hurriedly pulling aside so a truck can pass (was it following her?), the woman drives onward but eventually parks beside a river. There, she labors to remove the lifeless body from the backseat and dump it into the water. We later learn that the driver is Genessier's assistant/mistress and that the body is that of Simone Tessot, one of the surgeon's skin graft victims.

Given the previously mentioned fact that the production of *Eyes Without a Face* overlaps with that of *The 400 Blows* and that Truffaut frequently visited Franju's set, it is striking to note both the similarities and key differences between the openings of the two films. Truffaut's film, like Franju's, begins with a title sequence composed of tracking shots taken from a car. But in *The 400 Blows*, the shots occur during the day and forgo the disorienting, placeless motion of *Eyes Without a Face* in favor of more coherent, easily processed movement—each tracking shot features a different view of the same object, the Eiffel Tower. Jean Constantin's score, unlike Maurice Jarre's, is spare, soothing, and almost playful. Truffaut's first sequence after the titles preserves the sense of motion as a positive, familiar, and hopeful force. Young boys clandestinely pass around a female pinup during a class exam. Even when the pinup's quick circulation around the classroom is halted abruptly when the teacher demands that Antoine Doinel (Jean-Pierre Léaud) surrender it to him, Antoine's movement (as well as the camera's, not yet cutting away from the sequence's opening shot) continues. He proceeds to the front of the room and behind a small blackboard, where he has been sent as punishment, but still manages to make a face behind the teacher's back that draws laughter from his classmates. Again, Antoine is punished by an attempt to have his movement curtailed (he is forbidden from attending recess), but again, he regains the power of motion—he tosses an eraser, then scratches an angry ode to the teacher on the wall, which promises "it'll be an eye for an eye, a tooth for a tooth."

While Franju presents mobility as darkness, dread, and death, Truffaut presents it as the irrepressible energy of individual (and, via the icon of the Eiffel Tower, national) freedom. The difference is telling when placed in relation to what Kristin Ross describes as one of the central cultural fantasies in France during the 1950s and early 1960s: that the rapid capitalist modernization then shaping the postwar nation promised "timeless, even, and limitless development" that would permit "everyday life" to supersede the "eventfulness" of historical crises such as the Algerian War. According to Ross, "the arrival of the new consumer durables into French life—the repetitive, daily practices and new mediations they brought into being—helped create a break with the eventfulness of the past, or better, helped situate the temporality of the event itself as a thing of the past."[81] Modernization's focus on the daily practices of "everyday life" corresponds to a cultural shift toward privatization, toward the "withdrawal of the new middle classes to their newly comfortable domestic interiors, to the electric kitchens, to the enclosure of private automobiles . . . and to depoliticization as a response to the increase in bureaucratic control of daily life."[82]

The automobile, as Ross demonstrates, is crucial to this process of modernization as privatization and depoliticization. The newly accessible (for the middle class) experience of driving a car was incessantly described and advertised through a discourse "built around freezing time in the form of reconciling past and future, the old ways and the new."[83] The car was presented as the agent of "timeless" modernization's triumph over the historical time of the event. So pervasive and exhilarating was this discourse of auto-mated modernization that those who feared or fought its progress were sometimes perceived as backward, as antimodern. For example, witness the New Wave's response to French political and industrial rhetoric of the 1950s that often valorized antimodernization as a defense of the nation's "quality,"[84] of an age-old French national essence perceived as disappearing with the onset of modernization's Americanized mass-production techniques; this antimodern (or at least anti-standardization) discourse of "quality" would come to be opposed, to a certain extent, by the discourse of the "new wave" that was originally coined in 1958 to refer to a "modern" urban youth culture in France. It is no surprise that in 1954, while Truffaut was busy imagining the film movement that would later inherit the title of "New Wave," he chose to describe the New Wave's enemy as the "Tradition of Quality." When Truffaut condemns the Tradition of Quality, he is, in large part, condemning what he sees as antimodern French cinema, with its ties to an impossibly outdated conception of "Frenchness." But rather than questioning the construction of "Frenchness" itself, Truffaut finally advocates the substitution of a modern, New Wave national essence for the Tradition of Quality's antimodern national essence. Consequently, Truffaut and the New Wave will embrace the forces of modernization (if not always Americanization) with a rather uncritical enthusiasm that, while effective in terms of demolishing the dominance of the Tradition of Quality, ultimately elides the problems that modernization poses for politics, history, and the construction of national identity. In other words, there is a price to be paid for the New Wave's exciting role as a modern cinema of the private car, liberating motion, and the "timelessness" of everyday life.

The 400 Blows crystallizes the New Wave's embrace of a privatized, depoliticized, and "timeless" version of modernization. The emphasis on motion as freedom in the film's opening sequences continues throughout the film as a whole. For example, the one truly happy moment that Antoine experiences with his troubled family transpires inside the car, as they drive home from a night at the movies. The family's ability to laugh with and genuinely enjoy each other in this instant grants the car an almost magical aura—it is an idealized home in motion rather than the cramped, unhappy quarters of their actual apartment. Although his parents also indulge in forms of mobility that are potentially upsetting and alienating to Antoine (his father is always preoccupied with his auto club, while his mother uses her time outside the home to pursue extramarital affairs), it is Antoine who ultimately has the last laugh. He steals his father's beloved Guide Michelin (a testament to auto-mobility), thus pulling the strings of both his parents—his father suspects the mother of losing the guide, and his mother denies this accusation so defensively that we suspect she may well have lost it while traveling with a lover. Only later in the film do we see Antoine, the true master of mobility, using the Guide Michelin as raw material for spitballs.[85]

Similarly, Antoine's precious experiences of freedom are often portrayed as literal movement: his thrilling ride on the Rotor at an amusement park, his sly departure from a gym teacher's jogging class, and his escape from a harsh reformatory at the film's conclusion. (See fig. 1.2.) Each of these sequences acquires additional energy and endorsement within the film by pairing Antoine's movement with the camera's movement (spinning point-of-view shots from inside the Rotor, a breathtaking aerial perspective of the gym class, and long, uninterrupted tracking shots following Antoine's flight from the reformatory). Of course, the film's famous final shot, a freeze frame on Antoine with the ocean behind him, appears to represent mobility ambivalently; indeed, this shot is commonly referred to as an example of the art cinema's penchant for narrative ambiguity. On the one hand, this shot arrests Antoine's movement, abruptly halting his thrilling escape to the sea in a manner that may recall the images of imprisonment that recur throughout the film (Antoine's ride in a paddy wagon, for instance, can be seen as the imprisoning antithesis of the liberating ride in the family car).[86] On the other hand, the freeze frame can be seen as *protecting* Antoine from future imprisonment, allowing him to remain instead within a timeless moment of freedom through one last act of cinematic modernization. Cinema's ability to freeze time means that Antoine's ultimate triumph of movement—he has finally reached his long-desired destination of the sea—can be permanent, rather than fleeting. At last, history no longer intrudes.[87]

In *Eyes Without a Face*, however, history forms a prison from which modernization offers no real escape. While Truffaut highlights the "timeless," emancipating power of modernized movement, Franju reckons with the darker aspects of modernization as technologized mobility. The film's murderous narrative originates in a disastrous car *accident*, and it is this accident's ghostly legacy that haunts so much of the rest of the film. For example, Louise's drive in the film's opening sequence includes not only a potential accident of its own (the passing truck) but yet another maimed young woman who has died standing in for (and will later be falsely identified as) Christiane. Similarly, when Louise later drives another prospective victim, Edna Grüberg (Juliette Mayniel), to Genessier's house under the pretense of showing her an apartment for rent, the trip itself becomes long and vaguely menacing. By the time Louise and Edna reach a railroad crossing where they must stop for a passing train, Edna clearly feels trapped by a situation that on the surface offered only the liberating possibilities of modern mobility (a free car ride, a dream apartment with easy access to the passing train that Louise assures Edna will take her to Paris "in less than twenty minutes"). For Edna, mobility's promise ends in death, not freedom. As in *Blood of the Beasts*, the train is one of several war-related emblems of modernity's poisoned technological "progress" that appear prominently in the film. The noisy intrusions of yet another train following Genessier's identification of "Christiane" (actually Simone Tessot, one of his surgical failures) at the morgue, and an airplane during the illicit burial of Edna Grüberg in Christiane's false tomb, seem remarkably deliberate and disruptive. In the latter sequence, a distressed Louise shields her ears from a linked chain of assaultive sounds: Genessier's pick clanging against the tomb gate, the airplane passing overhead, a tolling church bell, and the dull thud of the dumped corpse. Louise's anguished reaction underlines the horror of disillusionment that binds these sounds together. Loss of faith in the values of medicine (Genessier), the progress of technology (airplane), and the comfort of religion (church bell) leaves only the terrifying materiality of the corpse.

FIGURE 1.2 *The 400 Blows* (François Truffaut, 1959): Antoine Doinel (Jean-Pierre Léaud) prepares to flee the prison of history. (Courtesy of Jerry Ohlinger's Movie Material)

Even at the conclusion of *Eyes Without a Face*, when Christiane gains control of the power of movement to free a potential skin graft victim, stab Louise, and unleash the dogs that have endured Genessier's awful experiments, any sense of true liberation is tainted. First of all, the fact that the dogs use their freedom to maul Genessier with ferocious savagery provides precious little satisfaction; Franju films Genessier's death with such chilling attention to the grim details of being eaten alive that we lose much of our sympathy for the dogs and develop a higher degree of compassion for the surgeon. Second, Christiane herself, although possessed of a certain macabre beauty that is enhanced by framing her with the doves she has uncaged, lacks the sense of accomplishment in mobility that characterizes Antoine at the conclusion of *The 400 Blows*. Antoine, having reached his goal of the sea, turns toward the audience to share his surprise and success—this is the image Truffaut freezes forever. *Eyes Without a Face* ends with Christiane walking *away* from the audience, disappearing into the night while still wearing the expressionless mask that hides her ruined face. When the screen fades to black, there is no sense of cure or resolution for Christiane. Her face remains the same and functions as an undeniable reminder that her features will never truly be her own, that she must always (as she says herself) "live for the others" who have died during the attempts to restore her face. Christiane discovers no source of mobility that will allow her to escape the burden of history and its demand that she live with the dead, that she see them every time she looks into her own face.

But who exactly are the dead that Christiane and, by extension, the audience of *Eyes Without a Face* must recognize? On one level, Christiane and the other horribly mutilated young women clearly evoke the victims of Nazi medical experiments conducted in concentration camps, just as Genessier's practices portray him as a Joseph Mengele-like figure. Christiane refers to herself as a "human guinea pig," and one scene even depicts Genessier leading a German shepherd into his medical compound where many scarred dogs are caged, awaiting further experimental surgery. The dogs, and this German shepherd in particular, are icons of both the Occupation and the Holocaust. Their insistent barking, which permeates much of the film's sound track, is both the pitiful cry of imprisoned victims as well as the threatening sound, heard so often during the Occupation, of the animals belonging to the police and the Nazis. When the dogs respond gently and lovingly to Christiane's affection, they seem to share in common her status as a victim of Genessier. But when they tear Genessier apart during the film's climax, the dogs remind us of their potential for the terrifying violence enforced by the Nazis.

Similarly, the roles of Christiane as victimized and Genessier as victimizer include complex, double-edged connotations. Although we pity and sympathize with Christiane for her wounds and her imprisonment, she tacitly condones the deaths of the young women sacrificed for her benefit and eventually becomes a murderer herself, killing Louise directly and her father indirectly. And Genessier, monstrous in so many ways, is also granted brief but significant moments of humanity. In a sequence that recalls some of Mengele's most infamous crimes, the experiments that attempted to change the eye color of children but resulted only in blindness, Genessier visits with one of his patients, a young boy recovering from recent surgery. When Genessier gauges the boy's progress by testing his eyesight, the boy fails to identify how many fingers Genessier holds up to him. Although Genessier, like Mengele, is responsible for this child's ruined vision, Genessier is visibly moved by this failure—it is an operation, like all of the surgeon's operations (no matter how misguided or unethical) and unlike Mengele's experiments, intended to heal rather than to harm. Part of Genessier's monstrousness stems from his inability to deal with the failure of his intentions, and indeed he lies to the boy's mother by telling her he has "high hopes" for her son's recovery. But the brief glimpse of anguish in Genessier's eyes when he realizes he has failed also occurs when he discovers the first signs of disintegration in one of Christiane's initially successful skin grafts. It is a look that conveys, despite all the surrounding condescension and deadly narcissism, real concern and vulnerability.

Franju's refusal in *Eyes Without a Face* to provide any easy, one-to-one index for his allegories of the Occupation and the Holocaust reflects a commitment to engaging history as a complicated force to be struggled with by the audience, rather than spoon-fed to them. This commitment extends to a willingness to intertwine the traumatic history of World War II with the contemporary history of the Algerian War. Christiane's fate in *Eyes Without a Face*, to recognize both herself and the dead she is responsible for in her own disfigured face, echoes the words Jean-Paul Sartre writes in 1958: "During the war . . . we watched the German soldiers walking inoffensively down the street, and would say to ourselves: 'They look like us. How can they act as they do?' And we were proud of ourselves for not understanding. . . . But now when we raise our heads and look into the mirror we see an unfamiliar and hideous reflection: ourselves."[88] The context of "now" to which Sartre refers is the context of the Algerian War, the bloody colonial conflict that rages between 1954 and 1962. By the time Algeria finally wins its independence, this war of "shattering divisiveness" has "on more than one occasion" threatened France with "civil war."[89] Because the Algerian War goes to the very heart of French national identity (a common slogan of the late 1950s was "No more French Algeria, no more France"),[90] it makes sense that it was understood at the time through the lens of that other recent battleground for French identity, the Occupation.[91] *Eyes Without a Face* enacts this connection by blending the iconography of World War II with the iconography of torture so central to French public perception of the Algerian War.

In his introduction to Henri Alleg's *La Question* (*The Question*, 1958), a harrowing autobiographical account of torture experienced at the hands of the French military in Algeria, Sartre warns that "one would not advise" Alleg's book "for weak stomachs."[92] The same could be said of *Eyes Without a Face*, and indeed, many of the tortures Alleg describes are mirrored by allegorical representations in the film, including burns, electric shock, and drowning. When Alleg recounts his torture by drowning, where his face is forced underwater while wrapped in a rag,[93] the imagery parallels the depictions of Genessier's surgical failures: Edna, her postoperative face wrapped completely in bandages; and Simone, her corpse reported by police as submerged underwater for ten days. The specter of electric shock surfaces during an electric scanning procedure performed in Genessier's hospital on Paulette Mérodon (Béatrice Altariba), a young woman whom we know Genessier is sizing up for a skin graft operation. The scanning procedure does in fact deliver a mild electric shock, but is ultimately harmless. However, our knowledge of the awful surgery to come (Genessier supervises Paulette's test personally) grants the procedure distinct overtones of torture (fig. 1.3). Although the burns Alleg suffers do not extend to his face, burns to the face were commonly reported by victims of torture in Algeria.[94] When Franju confronts us with an image of Christiane's unmasked face, it is revealed as a mass of burned and torn flesh. To be "without a face," the film seems to insist, is to acquire the face of traumatic history.

If *Eyes Without a Face* is capable, as I am arguing, of staging a reckoning with traumatic history, why does it resort to allegorical modes of representation to accomplish this? Part of the answer rests with censorship. During the years of the Algerian War, and particularly during the late 1950s and early 1960s, the French government exercised strict censorship policies with regard to the war's coverage. Articles and books critical of the war or reporting acts of torture might be published, but were often seized and banned shortly after publication—this was the fate of *The Question*. Films were also subject to censorship, resulting in many directors deliberately avoiding the subject of Algeria. Those who did not, even when they refrained from critiquing the government directly, could see their film banned.[95] Franju also complained that his producers attempted to curtail his vision of the film, but for rather different reasons: "When I shot *Eyes Without a Face* I was told: 'No sacrilege because of the Spanish market, no nudes because of the Italian market, no blood because of the French market, and no martyrized animals because of the English market.' And I was supposed to be making a horror film!"[96] To fully understand how Franju overcomes these two different kinds of censorship in *Eyes Without a Face* by employing an aesthetic of allegorical shock, it is necessary to revisit the crossroads of horror and Surrealism.

THE GRAND GUIGNOL APPROACH TO HISTORY

André Breton once described Surrealism as the "prehensile tail" of Romanticism,[97] but before Breton bestowed this title upon his own movement, it surely belonged to the Gothic novel. Breton even mentions M. G. Lewis's early Gothic horror sensation *The Monk* (1796) in the first Surrealist mani-

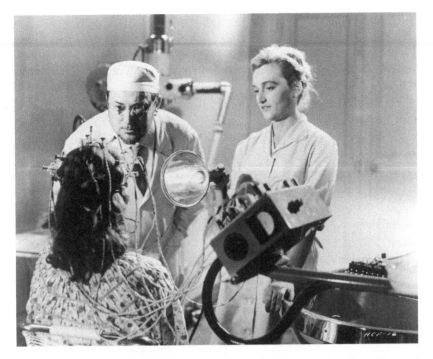

FIGURE 1.3 *Eyes Without a Face* (Georges Franju, 1960): Dr. Genessier (Pierre Brasseur) evokes shadows of torture and the Algerian War. (Courtesy of Photofest)

festo as embodying "an unforgettable intensity" where "there is no longer anything fantastic; there is only the real."[98]

The Gothic novel, with its original incarnation in Horace Walpole's *The Castle of Otranto* (1764), represented a particularly dark strain of Romanticism that intervened in eighteenth-century Enlightenment discourse in a manner not unlike Surrealism's confrontation with modernity.[99] Surrealism's response to the crisis of World War I is prefigured by the Gothic's delayed development after *Otranto*; all of the subsequent major Gothic texts appear *after* the French Revolution.[100] Gothic reacts to the need for an "aesthetics of embodiment" in the wake of the revolution's painful paradox: Rousseau's newly conceived "individual" comes to prominence as an autonomous, empowered body, but is simultaneously exposed as frail and vulnerable in the face of brutal state terror.[101] Michel Foucault also dates the birth of modern medical rationality to this historical moment, as clinical experience demarcates "as its field of origin and of manifestation of truth the discursive space of the corpse: the interior revealed."[102]

Gothic engages and contests these bodily discourses through a fascination with the violently ruptured body, and its status as a crucial site of personal and political meaning. In this sense, Gothic looks ahead to Surrealism, and beyond to the modern horror film. In Franju, the points on this trajectory converge.

Eyes Without a Face also owes a significant debt to the stage of the Théâtre du Grand Guignol. The Grand Guignol, a French theatrical phenomenon running from 1897 to 1962, featured the unflinchingly graphic depiction of sensational acts of violence. Stabbings, burnings, beheadings, dismemberments, and all other manner of carnage occurred onstage in vivid detail. Its variety format interspersed comedies, dramas, and slapstick with horror, but its primary progenitors were gory newspaper items chronicling true-life crime (the *faits divers*) and the naturalist theater of the late 1880s. Oscar Méténier, founder of the Grand Guignol, polished his playwrighting skills with the Théâtre Libre, a company that modeled itself on Emile Zola's "scientific" theater and its concern with the "methodical analysis of human behavior, heredity, and environment."[103] Naturalist realism reaches its extremes with the Grand Guignol, a theater where scientific objectivity ultimately implodes in much the same manner as in *Blood of the Beasts*. Given this connection, it is not surprising to find that Jean Redon's novel, *Eyes Without a Face* (the source for Franju's film), was also adapted for the Grand Guignol stage.

Eyes Without a Face seems tailor-made for Grand Guignol performance. Its motifs of bloody revenge, familial disintegration, and science gone awry closely resemble the plays authored by the Grand Guignol's most prolific writer, André de Lorde. De Lorde, the "Prince of Terror" who contributed over one hundred plays to the Grand Guignol between 1901 and 1926, was the son of a physician. His father, wishing "to convince his son, once and for all, not to be afraid of death or pain," forced the child to keep watch over his dead grandmother the night before her funeral. De Lorde, far from overcoming his fears, was traumatized by the event.[104] This anecdote lends a certain biographical resonance to de Lorde's challenge to the authority of rational clinical experience. The Grand Guignol adheres so literally to the logic of the penetrating clinical gaze that the power of this gaze crumbles amidst its faithful embodiment. As Tom Gunning observes, Foucault's clinical eye searches for higher truth within the body's interior, while de Lorde's plays reveal "not moral truth, but . . . corpse[s], madness, and speechlessness."[105]

Gunning, who argues cogently for the placement of the Grand Guignol within a melodramatic trajectory that stretches back to the Gothic and forward to the horror film, claims that de Lorde's horror ultimately represents "nothing beyond itself, except the *frisson*, the shudder, the knot in the pit of the stomach, the sensation experienced by the spectator" and "affirms itself as a terminus, a barrier with no beyond."[106] Gunning makes this claim in order to highlight the presence of *sensation* in a melodramatic tradition Peter Brooks characterizes chiefly by a "moral occult" dimension, or hidden significance of virtue.[107] I wish to extend Gunning's intervention and his emphasis on the visceral address of the spectator by suggesting there exists a significant "beyond" to de Lorde's horror that does not necessarily fall within the moral occult or pure sensation categories: the restoration of visceral yet politically engaged affect to public historical trauma.

Gunning's account of de Lorde's *L'Acquittée* (1919) notes its invocation of the landmark Jeanne Weber scandal in France that "shook public faith in legal and medical discourse."[108] Weber was acquitted twice of strangling infants in 1905 and 1906, then finally convicted in 1908 for attempting another infanticide. De Lorde does not tack on a moral resolution to this public trauma, but instead reenacts the event. The play concludes with a doctor and magistrate placing the Weber figure in a hypnotic trance. Although she then displays her guilt by performing the infanticides she has committed, this does not qualify as legal evidence and she walks away free.

I would argue that the horror of this spectacle, rather than being a dramatic dead end terminating only in sensation, returns personal and political audience affect to a traumatic public event—the kind of event subjected to the widespread exposure that threatens to overwhelm any meaningful response. At least for one charged moment, the spectators of *L'Acquittée* can reconnect their aroused senses and political sensibilities to a scandal anesthetized by overwhelming hype in its public incarnation. One should note that Weber's third trial coincided with a heated national debate over the death penalty, and that the case provided "excellent copy" for a French press eager to feed the fires of public hysteria over the issue.[109] At the time, noted French novelist and historian Paul Margueritte blamed sensationalist press coverage of the type lavished on the Weber case for influencing the legislative decision to retain the death penalty: "The yellow press, with its enormous headlines and its portraits of killers, the press blaring the most recent crimes to the four corners of the world in the voices of a thousand trumpets, . . . the press, I tell you, has inflamed public opinion and burdened the thoughts of our legislators."[110] In some plays of the Grand Guignol, cultural trauma viscerally reenters personal and political consciousness reinvested with an immediacy that may have slipped away from it through the abstractions of public dissemination.

This return of history through the gut seems echoed in de Lorde's own description of terror—it is ultimately "addressed less to the nerves than to the understanding."[III]

The scenes in Franju's *Eyes Without a Face* most directly indebted to the Grand Guignol enact this restoration of visceral political affect to public history. In the film's most infamous sequence, Genessier and his assistant Louise perform the surgical removal of young Edna Grüberg's face, while Christiane lies unconscious on an adjoining table. Franju again invokes the science film by dwelling on the clinical details of the procedure: the powerful surgical lamps, the adjustment of the gloves and masks, the metallic sheen of the operating tables, the sleek shape of the scalpel. The stony silence and methodical execution of the sequence greatly accentuates its horror. Franju first details the preliminary tracing of the scalpel's path in marker, and then the actual slicing of the skin. He inserts many shots displaying the sweat on Genessier's brow, the exchange of instruments and glances between himself and Louise, and the orientation of characters around the operating table. By the time the scene climaxes with a grisly close-up of the complete removal (in a single fleshy strip) of the facial skin, the spectator squirms from the sheer perceived duration of this ordeal. Shocking spectacles like this one reportedly caused seven people to faint during the screening of *Eyes Without a Face* at the Edinburgh Film Festival, a feat that would have made André de Lorde proud.[112] But Franju's "torture" of the audience during this scene is inseparable from an allegorical, politically charged iconography of torture that invites the connection of private affect with public history. Franju's spectacle ultimately combats what Simone de Beauvoir called, in December 1961, "a sort of tetanus of the imagination" that had set in for those French citizens politically committed to ending the Algerian War. For de Beauvoir, this "tetanus of the imagination" is "the final stage of demoralization for a nation: one gets used to it. But in 1957, the broken bones, the burns on the face, on the genitals, the torn-out nails, the impalements, the convulsions, they reached me, all right."[113] In *Eyes Without a Face*, this pain lives again through the mode of allegorical representation—a mode that holds out the promise of shock, of bursting through an audience's "tetanus of the imagination." (See fig. 1.4.)

As I noted earlier, Benjamin's conception of a Surrealist dialectical optics relies on shock to provide the necessary "profane illumination" of modern history. The interplay of shocks and countershocks could be described as a homeopathic enterprise, and indeed, Franju calls his films "horror in homeopathic doses."[114] As Eric L. Santner explains,

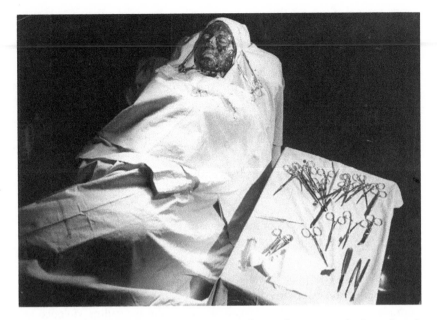

FIGURE 1.4 *Eyes Without a Face* (Georges Franju, 1960): Grisly operations that burst through the audience's "tetanus of the imagination." (Courtesy of Photofest)

In a homeopathic procedure the controlled introduction of a negative element—a symbolic, or in medical contexts, real poison—helps to heal a system infected by a similar poisonous substance. The poison becomes a cure by empowering the individual to master the potentially traumatic effects of large doses of the morphologically related poison.[115]

Santner theorizes Freud's famous *fort/da* episode from *Beyond the Pleasure Principle* (1920) as an instance of homeopathy. Freud describes a game played by his grandson with a reel of string that accustoms the child to his mother's unpleasurable absence. The child tosses the spool out of sight with an "expressive" utterance of "o-o-o-o" (interpreted as *"fort"* or gone) and then reels it back into view with a "joyful *'da'* (there)."[116] This game simulates the mother's departure and return in a homeopathic attempt to master the traumatic event.

Benjamin's homeopathic formulation of shock also draws on Freud's *Beyond the Pleasure Principle*, and he mirrors the ambivalence inherent in Freud's notion of "mastering" trauma—itself drawn from Freud's experience with shell-shocked soldiers during World War I. The centrality of *repetition* to both Benjamin and Freud—shocks remedied by counter-shocks, traumatic loss treated by simulated loss—underlines the vexed nature of the homeopathic project. The danger of parrying shocks with countershocks symbolically parallels the risk of homeopathy: too little of the reintroduced poison permits the spread of infection, while too much results in death. In fact, there is a "strangely intimate" relation between Freud's mastery instinct, which emphasizes the active mastery of trauma through the repetition of unpleasure, and the death drive, which manifests itself as the passive "compulsion to repeat experiences of an overwhelming and incapacitating sort."[117] The allegorical moment's redemptive potential exists in this volatile participation with the very poisons it could work to dissipate.

Benjamin reminds us that the allegorical moment is also always a "moment of danger" prone to potentially dangerous transformations and appropriations.[118] The allegorical encounter with historical trauma entails an opening out to complex and often contradictory representations, where unexpected recombinations and disfigurements of history can occur. For example, *Eyes Without a Face* largely displaces the masculine violence associated with war onto a network of violence exchanged between women. This network consists of Louise as stalker, caretaker, and disposer of young female victims; Christiane, as receiver of their sacrificed skin; and finally, a transformed Christiane as their savior and avenger. At the film's conclusion, when Christiane frees Paulette and kills Louise, she completes this circuit of violence. By stabbing Louise in the neck with a scalpel, she enacts her father while excluding him from the feminine circuit of exchange. Christiane's action reverses her father's surgical restoration of Louise's face (her neck bears the scar of this operation), and severs the tie that binds Louise to her father. The replacement of the bond between Louise and Genessier with a link between Louise and Christiane is also carried out at the level of the film's sound track. Maurice Jarre's score has two main themes—one associated with Louise, the other with Christiane. In the film's final sequence, as Christiane walks out alone into the night and past her father's corpse, her gentle theme combines with the more ominous tones of Louise's.

Though Genessier's shadow certainly haunts this feminine network, he stands outside its register of spectacle for most of the film; only women carry the wounds that shock our sensibilities. Genessier himself enters the economy of the spectacle only at the price of his life, as the unleashed dogs rip away his face. He is emasculated during this gory death, in the sense that he comes to resemble his faceless female victims. But why this insistent displacement of warfare's wounds and scarring from the masculine to the feminine? One possible answer lies at the heart of traumatic repetition: revenge. Freud notes that the active manipulation of maternal disappearance and reappearance in the *fort/da* game allows the child to defiantly "revenge himself on his mother for going away from him." The child says, "'All right, then, go away! I don't need you. I'm sending you away myself.'"[119] By the same token, representing women as the agents and casualties of violence in *Eyes Without a Face* exacts metaphorical revenge for female absence from the front, as well as for female failure to substantiate the national fantasy of women as warfare's "symbolic stakes, what war was fought for."[120]

This national fantasy of the feminine resonates powerfully with French cultural discourse surrounding the Occupation and the purge, where France's "feminized" position of defeat is often remasculinized by punishing those perceived as responsible for this disastrous "feminization." Noteworthy examples include the *tonte*, those incidents where French women suspected of having slept with the enemy during the Occupation were subjected to humiliating public head shavings (depicted in *Hiroshima, mon amour*), and the Occupation-era writings of collaborator Robert Brasillach that condemned him to death during the purge. It was not Brasillach's anti-Semitism that was most damning to him during his trial, but his "avowal of having given in to irrational sexual political feelings about Germany"—feelings likely perceived by his accusers as tinged with homosexuality.[121] The occurrence of rape and genital mutilation (of both men and women) as torture techniques practiced by the French military during the Algerian War seems similarly tied to a symbolic, remasculinizing discourse of punishment for "feminized" betrayal during wartime.[122]

Another possible reason for the displacement of violence from the masculine to the feminine in *Eyes Without a Face* has more to do with an evasion of threatening mortality. Elisabeth Bronfen notes that death and the feminine body share a cultural value as "superlative site[s] of alterity":

> Over representations of the dead [or wounded] feminine body, culture can repress and articulate its unconscious knowledge of death. . . . There is death, but it is not my own. The aesthetic representation of death lets us repress our knowledge of the reality of death precisely because here death occurs *at* someone else's body and *as* an image.[123]

According to Bronfen, the otherness of the feminine body allows death to be kept at a safe distance from "the masculine artist and the community of survivors"; "even as we are forced to acknowledge the ubiquitous presence of death in life, our belief in our own immortality is confirmed."[124] *Eyes Without a Face* both participates with and questions this othering of the feminine body in the cause of confirming male immortality. Genessier cannot bear the sight of Christiane's burned face or Louise's scarred neckline, so he hides the first behind a delicate white mask and the second behind a pearl necklace. These exaggerated signs of ideal femininity compensate for anxiety about the proximity of femininity and death, which always threatens to undermine Genessier's illusory masculine authority over immortality (he is, after all, a celebrated plastic surgeon).

Eyes Without a Face powerfully conveys the struggle between registers of mortal feminine spectacle and masculine clinical authority through a sequence of stills that detail the gradual infection of Christiane's initially successful skin graft. While Genessier's distant, rational voice-over narrates dates and clinical descriptions of the developing damage ("spots of pigmentation," "sub-cutaneous nodules," "ulcerations"), the progression of the photographs brings Christiane closer and closer to resembling her disfigured self, as well as the skinned faces of those victims who have died for her. Genessier's narration concludes with the statement that the infected graft must finally be removed, but there is no accompanying photograph to illustrate this statement. The chain of signification disintegrates as the spectacle of feminine mortality overwhelms rational masculine distance from death. On the one hand, the absence of the final photograph fetishistically preserves the illusion of masculine wholeness and immortality. But on the other hand, the abrupt breakdown of the clinical masculine discourse of visibility betrays an inability to conceal successfully the wounded feminine body behind false masks acquired by modern technological expertise. In fact, the only time we fully glimpse Christiane's ruined face is through the eyes of another woman, when Edna Grüberg is granted a point-of-view shot as an unmasked Christiane stands over her.

Franju's own experience during the Occupation may inform the decidedly double-edged treatment of historical trauma during the allegorical moments of *Eyes Without a Face*. The specter of collaboration haunts the partnership of Franju and Henri Langlois with a German army and government official, Frank Hensel, that kept alive the Fédération Internationale des Archives du Film (FIAF) during the Occupation. Although Franju describes Hensel as an extraordinary man who usually aided him and Langlois in their valiant attempts to preserve films during Nazi raids, the director seems aware of the need to acknowledge the moral dilemmas of this alliance: "It would have been so much easier for me to leave FIAF, to go underground, but I think I did more for France where I was."[125] Franju also grew painfully aware of the blind spots in his own leftist, Popular Front ideological stance preceding the war: "During the Popular Front, we voted against a war or defense budget. Later I realized we had been stupid. The Right is hateful, but it was they who were correct [in advocating war] and we who were wrong. They saw clearly."[126] Such experiences may inflect the anguished tone of *Eyes Without a Face*, where even a shocking reckoning with history cannot dissipate a lingering sense of unresolved conflict, even madness.

In a curious instance of the return of the repressed, *Eyes Without a Face* has recently exacted a bit of its own revenge on the critical establishment that largely reviled it upon its initial release. *Sight and Sound*, part of the British press that originally gave the film a "unanimously shocked, or contemptuous" reception, ran a feature story on the film's international rerelease in 1995.[127] Franju's film, which departed in so many significant ways from the emergent national cinema of the French New Wave at the time, now fits rather majestically into a very different cinematic context: the modern horror film.[128] *Eyes Without a Face* has finally begun to take its place alongside Alfred Hitchcock's *Psycho* (1960) and Michael Powell's *Peeping Tom* (1960) as the early, influential breakthroughs that opened the doors of modern cinematic horror. *Eyes Without a Face* in particular points the way toward the genre's complex engagement with "splatter" or "gross-out" visual effects.[129] In an era when many observers dismiss splatter as the last gasps of the newest *Halloween* (John Carpenter, 1978) or *Friday the 13th* (Sean Cunningham, 1980) slasher series entry (or knowing parodies of them), it is important to recall Franju's pioneering work as an example of the form's potential. Franju's films remind us that splatter does not preclude (and may sometimes even encourage) an allegorical confrontation with the historical trauma of modernity.

"DIRECT EMOTIONAL REALISM"

The People's War, Classlessness, and Michael Powell's *Peeping Tom*

Isabel Quigly, film critic for the British magazine *The Spectator*, had disposed of Georges Franju's *Eyes Without a Face* in February 1960 with two sentences: "*Eyes Without a Face* gets my prize as the sickest film since I started film criticism. Sad to see Alida Valli mixed up in it; or Pierre Brasseur either, though his deadpan manner is better suited to necromancy and surgical horror than her subtle and nervous expressiveness."[1] But in April, with the release of Michael Powell's *Peeping Tom*, she revises her earlier judgment:

> [*Peeping Tom*] turns out to be the sickest and filthiest film I remember seeing. Some weeks ago we had Franju's *Eyes Without a Face*, which I thought set a record for highbrow horrors. It was perhaps more directly ghastly—there were worse visual horrors (the operating scenes)—but it didn't involve you, it made little attempt at direct emotional realism, as *Peeping Tom* does; you had the creeps, but

remotely, and often with amusement. *Peeping Tom* didn't make me want to streak out of the cinema shrieking, as Franju's film did at times; it gives me the creeps in retrospect, in my heart and mind more than in my eyes. We have had glossy horrors before . . . but never such insinuating, under-the-skin horrors, and never quite such a bland effort to make it look as if this isn't for nuts but for normal homely filmgoers like you and me.[2]

Quigly is quite representative of the British critical reaction to *Peeping Tom*—an overwhelming expression of outrage that remains "a landmark in British cinema."[3] At the time, critics simply could not stomach Powell's masterful portrait (from a brilliant screenplay by Leo Marks) of a disturbed young man whose childhood subjection to his father's cruel psychological experiments leads him to film/murder women with a spiked camera tripod apparatus. Today, with *Peeping Tom* now widely hailed as one of the towering achievements of British filmmaking (a transformation substantially indebted to Martin Scorsese's tireless championing of Powell, including his backing of a theatrical rerelease of *Peeping Tom* in 1980), at least one prominent British critic has gone so far as to recant her original declaration of seething hatred for the film.[4] But as Ian Christie warns, just to dismiss the 1960 reviews as hysterical or dim-witted is to "run the risk of merely incorporating [*Peeping Tom*] into a cultish nostalgia."[5] Taking a reviewer like Quigly seriously is the first step toward a project left largely untouched by the critical redemption of *Peeping Tom*: restoring the film to its cultural context and revealing its allegorical significance at a flashpoint in British social history—an era characterized by interlaced struggles over class definition and the national legacy of World War II, Britain's traumatic "people's war."[6]

Quigly's distinction between the remote, amusing thrills of *Eyes Without a Face* and the direct, under-the-skin insinuations of *Peeping Tom* does not rest on the use of graphic gore. How then, in her view, is Powell able to achieve the confrontational address of the allegorical moment—to get under the skin of his audience—without following Franju in literally peeling away the skin of his onscreen victims? For Quigly, the charged term of difference is "direct emotional realism." She feels directly addressed by a film that she believes *should* have been speaking to the "nuts" in the crowd rather than to the "normal homely filmgoers." She responds to an unnerving sense of inclusion, of collapsed boundaries between herself and an imagined audience of pathologized others. *Peeping Tom*'s "realism" blurs distinctions of intended audience address—indeed, the film's status as "the sickest and filthiest" in memory lends it the air of a communicable disease, capable of spreading infection from one type of viewer to another. The jolt that accompanies this new kind of realism results from its painful demand that "normal" viewers recognize *themselves* as the "nuts" they have constructed as their opposites.

The allegorical dimension of *Peeping Tom*'s "direct emotional realism" begins to take shape when Quigly's apprehensive review is juxtaposed with Richard Hoggart's contemporaneous sociological study of British mass culture, *The Uses of Literacy* (1957). In Hoggart's analysis of postwar British society, "the great majority of us are being merged into one class." For Hoggart, an emergent mass culture is erasing traditional class-specific cultures (particularly those belonging to the working class) and creating a "faceless" and "classless" mass society that is in many ways "less healthy" than the one it is replacing.[7] Prime Minister Harold Macmillan, on the other hand, could afford to portray this apparent social trend toward class-lessness as a source of political triumph rather than sociological anxiety. "The class war is over and we have won it," declared Macmillan in 1959, as his Conservative Party defeated Labor in national elections for the third consecutive time.[8] In many ways, the Conservatives owed their victories to Britain's substantial economic growth during the 1950s—what has been referred to commonly as the country's transition from a wartime and early postwar "age of austerity" (1939–1951) to an "age of affluence" (1951–1964). This transition from austerity to affluence meant marked increases in national production, average earnings, and personal consumption of products such as cars, televisions, and household appliances.[9] But the new affluent society was hardly a classless utopia where the traditional hierarchies of privilege simply disappeared, nor was it ever really designed to be so by the Conservatives. When Macmillan explains that his vision of the class war's end has nothing to do with "dreary equality,"[10] he signals how the notion of "classlessness" also implies a potentially threatening inability to maintain the usual distinctions that allowed the middle class and upper class to differentiate themselves from the working class. Of course, the threat accompanying this sort of classlessness is mistaking those who count as the dominant "us" with those who count as the subordinate "them" when it comes to political and cultural power. In his conclusion to *Culture and Society* (1958), Raymond Williams eloquently captures this shifting sense of "us" and "them," along with the potent challenge it presents to the ruling classes: "The masses are always the others, whom we don't know, and can't know. Yet now, in our kind of society, we see these others regularly, in their myriad variations; stand, physically, beside them. They are here, and we are here with them."[11] In other words, the class war has not been "won" in the age of affluence—only transformed in relation to discourses of classlessness.

A primary source for the concepts of classlessness that animate the social fantasies and nightmares of Britain's age of affluence (and that haunt the critical reception of *Peeping Tom*) can be found in the historical trauma of World War II.[12] For Britain, the war was an all-encompassing "total war"—a fact made vividly clear by the grim statistic that the roughly 300,000 British soldiers killed in combat "were matched by a similar number of civilians, most of them casualties of aerial bombardment."[13] So it is not surprising that the notion of World War II as "the people's war," a time when Britain must fight as one united nation devoid of class antagonisms, would be a powerful ideological construction mobilized by Prime Minister Winston Churchill during wartime. Indeed, the myth of the people's war persists to this day, despite the fact that the myth minimizes or erases as much actual wartime experience as it describes.[14] Part of the myth's staying power must be attributed to its compelling articulation of a cohesive national identity, a democratic vision of a "real" Britain beyond the veil of class conflict. This image of the people's war was actively pursued in the influential wartime policies of Britian's Ministry of Information, so that "if there was one theme which was prominent above all others in film propaganda, it was the part played in the war by ordinary men and women."[15] This cinematic address of the "ordinary" as the "real" during wartime meant speaking to and incorporating those populations—most notably the working class and women—who were not normally included in the dominant "us" of the nation. But how could such an address, with its demand for a new vision of an explicitly national cinema, be effectively achieved?

As Antonia Lant observes, "documentary filmmaking in Britain since the 1930s had been directly associated with 'ordinariness' as a euphemism for working-class subject matter," so there already existed a cinematic tradition well-suited to the need presented by World War II to project this particular national identity.[16] John Grierson, the figure perhaps most central to the conception of Britian's documentary film movement in the late 1920s and 1930s, imagined the documentary as a tool for building national culture by speaking *to* the middle class *about* the working class, so that "we" look at "them."[17] This is the philosophy of documentary realism, or "responsible" documentary, that characterizes the important British documentaries of the 1930s, such as *Housing Problems* (Edgar Anstey and Arthur Elton, 1935), and that continues through much of the extraordinary British documentary production during the war, including such "story documentaries" as *Target for Tonight* (Harry Watt, 1941) and *Fires Were Started* (Humphrey Jennings, 1943).[18] This is not to say that certain key craftsmen of the wartime documentaries (most notably, Humphrey Jennings) did not offer their own unique variations on and occasional subversions of such a philosophy, but the intersection of national emergency and documentary realist ideology forged a powerful equivalence between a realist cinematic aesthetic and a national cinematic aesthetic during wartime that lasted long after 1945.

This significant interchange between the realist and the national is already apparent in the Ministry of Information's wartime practice of mixing "what had been before the war two mutually exclusive groups"[19]—documentary filmmakers and fiction filmmakers—but it is also present in the common critical endorsement of wartime realism as the origin of an authentic, "traditional English style" that holds out the promise for "the serious British film" to "find not only merely a national, but an international audience" in the postwar era.[20] Producer Michael Balcon helped set these terms in his pamphlet *Realism or Tinsel* (1944), where he advocated the British film industry's investment in realism and warned that there might be "a violent reaction toward tinsel once hostilities have ceased."[21] Of course, as head of production at Ealing studios, Balcon himself would oversee a number of films after the war that did not exactly adhere to the realism he championed, but the rhetorical stance that realism is the proper, heavily favored course for British national cinema has remained until quite recently a remarkably influential critical paradigm. Julian Petley's complaint (circa 1986) that "the realist aesthetic is so deeply ingrained in British film culture that it not only renders 'deviant' movies either marginal or completely invisible . . . but also imposes a 'realist' framework of interpretation like a stifling blanket over the entire area of British cinema"[22] has finally begun to be remedied. The correctives include not only an impressive array of new scholarship on such "deviant" areas of British cinema as the horror film and the melodrama, but also Charles Barr's valuable insight that "perhaps the conventional binary opposition of realist and non-realist is a too rigid one: at any rate, the terms of its application to British films needs reworking"[23] and Christine Gledhill's related argument that in British wartime cinema, "documentary is not immune to the investment of melodramatic meaning, nor is the costume melodrama remote from social reference."[24] Still, these developments in criticism come from the quarters of academia, not the mainstream press, and are of recent vintage. So when Quigly decries *Peeping Tom*'s use of "direct emotional realism" in 1960, she evokes not only contemporary issues of classlessness, but the adjoining specter of World War II, with its conflation of discourses of realism and national identity—a reference apparent in her question, "What *are* we coming to, what sort of people are we in this country, to make, or see, or seem to want (so it gets made) a film like [*Peeping Tom*]?"[25]

Quigly's question returns us to the central term that binds discourses of wartime realism with those of postwar classlessness: "the people." The notion of "the people" also arises during a BBC radio interview in 1959, when Powell recounts how he and Leo Marks decided on the title *Peeping Tom* for their upcoming film. According to Powell, Marks was discussing the term "peeping tom" with him when Powell exclaimed, "Well that's a good title!" Marks, "rather shocked," replied, "Oh, it's not that kind of film. Won't that get all the wrong people in?" To which Powell answered, "Well, let's get the wrong people in as well as the right ones."[26] In this sense, Quigly does not misread *Peeping Tom* at all—she responds directly to the film's refusal to distinguish the "right" people from the "wrong" people when addressing its audience.

For Powell and Marks, the commitment to this kind of refusal is intimately tied to their own experiences connected to World War II. Marks, who spent the war as a cryptographer for Britain's Special Operations Executive (SOE), maintains that "the idea of writing *Peeping Tom* was born in the briefing rooms of SOE."[27] Much of *Peeping Tom*'s disturbing tone emanates from Marks's work at SOE, where he was responsible for designing the secret codes carried into the field by British intelligence agents—codes upon which the agents' lives literally depended, and for which they would be tortured to divulge if captured by the enemy. Marks imagined *Peeping Tom*'s similarly named protagonist, the murderous but tragically anguished voyeur Mark Lewis (Carl Boehm), as an amalgam of himself and the SOE agents he felt so powerfully responsible for: "I became convinced that all cryptographers are basically voyeurs. And in my case, I was staring at these agents. I wanted to remember them—in case they sent an indecipherable message back—watching them, probing them, *trying* to belong to them." Marks adds, "At the very end of the war, many agents had been tortured. This was a new experience for British intelligence. The problem was, how to help them? We . . . learnt the hard way what did and did not work in psychotherapy."[28] Mark Lewis, like Leo Marks, is a voyeur; like the SOE agents, he is tortured (by his father's psychological experiments) and cannot find the help that would heal his suffering.

Powell also saw himself in Mark Lewis: "I felt very close to the hero [of *Peeping Tom*] who is an 'absolute' director, someone who approaches life as a director, who is conscious of and suffers from it. He is a technician of emotion ... I was able to share his anguish."[29] (See fig. 2.1.) In fact, Powell's identification with Mark went far enough that he cast himself as Mark's father and his own son Columba as the young Mark in the film. "I don't approve of directors acting in their own films, but this was a family affair," said Powell.[30] Clearly, Powell insists on making Mark painfully familiar, painfully human. In this sense, *Peeping Tom* is not so much a radical departure from Powell's previous, more warmly received (but still frequently misunderstood) films—so many of them produced in collaboration with screenwriter Emeric Pressburger—as a bold extension of their often "anti-consensual themes"[31] and unorthodox visions of World War II. Powell and Pressburger's celebrated partnership began in 1939, when Pressburger, a Hungarian Jew whose mother would die at Auschwitz, had already fled Hitler's Germany for France and then England. Together Powell and Pressburger would create a number of magnificent films on diverse subjects, including *The Red Shoes* (1948) and *The Tales of Hoffmann* (1951), but again and again they would return to World War II and the problem of national identity. Films such as *49th Parallel* (1941), *The Life and Death of Colonel Blimp* (1943), *A Canterbury Tale* (1944), *A Matter of Life and Death* (1946), and *The Battle of the River Plate* (1956) vary widely in terms of the degree to which they interrogate conventional ideas of patriotism and nationhood as they pertain to World War II, but some sense of interrogation always surfaces.[32] Indeed, Andrew Moor describes the key themes of Powell and Pressburger's films as "the journey, the trauma of enforced displacement, the encounter with alien territory, the curious way in which the existence of borders is admitted yet disavowed,"[33] while Antonia Lant adds "the loss of nationality, the masquerade of nationality, and the difficulties of being alien but not enemy, of being non-national."[34] This is the context that must be considered when pondering Powell's decision to cast the Austrian-born actor Karl-Heinz Böhm (anglicized as "Carl Boehm") as *Peeping Tom*'s British protagonist Mark Lewis.

Boehm, an actor virtually unknown in Britain at the time but famous in Germany for his role in the *Sissi* films opposite Romy Schneider, was selected by Powell after he failed to sign British actor Laurence Harvey. Although Powell has claimed that to his own ear, Boehm "spoke English with hardly any accent," most viewers cannot overlook his pronounced German inflection.[35] To turn once more to Quigly:

> Someone suggested that the absurdity of having a German actor with
> a thickish accent playing a British hero might be explained by the
> idea that no one would want to see a local boy in such a part, but

FIGURE 2.1 *Peeping Tom* (Michael Powell, 1960): Mark Lewis (Carl Boehm), the filmmaker/ murderer as "'absolute' director," with Helen Stephens (Anna Massey). (Courtesy of Thomas Doherty)

> that if it could be shoved off on to someone else (and ideally, on to a German) it would be consoling to know that although in the *story* the hero was a Londoner from birth, in 'real life' . . . he is an outsider, as you know the minute . . . he opens his mouth to say a word.[36]

Quigly's attempt to explain away the troubling presence of Boehm is not very effective—after all, she simultaneously describes Mark as a "hero" (and, earlier in the review, even "handsome, tormented, lovable").[37] Mark's accent may code him as an outsider, but audience sympathy grants him the status of insider as well. His frightening but deeply felt humanity stems from his ability to blur the lines between a British "us" and a German "them," between a heroic victim and a murderous predator. The character of Mark joins Powell's long line of human hero/villains, which includes even the Nazis of *49th Parallel*. When Powell pitched the script of *49th Parallel* to the Ministry of Information during the thick of World War II, he said, "This is a propaganda picture in which the only good Nazi is a dead Nazi. . . . But as that kind of propaganda can be self-defeating, we have started out by making them human beings."[38]

Mark also muddies distinctions between the culturally powerful and the culturally powerless. He owns his deceased father's house in which much of the film takes place, but as one of his tenants tells him, "you walk about as if you hadn't paid the rent." With a nervous absence of irony, Mark replies, "I haven't," and then worries aloud about whether he overcharges the tenants. Similarly, Mark is both the powerful producer of images and the powerless consumer of them, master and slave of the endless process of filming his murders so that he may complete his father's research and watch a perfect image of fear at the moment of death. In other words, Mark, like *Peeping Tom* itself, is both of "the people" and apart from them. Appropriately enough, he refers to his own lethal film project as "a documentary."

So when Quigly asks, "what sort of people are we in this country, to make, or see, or seem to want (so it gets made) a film like [*Peeping Tom*]?" the seeds of several other anxious questions can be detected behind it. If World War II was indeed a people's war, just who is it that counts as "the people" when one looks back at that traumatic event from the vantage point of 1960? Are these also "the people" of this newly affluent, "classless" present? How dare *Peeping Tom* pose this problem of defining "the people" by denaturalizing precisely that aesthetic mode—"direct emotional realism"—associated with constructing "the nation" and documenting those class distinctions that ultimately demarcate "us" from "them"? And what, then, does *Peeping Tom*'s allegorical "realism" have to do with the "kitchen sink realism" of the contemporaneous art films belonging to the British New Wave?

CONFLICTING REALISMS: *PEEPING TOM* AND THE BRITISH NEW WAVE

As mentioned earlier, Powell first offered the role of Mark Lewis to Laurence Harvey, star of one of the definitive and most successful films of the British New Wave, Jack Clayton's *Room at the Top* (1959).[39] But this is not the only connection between the two films. Critical reactions to *Room at the Top* in Britain echo the concern with realism present in Quigly's review of *Peeping Tom*, though to a very different end. In a typical example from the *Daily Express*, Leonard Mosley states that

> *Room at the Top* was the real eye-opener for me—the real proof that something had happened in the cinema. For here was a British film which, at long last, got its teeth into those subjects which have always been part and parcel of our lives, but have hitherto been taboo subjects on the prissy British screen. . . . It is savagely frank and brutally truthful.[40]

Quigly herself heralded *Room at the Top* by proclaiming, "At last, at long, long last, a British film that talks about life here today . . . slap in the middle of the dissolving and reforming social patterns of our time and place."[41] Even *Room at the Top*'s X certificate from the British Board of Film Censors, a rating then evoking an "aura of disreputability" associated with horror and exploitation fare, could not dampen critical enthusiasm for the film.[42] Derek Monsey, in the *Sunday Express*, claimed that *Room at the Top* had "earned" its rating, "not for meretricious horror or peek-hole sex: but for sheer, blatant honesty. . . . In this case at least, and at last, the X certificate looks like a badge of honour."[43] The realism of *Room at the Top*, though "savage" and "brutal," clearly managed to sway the critics in a way *Peeping Tom* could not.

In *Room at the Top*, a working-class clerk, Joe Lampton (Laurence Harvey), leaves the depressed northern industrial town of Dufton for the more prosperous Yorkshire city of Warnley and resolves to procure there all the trappings of a more privileged lifestyle: the right car, the right home, and most importantly, the right woman. He sets his sights on Susan Brown (Heather Sears), the daughter of one of Warnley's wealthiest men. He wins her, but along the way he falls in love with the older, married, and penniless Alice Aisgill (Simone Signoret). Susan becomes pregnant by Joe, and he agrees to marry her in a bargain with her father that avoids the humiliation of Susan having a child out of wedlock in exchange for Joe's promotion to a comfortable company position. As part of the arrangement, Joe must also abandon Alice. Alice reacts by committing suicide, and Joe's wedding is poisoned by regret over a life passed up, and dread of the life to come.

The jumble of elements comprising social realism in *Room at the Top* reflects the somewhat complex prehistory of the New Wave.[44] In one sense, the New Wave grew out of "The Movement," a literary circle of the early and mid-1950s that included John Wain and Kingsley Amis. Literary editor J. D. Scott coined the term "The Movement" in a 1954 column for *The Spectator*, where he characterized it as "anti-phoney . . . sceptical, robust, ironic, prepared to be as comfortable as possible in a wicked, commercial, threatened world," and a vital component of "that tide which is pulling us through the Fifties and towards the Sixties."[45] The Movement gained a mythical dimension with the addition of the Angry Young Man, a disillusioned working-class figure brought to life in plays such as John Osborne's *Look Back in Anger* (first performed in 1956, then filmed in 1959 by Tony Richardson) and in literature like John Braine's novel *Room at the Top* (1957).

In another sense, the New Wave drew on Free Cinema, a documentary film movement represented by an important series of screenings at the

National Film Theatre in London between 1956 and 1959 and led by Lindsay Anderson, Karel Reisz, and Tony Richardson—all of whom went on to direct key New Wave features. The New Wave's gritty, spare aesthetic of "kitchen sink realism" is heavily indebted to the documentary approach of Free Cinema, which itself follows in the footsteps of Griersonian documentary realism by focusing on "authentic" depictions of the British working class. The realist impulse behind Free Cinema, later imported to the New Wave, is outlined by Lindsay Anderson in his strident essay "Get Out and Push!" (1957). For Anderson, the Conservative contention that the class war is at an end in the age of affluence is hopelessly false: "The grim truth is that we still live in one of the most class-conscious societies in the world, and I see nothing to be gained from the pretence that this is no longer so." Anderson accuses the British cinema of colluding with the Conservative "flight from contemporary reality" by ignoring class divisions and opting instead to portray Britain as

> a country without problems, in which no essential changes have occurred for the last fifty years, and which still remains the centre of an Empire on which the sun will never have the bad manners to set. Nothing is more significant of this determination to go on living in the past than the succession of war films which British studios have been turning out for the last four or five years, and which shows no sign of coming to an end.[46]

Film historians have borne out the validity of Anderson's observation by designating the 1950s as "the heyday of the British war film"[47] and noting how 1950s war films such as *The Dam Busters* (Michael Anderson, 1955) and *Reach for the Sky* (Lewis Gilbert, 1956) tend to revise the class-transcending thrust of many 1940s war films. According to Christine Geraghty, the war films of the 1950s emphasize a "return to normal," which "means that it is no longer important to represent women or working-class men as taking part in the war" and that instead middle-class officers "are seen to be fighting the war on behalf of rather than as part of the nation."[48] Or as Neil Rattigan puts it, "1950s war films are concerned with putting the 'people' back in their place" after the urgency to construct World War II as the people's war has passed.[49] What Anderson calls for in 1957, on the eve of the New Wave, is a return to the Griersonian tradition of documentary realism that flowered in the 1930s and, especially, during the war years of the 1940s. "During a war it is useful to be able to appeal to national democratic sentiments," Anderson explains. "But after a war, when the slogan is 'Back to Business as Usual!' democratic sentiments are apt to seem unnecessary, and such appeals are discontinued." Anderson accurately diagnoses a problem in contemporary British cinema, but his solution—to return to Grierson and ensure that "those good and friendly faces" of the British working class secure "a place of pride on the screens of their country"—however well-intentioned, does not fully reckon with the dissonance produced by maintaining the ideological viewpoint of a middle-class "us" observing a working-class "them." To Anderson's credit, he is not unaware of such dissonance—he mentions the "unfortunate" wartime poster that proclaimed, "Your courage, your hard work, your cheerfulness will bring Us victory!"[50]—but he still believes documentary realism is the answer. Many British critics would go on to endorse some form of Anderson's answer by embracing the "brutally truthful" realism of the New Wave while vilifying the "under-the-skin" realism of *Peeping Tom*. Powell, however, remained steadfast during the New Wave's success about the fact that "neorealism doesn't really interest me much" as a cinematic mode for engaging "English problems."[51] Indeed, comparing the openings of *Room at the Top* and *Peeping Tom* reveals a telling insistence on upholding soothing class definitions for spectators in the former, and a tendency to violate comforting spectator boundaries in the latter.

Room at the Top begins with a journey that quite literally provides viewers with a well-marked road map to Joe Lampton's working-class identity. Joe sits and smokes in a railway car, with his shoeless feet elevated. The bleak succession of factories passing outside the window verifies the locale as Britain's industrial north. In a heavily symbolic gesture, Joe dons a new pair of shoes in preparation for his arrival at Warnley. Once reaching the Warnley station, he takes a taxi to town hall, catches the eye of every secretary in the outer office of the treasurer's department, and finally meets privately with his boss. The sequence ends with Joe's first hungry glimpse of an obviously wealthy Susan Brown, whom he spies in the street from an office window. Joe's colleague, Charles Soames (Donald Houston), follows his gaze and cautions, "That's not for you, lad." Joe responds, "That's what I'm going to have."

The sequence carefully defines Joe's class status by contrasting his comfort and belonging in certain spaces (the train as it passes through the industrial landscape; the outer office while the secretaries ogle him) with his awkward exclusion from others (the private office, where he cringes at his boss's suggestion that the people of Warnley are more "civilized" than those of Dufton; the affluent world conveyed by Susan's clothing, car, and boyfriend). This meticulous spatialization of Joe's working-class identity produces a spectator position characteristic of the New Wave films, which

John Hill (partially paraphrasing Andrew Higson) describes as a view-point "'outside and above,' marking a separation between spectator and subject, [where] the pleasures delivered may well rely less on recognition than the very sensation of class difference."[52] Joe Lampton may signify the arrival of a new kind of character on the British screen, but the film's inscription of the viewer's relation to him resembles the ethnographic stance of an observer peering curiously at an unusual species, captured in all its "genuine" detail. Reviewer praise for the "accuracy" of Harvey's performance as Joe attests to the pleasure possible in understanding him as an ethnographic specimen: "every movement, every intonation, the way he holds his cigarette, sits, speaks, has his hair cut, wears his clothes, jumps on a bus, everything convinces one not just of Joe, but of what Joe stands for."[53] The middle class watches an impeccably "realistic" representation of a working-class character, but the film's insistence on the viewer's distance from him (and from the "working-class" spaces he inhabits) bypasses any sort of meaningful social recognition of working-class subjects. Instead, the dominant sensation evoked by the middle-class encounter with Joe is closer to what Higson calls "cultural tourism," where a "self-conscious aestheticization . . . erases the danger, the traces of the otherness, rendering [him] exotic and spectacular . . . like so [much else] with which 'we' are familiar."[54]

The opening of *Peeping Tom*, on the other hand, disorients and unsettles viewers as thoroughly as *Room at the Top*'s introduction reassures and guides them. The film begins with a close-up of a closed eye, which opens with the sound of a camera shutter click.[55] Already Powell has set in motion the questions that will lead viewers to approach the film with a profound unease, and not a little distrust. Whose eye is this? Is it wide-eyed with fright or excitement? Does it open *because* it is being photographed, or is the camera click inseparable from the physical functioning of the eye itself, as involuntary as blinking? Is this the gaze of the filmmaker, looking out at the spectators, or a reflection of the audience's own gaze, as they open their eyes to begin watching the film?

The next shot relieves viewers from these disconcerting questions of motivation and agency by establishing a concrete setting: an empty street at night, the uneven glow of street lamps, a woman standing outside a shop window, a man whistling as he approaches her. On the surface, this is exactly the kind of "realistic" setting so fetishized by the New Wave—contemporary, gritty (or "working-class"), evocative of social issues (here, of course, prostitution). And yet, the aura of unease introduced by the film's first shot lingers. For this is not the authentic location shot characteristic of the New Wave; it is clearly a self-consciously "cinematic" phantasma-goria, with its garish lighting and shadowy scenery more reminiscent of German Expressionist studio sets than anything else.[56] As if to confirm an impression of artificial construction, the next shot is a close-up of another "eye"—a movie camera cradled inside a jacket lapel, whirring quietly as it is switched on. The camera approaches the spectator directly, blurring out of focus as it draws too close—to the screen, to the audience, to the film-maker filming the filmmaker.

The camera's subsequent, unforgiving inspection of the body, clothing, and apartment interior of the prostitute victim Dora (Brenda Bruce) seems just as invasive as the most weakly motivated working-class location or character study in a New Wave film, but there are key differences in *Peeping Tom*. The audience's initial investigation of Dora comes through the literal crosshairs of Mark's viewfinder, and spectators immediately reexperience their deliberate participation in this spectacle as they watch Mark (still faceless, just another anonymous filmgoer) watching his black-and-white footage of the murder. The sequence lays bare the potential violence inherent in the social realism adopted so unproblematically by the New Wave. Not only is the camera's subject explicitly rendered as a vulnerable target, but the black-and-white film itself (a stylistic hallmark of every New Wave production) is revealed as a fetishized construction of reality with no privileged claim on any social truth. Even Mark's private screening does not reproduce all the images glimpsed only seconds before in color during the "live" encounter. The insistent implication of viewer and filmmaker in this sequence's construction concludes, appropriately enough, with the credit "Directed by Michael Powell" superimposed over Mark's projector. Here, then, is a model for the "direct emotional realism" which strikes Quigly as so "insinuating"—an allegorical realism that locates the viewer squarely in the field of the other, not somehow "outside and above" it.

By contrast, Joe's vision in *Room at the Top* of Susan as a commodity he decides he is "going to have" after seeing her on display outside the office window displaces a naive sensibility of compulsive consumption to a thoroughly working-class point of view. Middle-class viewers threatened by the new "classlessness" need not feel spoken to by Joe's immersion in this alien sensibility, which begins as an expression of masculine desire but is ultimately emasculating. Later in the film, Joe again spots Susan through a window, only this time the window belongs to a women's lingerie shop. Oblivious to the surroundings and fascinated only by the pursuit of his "product," Joe is startled outside the shop by Susan's wealthy boyfriend, Jack Wales (John Westbrook), who says sarcastically, "Hello,

Sergeant. Shopping for lingerie? What size are you? Forty-four?" Jack, a decorated squadron leader in the RAF during the war who escaped from a POW camp, belittles Joe not only by pointing out how out of place he is, but by addressing him as "Sergeant"—a means of calling attention to the disparity in their wartime rank and service record. Joe, who also served in the RAF, was shot down early in the war and never attempted to escape from the POW camp because he felt it was the only time he would ever have to study for the accounting exams that promised a ticket out of factory labor back home. During their standoff outside the lingerie shop, Joe spits at Jack, "Just do me a favor. The war is over. Stop calling me Sergeant!"

One of the most provocative ideas suggested by *Room at the Top* is that the war is not entirely over.[57] When Joe relates the tale of his humiliating encounter with Jack to Charles Soames and one other working-class colleague, Charles points out that if any of them had performed the wartime feats attributed to Jack, they would not have received the same prestigious honors bestowed upon him. Joe agrees and says bitterly, "Different brands of courage, don't you know?" What Joe means, of course, is different *classes* of courage—a critique of precisely the kind of revision of the people's war occurring in the war films of the 1950s. But by the end of *Room at the Top*, this critique has been emptied out. At the film's conclusion, Joe "has" exactly what he set out to obtain and it leaves him impotent—shorn of working-class virility (beat up by working-class men who reflect back Joe's own sense of self-abandonment by no longer recognizing him as one of their own) and emotionally broken (crying helplessly in the car as he leaves his wedding with his "prize" bride, Susan). In a drunken stupor, Joe even refers to himself as "Jack Wales," intimating how much he has become the very thing he once despised. What began as an attack on the hypocrisy of the myth of the people's war as well as its postwar retelling ends with the message that Joe's desires for class mobility and the recognition of class injustice are deluded weaknesses, not visionary strengths. The film underlines this conclusion by portraying Joe's loss of his parents in a wartime bombing not as a political event but as a metaphorical means of showing how Joe's refusal to "just be himself" and "stick to his own kind" (as he is reminded frequently by an assortment of characters) winds up "murdering" the soul given to him by his parents as well as the soul offered to him by Alice.

When Joe fixates on a child's toy car as a symbol of Alice's automobile suicide, the image echoes an earlier scene depicting Joe's pilgrimage to the ruins of his bombed childhood home in Dufton. There he meets another child, a destitute young girl whom he tells that this was once his home as it is now hers. But before he can speak much further with this young mirror of his own former working-class self, her mother snatches her away from Joe because he is a "stranger." Joe's protest that he is "not *really* a stranger" falls on deaf ears, and the point that he has lost his innocent, childlike, working-class identity is hammered home when other children of Dufton appear to follow him down the street as more of a curiosity than a community member. In the film's visual and thematic logic then, Joe's pained clutching of the toy car (another encounter with the loss of his childlike, "authentic" identity) collapses the wartime deaths of his parents into his indirect murder of Alice. This reduces Joe's wrenching experience to a cautionary fairy tale about the price paid in innocence and genuine selfhood through a tragic but elementary misunderstanding of class difference. In this manner, the possibilities of Joe embodying any real threat to middle-class subjectivity are carefully contained. Joe's character ultimately calms middle-class anxieties concerning classlessness and the legacy of the people's war by reassuring "us" that any attempt to ascend in class status or question class hierarchies can only result in emasculated misery and the loss of that "genuine" class identity ("them") forged in childhood. (See fig. 2.2.)

In certain important ways, *Peeping Tom*'s ending inverts the conclusion of *Room at the Top*. Mark, finally cornered in his home by the police, faces the forced termination of his "documentary" film project. But rather than add one last female victim to the final reel, Mark spares Helen Stephens (Anna Massey) and instead turns the camera on himself. "Helen, I'm afraid . . . and I'm glad I'm afraid," are Mark's final words to the woman who found a way to love him, and whom he loves in return by valuing her life above his own. She tries to prevent his often-rehearsed act of suicide, but he proceeds to film the image of his own face as the camera tripod spike pierces his throat. Unlike Joe, who causes Alice's suicide, Mark takes his own life in order to preserve Helen's. And whereas Joe's association with children serves to contain his challenge to class definitions attached to the mythology of the people's war, Mark's return in death to his childhood self (once again father's test subject) frustrates audience attempts to pin down the "true" Mark as "us" or "them." In fact, the film's last lines of dialogue—a child softly whispering, "Goodnight, Daddy. Hold my hand."—does not belong to any easily identifiable onscreen source. Is this the recorded voice of a young Mark, part of the cacophony of sounds taped by his father (and later, himself) through hidden microphones in all the house's rooms? If so, then why is this voice so clearly isolated from all the other sounds con-

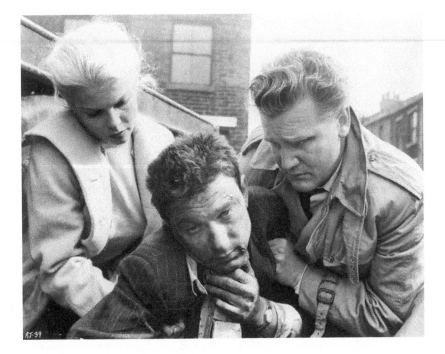

FIGURE 2.2 *Room at the Top* (Jack Clayton, 1959): The miserable, emasculated end of Joe Lampton's (Laurence Harvey) class mobility fantasies. (Courtesy of Jerry Ohlinger's Movie Material)

nected with these tapes, as played by Mark in his last living moments? Why does the child's voice emerge from complete darkness, masking any possible visual source?

Such questions return spectators to the ambiguous opening of *Peeping Tom*, with its uneasy absence of agency. The projector that provides the final image in that initial sequence (the one upon which Powell's directorial credit was superimposed) is glimpsed again here, but only to show the last reel of film run out and the projector fall silent. It is as if the things that spectators see and hear afterward—the child's voice in the darkness, then a fade-in to Mark's private projection screen, now blank but half-bathed in the red illumination of a darkroom—cannot be attributed fully to Mark, or even to Powell himself. We are left staring at a screen of our own that waits to reflect the images we are developing in the wake of all that *Peeping Tom*'s allegorical moments have confronted us with. These will be, inevitably, images of ourselves.

CHILDREN OF "THE CLINICAL CULT"

The centrality of children to the conclusions of both *Peeping Tom* and *Room at the Top* resonates with other contemporary British reactions to classlessness and World War II that infantilize the working class as well as those audiences attracted to the boom in British horror films beginning in the late 1950s. At the center of this boom are the productions of Hammer Films, a small but influential British studio specializing in low-budget horror and science fiction fare. Hammer's remarkable commercial success in the late 1950s and 1960s depended heavily on their series of Gothic horror films that revamped (in color) the Universal versions of the 1930s, commencing with *The Curse of Frankenstein* (Terence Fisher, 1957) and *Dracula* (Terence Fisher, 1958). Ian Christie notes that "the immediate background" behind *Peeping Tom*'s production and reception is the box office success of the Hammer horror films and "the implacable hostility of most reviewers toward these."[58] But Peter Hutchings observes that the contemporary critical reception of Hammer's horror efforts, often accepted as uniformly scathing, was actually not nearly as dismissive as the treatment accorded *Peeping Tom*. As Hutchings demonstrates, reviewers of the Hammer productions were relatively successful at distancing themselves from the films by designating them as fanciful, and their audiences as "primitive, childlike, easily exploited, possibly in need of an analyst."[59]

For example, Derek Granger of the *Financial Times* is able to dismiss *The Curse of Frankenstein* as "hilarious" by pathologizing its audience: "Only the saddest of simpletons, one feels, could ever really get a satisfying *frisson*. For the rest of us, [horror films] have just become a rather eccentric and specialised form of light entertainment and possibly a useful means of escape for a housewife harrowed by the shopping."[60] This detached, feminized, and infantilized portrait of a Hammer audience succeeds at laughing off *The Curse of Frankenstein* as thoroughly as Quigly's attempts to dissociate herself from *Peeping Tom* fail. Yet even Quigly manages to infantilize the surrounding horror film phenomenon by using *Peeping Tom* to demote Powell from his status as a "respected" director possessing "remarkable technical gifts" to the ranks of "British film-makers with a stake in horror," who are not considered filmmakers at all, but "children playing 'dares.'"[61]

A particularly striking example of this infantlizing discourse can be found in Derek Hill's article "The Face of Horror," published in a 1958 issue of the British film journal *Sight and Sound*. "The Face of Horror" supplies a vital context for Hill's vicious review of *Peeping Tom*; in fact, Hill's oft-quoted salvo against Powell's film (which begins, "The only really satisfactory way to dispose of *Peeping Tom* would be to shovel it up and flush it swiftly down the nearest sewer. Even then the stench would remain")[62] can be read as a frustrated postscript to his lengthier article of two years earlier. In "The Face of Horror," Hill describes a disturbing trend he detects in the recent wave of horror films distributed in Britain, both Hammer and non-Hammer. He dubs this trend "the clinical cult," and characterizes it as "the worst the industry has ever offered"—films designed "to disgust," relying "almost entirely on a percentage of shots of repugnant clinical detail." Hill goes on to attack most psychologists for irresponsibly defending the cathartic possibilities of these films, rather than attending to "their long-range effect on public mentality" and their contribution to "a steadily accelerating corruption of the public's appetite."[63]

The one psychologist quoted approvingly by Hill is Dr. Fredric Wertham, who emigrated from Germany to America in the 1920s and rose to public prominence with the publication of his *Seduction of the Innocent* in 1954. The book's thesis, that sensational comic books cause juvenile degeneracy of every stripe, struck a powerful chord in America as well as Britain.[64] Wertham shares Hill's anxieties about the proximity of violent mass culture and war trauma, as well as his tendency to channel those anxieties through figures of children and infantilized viewers. For example, Wertham claims that in *Superman* comics, "there is an exact parallel to the blunting of sensibilities in the direction of cruelty that has characterized a whole generation of central European youth fed on the Nietzsche-Nazi myth of the exceptional man who is beyond good and evil,"[65] while Hill comments, "Perhaps adult cinemagoers should be more resistant than children. But the corruption of taste is, after all, a pretty insidious business. Given the Bomb, given the insecurity, producers have relentlessly used the fallacious old argument about giving the people what it wants . . . [but] cinemagoers' appetites harden on what they are fed."[66]

For Hill, much of the threat posed to an impressionable, childlike "people" by the clinical cult stems from the films' imitation of, and outgrowth from, trauma related to World War II: "Every horror film cycle has coincided with economic depression or war. Now we have the biggest, ugliest threat of them all, and a bigger, uglier horror boom than ever before." Although Hill criticizes the films of the clinical cult for including "details immediately reminiscent of concentration camp atrocities," the specific threat Hill refers to is atomic warfare. He claims that the existence of the atomic bomb

has fostered an atmosphere in which the horror film has been able to develop in disturbing directions and on an unprecedented scale.

The final analysis will find us a nation, probably a world, of quiet, controlled, largely unconscious hysterics, driven to that condition by submerged impotence and fear. The links between insecurity, hidden hysteria, and the current appetite for aggressive violence are not going to be easily broken.[67]

The national atmosphere Hill evokes is instantly recognizable as the fearful mood of the age of affluence, with its ghosts of classlessness and the people's war. Hill's concern with the corrupting "influence on public taste"[68] exercised by the clinical cult echoes Quigly's distinction between "nuts" and "normal homely filmgoers like you and me"—both reflect the same need to separate a reasonable and responsible "us" from an infantile and potentially violent "them."

When Hill mentions "the alarming parade of the perverted and the cranky . . . in the queues and foyers" of movie theaters screening the films of the clinical cult and quotes Hammer actor Christopher Lee defending horror films against charges of inciting "hooliganism,"[69] he conjures a cultural icon around which the age of affluence's fantasies of an infantilized and othered working class collected: the Teddy Boy. According to Paul Rock and Stanley Cohen, the Teddy Boy "seems to stalk like some atavistic monster through much of the otherwise prosaic newspaper reporting of the fifties." Teddy Boys were those working-class youths who, beginning in the early 1950s and ending in the early 1960s, donned the Edwardian suits previously associated with the middle class as a fashion statement reflecting their "relative economic emancipation" during the age of affluence. Almost instantly, it seems, the Teddy Boys were perceived by the public and the press (usually erroneously) as dangerous social deviants, prone to gang violence and wanton cruelty. By 1956, Teddy Boys were blamed for an outbreak of "rock 'n' roll riots" at movie theaters; the "fighting, slashing of seats, and other types of vandalism"[70] were severe enough to cause some theaters to hire ex-soldiers, ex-boxers, and even professional wrestlers to maintain order, while many others banned Teddy Boys outright.

Why did the Teddy Boy emerge as a "monster" during the age of affluence? Much of the Teddy Boy's threat begins (and ends) with his clothing—he is a living, breathing embodiment of precisely that sort of classlessness (the working class appropriating those cultural markers that once set off the middle class as distinct) which haunts 1950s and early 1960s British society. There is also the Teddy Boy's youth to consider. He is not the helpless, infantilized symbol of the working class, but rather its economically empowered alter ego. It is not surprising to discover that "one of the most common reasons given for the Teddy Boy phenomenon was the effect of the war,"[71] because it is the trauma of the people's war and its consequences for class definition that the Teddy Boy crystallizes. Given the cultural climate of the age of affluence, the Teddy Boy, like the infantilized audience of the clinical cult, must be seen as an amalgam of the monsters depicted on the cinema screen and those "monsters" imagined to be watching the films projected on these screens. Perhaps the audiences that "reacted with scorn and derision"[72] to *Room at the Top* when it was substituted for *The Curse of Frankenstein* or *Dracula* during a preview run at a theater in Tottenham, a working-class section of north London, were expressing some form of protest against how this amalgamation tends to occur—and pointing out what kind of film may *actually* contribute to Hill's reported "corruption of the public's appetite."

CONSUMING THE NEW WOMAN, DEVOURING MASS CULTURE

Alongside the Teddy Boy, another "monstrous" cultural icon central to the age of affluence is the "new woman": the wife and mother who works outside the home while simultaneously acquiring the new domestic appliances and managing the new household of the affluent economy. The new woman was often demonized through popular notions (influentially disseminated via the work of psychologist John Bowlby) of "maternal deprivation" as the culprit for everything from juvenile delinquency to divorce. Christine Geraghty explains that "the biggest debates about the new woman centered on her role in the public world of work and the psychological effects on children of the working mother,"[73] while John Hill adds that such debates never reckoned with how Britain's postwar economic growth "depended on the availability of female labor" or how "it was also women's work which underpinned the rises in household income and patterns of consumption characteristic of the 'affluent society.'"[74] The new woman resembles the Teddy Boy in terms of her cultural position—a threatening sign for the ruling classes that "the people" (women and the working class) incorporated as invaluable components of the nation during the people's war may not wish to return to "business as usual" in the postwar era. If the Teddy Boy challenges discourses of infantilization meant to contain the working class, does the new woman offer a similar resistance to the containment of women in the age of affluence? Revisiting the conflicting realisms of *Peeping Tom* and the art films of the New Wave permits an engagement with this question of national identity within the frame of national cinema.

The literary precursors of the New Wave, particularly those plays and novels of The Movement portraying the character of the Angry Young Man, tend to attack not so much the new woman specifically, but rather "the sum of those qualities which are supposed traditionally . . . to exude from the worst in women: pettiness, snobbery, flippancy, voluptuousness, superficiality, materialism."[75] John Hill points out that the New Wave films inherit from their literary sources an assumption of a " 'male norm' in their narrative organization, employment of subjective techniques and patterns of identification," resulting in "the dramatic and thematic subordination of the female characters."[76] Women tend to figure most prominently as placeholders for the almost always pessimistic fate of the male protagonist, rather than individuals with independent existences—a pattern on full display in *Room at the Top*, but also detectable in *Look Back in Anger, Saturday Night and Sunday Morning* (Karel Reisz, 1960), *A Kind of Loving* (John Schlesinger, 1962), and *This Sporting Life* (Lindsay Anderson, 1963).

Even *A Taste of Honey* (Tony Richardson, 1961), the notable exception in its use of a female rather than a male protagonist, still denies Jo (Rita Tushingham) much of her own agency by anchoring her (like so many of the women depicted by the New Wave) to a doomed, life-draining marriage. Only for Jo, the inescapable "marriage" is to her mother, Helen (Dora Bryan). Jo, for all her attempts at rebellious individuation (studying art, dating a black man, living with a homosexual), winds up reproducing herself as her mother—poor, unmarried, and pregnant at too young an age. The film even ends with Jo's gay roommate Geoffrey (Murray Melvin) moving out and her mother moving in. The fantasy of a family comprised of Geoffrey, Jo, and her unborn child crumbles with the arrival of Helen and her devotion to crass consumerism. Helen sends Geoffrey out of the apartment with the traditional wicker baby basket he had given to Jo—a basket Helen dismisses as "old-fashioned" and which will soon be replaced by a baby cart that she has ordered "with lambs and poodles all over it." In this manner, Jo's final union with her mother also signals a resignation to Helen's abandonment of traditional working-class culture for a repugnant consumerism associated with the new mass culture and, by extension, the new woman. Earlier in the film, Jo insistently distances herself from her mother in a sequence set at a Blackpool fairground, where Helen and her "fancy man" Peter (Robert Stephens) indulge gleefully in hot dog eating, rollercoaster riding, and other amusements indicative of what Terry Lovell calls "the shoddy new consumerism." Lovell also observes that Richardson films the sequence with an emphasis on the grotesque, using "an angle of vision and closeness to the face that produce similar visual distortions to those of the hall of mirrors."[77] *A Taste of Honey* ultimately affirms its similarity to the other New Wave films by linking a shallow, repellent consumption of mass culture to the feminized dissolution of working-class identity. In this sense, the film, despite its focus on a female character, does not transcend the New Wave's failure to interrogate a male, middle-class viewing position.

A Taste of Honey is not the only British film at this moment that utilizes the fairground as a privileged site for shifting representations of class, mass culture, and the feminine/feminizing gender roles set in motion by the new woman's emergence. The fair is a setting as significant to the New Wave as the kindred "attractions" of pinup photography and cinema are to *Peeping Tom*.[78] Richard Hoggart discusses the fair as one of those working-class sites caught in flux between "the older, the more narrow but also more genuine class culture" and "the mass opinion, the mass recreational product and the generalised emotional response." For Hoggart, the contemporary fair evokes both mass cultural decay and the resilience of traditional working-class culture: "The lovely stylised horses have almost gone, and so have the fantastic mechanical organs; each year bigger and louder relay systems and more and more Coney-Island-style colored lights appear. But again the new materials are adapted to the old demands for a huge complication and exotic involution of color, noise and movement."[79]

Hoggart's sense of the fair as a volatile space where competing cultural forces ignite the senses is strikingly realized in *Saturday Night and Sunday Morning*. Angry young factory worker Arthur Seaton (Albert Finney) is enjoying a date at the fair with Doreen (Shirley Anne Field) and friends when he sees Brenda (Rachel Roberts), the older married woman he is also romantically involved with. Arthur's choice between two generations of working-class culture is reflected not only in his two love interests, but in the fair around him, where both organ music and pop tunes clamor for supremacy and whirling, motorized rides stand alongside old-fashioned game booths. Arthur attempts to bridge the two worlds by exiting a ride with Doreen and then stepping onto another with Brenda, but he cannot simply recede into the noise and motion of the amusements. Brenda's husband sends two soldiers after him, who eventually overtake him and beat him severely. Although Arthur is now far from the fair, the organ music returns on the sound track to accompany his staggering figure, transforming his bruised and bloodied features into a cruel caricature resembling a drunken clown. As the music ceases, his sad "act" of inhabiting traditional working-class culture with Brenda ends—Arthur falls to the ground and the screen fades to black. The next morning he surveys his bruises in the mirror and tries to reassure himself that he is still an Angry Young Man, but he must finally admit, like Joe in *Room at the Top*, that his identity has been beaten out of him and that he no longer knows who he is. Just a few minutes later he proposes to Doreen, resigning himself to the domestic stagnation of his parents and their enslavement to mass culture—procuring what Arthur describes as "a television set and a packet of fags" in exchange for an existence "dead from the neck up." Arthur's final conversation with Doreen, where he concedes his masculine, traditional working-class preference for an older house to her new woman-ish, mass culture-driven desire for "a new one, with a bathroom and everything," completes a surrender understood as feminizing self-negation and closes down the alternatives suggested by the kaleidoscopic chaos of the fair.

Saturday Night and Sunday Morning is emblematic of the New Wave in its suggestion of the dynamic possibilities for cultural contestation and sensory exhilaration within the fairground space, as well as its subsequent termination of those "fantastic" possibilities in the face of the "realistic" encroachment of a mass culture that feminizes and entraps the protagonist (even when, as in *A Taste of Honey*, the protagonist is female). This narrative arc mirrors the one already present in *The Uses of Literacy*, where despite certain possibilities for adaptation and resilience, the dominant thrust of Hoggart's account charts an unmistakable decline from traditional working-class culture to faceless mass culture. Hoggart maps his narrative of decline onto a social transformation of the working-class woman where upstanding, resourceful mothers are being replaced by "flighty, careless and inane" teenage girls enslaved to the hollow pleasures of mass culture.[80] *A Taste of Honey* vividly depicts this transformation (but reverses the generations in order to accentuate Helen's monstrousness) by juxtaposing the previously described Blackpool fiasco with a second, idyllic visit to the fair by Jo and Geoffrey. This second visit is as romantic and peaceful as the earlier one was nightmarish and conflicted—Jo and Geoffrey smile happily at each other as they enjoy the rides and win game prizes together, all to the accompaniment of a melodic orchestral score which covers all onscreen sound. During the original Blackpool outing, by contrast, Jo looked on in disgust at the grotesque revelry of Peter and her mother and screamed at them after she could no longer stomach their company, while mechanical laughter and jangling pop tunes like "Grab It" blared on the sound track. *A Taste of Honey*, like *Saturday Night and Sunday Morning*, ultimately forsakes the promise held out by the fair as a site for struggle over definitions of culture as well as womanhood and insists instead on the fair's "unreality" when confronted with the "reality" of mass culture's suffocating, feminizing grip. Just as Arthur must wake up on "Sunday morning," Jo's genuine (platonic) relationship with Geoffrey must end with the return of her superficial, consumption-obsessed mother. Jo's farewell to Geoff, spoken tenderly after he has already gone, underlines the lost promise of the fair: "You clown, Geoff. You clown."

In *Peeping Tom*, there is no "Sunday morning," no awakening to the "reality" of mass culture's attractions as feminizing and self-erasing. Powell presents mass cultural spectacles not as fantasy to be dismissed or decried as "unhealthy," but as the very forms in which issues of national identity revolving around the people's war, classlessness, and the new woman must be understood and negotiated. Getting "outside" or "above" the space of mass culture, with its unpredictable possibilities for class (re)definition and sensational excess, proves virtually impossible. *Peeping Tom* discourages such attempts by consistently implicating its own status as a movie with the mass cultural forms of pinup photography and popular cinema that it represents so prominently. Powell provides no escape hatch for middle-class viewers to separate their own experience watching *Peeping Tom* from the various acts of "peeping" (at pornographic photography, at violent cinema) depicted within the film—acts shorn of their usual framing as a regrettable degeneration of working-class culture. *Peeping Tom* foregrounds this confrontational strategy in an early scene where an older, eminently proper middle-class man enters a news shop—purportedly to purchase the appropriately respectable *Times* and *Daily Telegraph* newspapers—only to leave with a series of pornographic pinup "views" Mark has photographed tucked inside an envelope labeled "educational books." This humorous lampooning of middle-class propriety, which extends to the shop owner's reminder to the hastily departing customer that he has forgotten his newspapers, carries the dark edge of allegorical implication; after all, Mark's "views" also comprise the substance of the film called *Peeping Tom* watched by the audience.

Similarly, women are not merely objects to be photographed for Mark, but points of complicated identification. For example, after snapping pinup shots of Milly (played by Pamela Green, a real-life nude model who became "Britain's answer to Betty Page")[81] in the news shop's makeshift upstairs studio, Mark approaches a second model, Lorraine (Susan Travers), who has been standing in profile at the window. Milly tells Mark that this is Lorraine's "first time," and she urges her not to be shy. When Lorraine turns to face Mark, she reveals her horribly scarred cleft palate. She tells him that he doesn't have to photograph her face (only her body), but Mark is already lost in her. "I want to," he says dreamily. "Don't be shy . . . for

me it's my first time, too . . . in front of eyes like . . . eyes as full of . . . "
As language fails him, Mark begins filming her with his personal camera
rather than the professional house camera. Of course, it is not Mark's "first
time" in terms of photographing a young woman with his camera, but this
is the first time the audience witnesses him resist using the deadly tripod
attachment. "Maybe you can fix my bruises," Lorraine suggests with bitter
sarcasm. When Mark replies again, "I want to," he means it very seriously.
In Lorraine's disfigured face he recognizes eyes as full of sadness and pain
as his own—he sees himself, not a hated stand-in for his stepmother or
another subject to offer as a sacrifice to his father's research. He identifies
with Lorraine and, in a poignant moment of childlike magical thinking,
hopes the camera that kills can become a camera that heals.

This powerful scene, with its disarming sense of emotional identification
and doomed hope, subverts Hoggart's characterization of pinup photography as yet another manifestation of mass culture that inhabits "regions so
stylised, so pasteurised, that the real physical quality has left them."[82] This
scene illustrates instead a mass cultural medium that transmits a sense of
"real physical" pain through a series of recognitions between Lorraine and
Mark. These recognitions frustrate any attempt to demonize Lorraine for
her femininity, her work, or her embodiment of mass culture. Viewers,
rather than dwelling in the sterile emptiness of Hoggart's pinups, experience something closer to that sense of aliveness and implication Carolyn
Kay Steedman conveys in *Landscape for a Good Woman* (1986). Steedman's
book, a remarkable historical and autobiographical account of British female working-class identity in the 1950s, is animated by a desire to remove
"passivity from the figures in Hoggart's . . . landscape, [and to suggest]
what desperations may lie behind the doors of the terraced houses."[83]

Still, *Peeping Tom* does seem to contain the new woman by policing the
division between working and mothering quite thoroughly. All the film's
victims (prostitute, model, actress) are working women who market their
appearance and sexuality as public spectacle, while Helen, the spared virginal heroine, works only in the most "motherly" profession of children's
librarian. Helen even drinks milk when she first meets Mark, scolds him
for his naughty tendency to peep, and most importantly, lives in Mark's
mother's old room. Yet Helen is also the active female agent who performs
the most daring work in the film by forging a sense of recognition between
herself and Mark that acknowledges his diseased attachment to the camera, but still regards her relationship with him as an act of creative collaboration. (See fig. 2.3.) Indeed, Helen and Mark truly do *work* together in a
manner unimaginable for most couples of the New Wave. Helen, thinking

FIGURE 2.3 *Peeping Tom* (Michael Powell, 1960): Mark Lewis (Carl Boehm) and Helen Stephens (Anna Massey) are able to collaborate despite the violent threat presented by Mark. (Courtesy of Jerry Ohlinger's Movie Material)

of Mark, writes (and has accepted for publication) a children's book entitled *The Magic Camera* for which Mark agrees to provide photographic illustrations. Even though Mark does not live long enough to take these photographs, the project's value as a genuine collaboration has already been registered. When Mark's lifeless body falls to the floor, he is surrounded not only by a weeping Helen, but by the manuscript of *The Magic Camera* that she has inscribed to him. It reads, "From One Magic Camera which needs the help of Another!"

Helen's manuscript testifies to the tangible existence of women's work, while her inscription poignantly enacts what Quigly condemns in *Peeping Tom*'s "under-the-skin horrors" and "direct emotional realism"—the sensation of recognition, of acknowledging "them" as "us." While many films of the New Wave won lavish critical praise for their "frankness" and "truthfulness," *Peeping Tom* paid a heavy price for pushing "realism" from comfortable contemplation to allegorical confrontation. At the time of *Peeping Tom*'s release, only the critic Jean-Paul Török, writing in the French film journal *Positif*, sensed the deep displacement underpinning the critical reception of the British horror film and the British New Wave: "There is much talk now of Free Cinema. However, by its power of suggestion, its frenzy, its invitation to voyage towards the land of dark marvels and erotic fantasy, isn't the English horror film the real Free Cinema?"[84] Today, many critics have discovered in *Peeping Tom* the reason for answering Török's question with a resounding affirmative. Jonathan Rosenbaum has called *Peeping Tom* "the *only* English New Wave film,"[85] and Tony Rayns has claimed, "In the early '60s, there was one brave film (which had nothing to do with kitchen sinks or working class tragedies) which struggled single-handed to drag the British cinema into the present tense: Michael Powell's phenomenal *Peeping Tom*."[86] Powell was unfortunate enough to see his film "forgotten . . . along with its director, for twenty years,"[87] but lucky enough to witness its resurrection. In 1960, however, during a British age of affluence at pains to rewrite the trauma of the people's war, it is no wonder that, as Powell himself so aptly puts it, "when [the critics] got me alone and out on a limb with *Peeping Tom*, they gleefully sawed off the limb and jumped up and down on the corpse."[88]

UNMASKING HIROSHIMA

Demons, Human Beings, and Shindo Kaneto's *Onibaba*

Shindo Kaneto dreams of writing and directing a feature-length film that transpires entirely during the split second of the atomic detonation over Hiroshima on August 6, 1945.[1] Whether or not this ambitious project is ever completed, Shindo's dream testifies to a remarkable artistic commitment that has already produced what is arguably the most important and under-valued body of work dealing with the atomic bomb in Japanese cinema. This chapter examines Shindo's horror film *Onibaba* (1964) as a means of refiguring how cinematic representations of Hiroshima[2] are legislated theoretically, with particular attention to the political issues of victim consciousness, war responsibility, and the construction of gendered models of Japanese national identity. In other words, I wish to posit *Onibaba* as a trauma text alongside the other films discussed in this book—films about historical trauma as well as cases for rethinking how relations between film and the representation of trauma are mapped. In the chapter's second half, these issues are extended to conceptions of Japanese national cinema, with a special emphasis on *Onibaba*'s relation to the seminal, nationally iconic directors Kurosawa Akira and Oshima Nagisa.

The decision to explore these concerns through *Onibaba*, a horror film set in fourteenth-century Japan with no explicit reference to Hiroshima, may seem somewhat puzzling. After all, Shindo, who was born in Hiroshima in 1912 but who is not himself *hibakusha* ("atom bomb–affected person/s"), contributes to a number of films that *do* address atomic destruction directly—films that reflect the complex struggle to depict the Japanese nuclear experience explicitly. In 1949, during an American occupation[3] that applied rigid censorship policies to Japanese films representing the war and particularly the atomic bomb, Shindo cowrote the screenplay for director Oba Hideo's *Nagasaki no kane* (*The Bell of Nagasaki*, 1950), based on the popular memoir of the same name (completed in 1946, but not published until 1949) by nuclear physicist and *hibakusha* Nagai Takashi. Although the film was eventually able to be produced, Shindo first had to endure major story revisions imposed by American censors—the result was a film that could incorporate Nagasaki only as a backdrop for a tragic romance.[4] When the occupation ended in 1952, Shindo returned to Hiroshima to shoot *Genbaku no ko* (*Children of Hiroshima*, 1952) a drama he wrote and directed concerning a young *hibakusha* schoolteacher who returns to Hiroshima several years after the bombing to revisit the lives of her former kindergarten students. Again, Shindo encountered disapproval, only this time the complaints came from very different quarters: one of the film's sponsors, the Japan Teachers Union, felt *Children of Hiroshima* was merely a "tearjerker" without an effective "political orientation" (the union subsequently endorsed Sekigawa Hideo's more didactically leftist and anti-American 1953 film *Hiroshima*).[5] Shindo is also the writer-director of *Daigo fukuryu-maru* (*Lucky Dragon No. 5*, 1958), a drama based on an actual 1954 incident involving a Japanese fishing boat (the *Lucky Dragon*) exposed to deadly radioactive fallout following American nuclear tests at Bikini atoll, as well as *Honno* (*Lost Sex*, 1966), the story of a man made impotent by the atomic bomb. In addition, Shindo continues to work on a long documentary project focusing on *hibakusha* experience entitled *August 6th*.[6]

Why not focus on these films, rather than "read into" *Onibaba* as a Hiroshima allegory? Precisely because the criticism concerned with Japan's cinematic engagements of Hiroshima tends to favor "realist" representations over "allegorical" ones, without a sufficient sense of what allegory might mean in this particular context. For example, Carole Cavanaugh's analysis of Japan's most canonized Hiroshima film to date, Imamura Shohei's *Kuroi ame* (*Black Rain*, 1989) (an adaptation of Ibuse Masuji's 1966 novel of the same name), notes the troubling absence of "an honest reconnection with history beyond allegory" in most Japanese films that touch on Hiroshima.[7] Cavanaugh echoes previous accounts by David Desser, who comments that "the number of [Japanese] films which overtly take the bomb as its subject is less than miniscule . . . the bomb cinema hardly deserves the name,"[8] and Donald Richie, who laments the fact that a "responsible attitude toward Hiroshima is seldom seen on the screen."[9] Cavanaugh, Desser, and Richie all mention the phenomenally successful franchise spawned by *Gojira* (*Godzilla*, Honda Ishiro, 1954) as a particularly problematic example of allegorical treatments of Hiroshima, evidence that Japanese film opts to "engage in a fantasy of futuristic monsters, at the cost of confronting the monstrous reality of the past."[10] Richie also takes to task allegory of a more modernist kind in what remains the most internationally well-known Hiroshima film, Alain Resnais's *Hiroshima, mon amour* (1959)—a French-Japanese coproduction, incidentally, but a decidedly French film in terms of key production personnel. Although he praises the film's various strengths, Richie asks, "Why Hiroshima? Why not *Yokohama mon amour*? The fact of the atomic destruction of the city has little to do with the film (though to be sure the fact of wanton destruction does)."[11]

Before turning to my own refiguration of allegory through *Onibaba*, I want to signal an important degree of sympathy with the impulse to legislate the representation of Hiroshima through terms such as "honest," "overt," and "responsible." The overwhelming fact of the atomic destruction itself, along with the intricate and controversial political issues of war responsibility, victim consciousness, *hibakusha* discrimination, and censorship exercised by both American and Japanese authorities demands that representation answer to the traumatic significance of the event.[12] But as I argued earlier in this book's introduction, too often a well-intended respect for trauma enables a reductive legislation of representation itself. The result, paradoxically, is a closing down of the very discussion that attempts to imagine and interpret representation in ways that might answer to the cultural and historical complexity of traumatic events. In the case of Hiroshima and Japanese cinema, "realism" trumps "allegory" as the critical discourse's preferred representational mode; in other cases, such as Holocaust cinema, "modernism" often trumps "realism."[13] Again, I want to shift such discussions to *moments* of representation rather than entire modes, and to conceptualize representation beyond legislation. In other words, I wish to reinvest allegory with a complexity that exceeds definitions reducible to realism's other or modernism's weaker ancestor. This is not an evasion of representation's connection to discourses of responsibility, but an attempt to refigure how we interpret that relation. By tracing signs of the allegorical moment in *Onibaba*, I once again strive to "blast open the continuum of history" and "seize hold of a memory as it flashes up at a moment of danger."[14]

What would such a "blasting open" mean in the context of Hiroshima and Japanese cinema? Recent studies have drawn attention to the vast political and cultural complexities involved with constructing a collective memory of World War II and the atomic bombings in Japan. Lisa Yoneyama investigates a pronounced shift in postwar Japanese cultural representation that covers over Japan's pre-Hiroshima imperial aggressions in favor of post-Hiroshima national victimhood, where national iconic images of the militarized male are replaced with images of the blameless, self-sacrificing maternal female. Through such a substitution, Yoneyama explains, "postwar Japanese womanhood became fully implicated in sustaining the myth of national innocence and victimology."[15] Central to this myth are figures such as the Japanese "A-bomb maiden," a tragic young heroine suffering from atomic-related illness. Although the "A-bomb maiden" came to prominent international media attention in 1955, when twenty-five young, single *hibakusha* women were sent to the United States for plastic surgery and medical attention, similar women have continued to inhabit Japanese literary, televisual, and cinematic renderings of Hiroshima up until the present day.[16] Through female characters such as the "A- bomb maiden," Yoneyama claims, "conventional gender distinctions [become] the 'other' of the violent, cataclysmic, and extraordinary time of structural crisis and liminality."[17] In short, traditional gender roles are deployed not only to provide a source of stability in the face of trauma, but to displace Japanese national responsibility for the trauma itself. In this sense, the figure of woman enables a historical narrative of forgetting, where victimization replaces responsibility for aggression. This is exactly the sort of narrative that must be blasted open, and I will argue that Shindo's *Onibaba* begins to perform this work as it allegorizes Hiroshima.

BETWEEN VICTIMIZATION AND WAR RESPONSIBILITY

Onibaba tells the story of two nameless peasant women, a mother (Otowa Nobuko) and her daughter-in-law (Yoshimura Jitsuko), who survive in war-torn fourteenth-century Japan by murdering stray samurai and then selling their armor on the black market. (See fig. 3.1.) When the younger woman desires to live with Hachi (Sato Kei), a shady fellow peasant recently escaped from military service, the old woman immediately recognizes the

FIGURE 3.1 *Onibaba* (Shindo Kaneto, 1964): The old woman (Otowa Nobuko) and her daughter-in-law (Yoshimura Jitsuko), survivors in the chaos of wartime. (Courtesy of Jerry Ohlinger's Movie Material)

disastrous implications of this wish—if realized, it would in effect elimi-nate her own means of survival. In an act of defensive manipulation, the old woman dons a demon mask stolen from a fallen samurai in order to frighten her daughter-in-law into staying with her. But the mask is cursed; it eventually fuses with the old woman's face, and when it is finally re-moved, scars reminiscent of atomic radiation burns disfigure her skin.

It is not entirely surprising to learn that Shindo did indeed base the makeup design for the brutal unmasking scene of *Onibaba* on photographs of maimed *hibakusha*.[18] After all, the old woman, the "demon hag"[19] who provides the film with its title, is at once the film's central victim and central aggressor. She is the key that unlocks the film's ambivalent presentation of victimization and war responsibility, as well as the anchor for the film's recasting of traditional gender iconography surrounding these issues. Neither masculinized mon-ster nor feminized victim, but displaying important attributes of both, she is realized in a bravura performance by Otowa Nobuko (also Shindo's wife at the time). Otowa had previously portrayed Takoko, the *hibakusha* schoolteacher and "A-bomb maiden"-like heroine of *Children of Hiroshima*. Part of the brilliance of Otowa's performance as the menacing *onibaba* is that echoes of Takoko remain. This is powerfully apparent in the final moments of the film, when the old woman, trapped beneath her demon mask, confesses to the young woman that it was she, and not an actual demon, that has been frightening her away from her lover. The old woman begs the young woman to help her remove the mask. After offering her unconditional agreement to the young woman's terms, the old woman must endure unbearable pain while the mask is shattered. When the old woman's face is revealed, the young woman recoils in horror and calls her a "demon." She flees from the woman she once recognized as her mother-in-law, but the old woman pursues her while pleading desperately, "I'm not a demon! I'm a human being!"

How, then, do we finally categorize the old woman? Is she a demon or a human being? The film's conclusion exists between the two terms, both thematically and cinematically. The young woman jumps over the deep hole hidden in the reeds where she and her partner have disposed of the bodies of ambushed samurai. The old woman, following close behind, attempts the same leap, but we never learn where she lands. Her jump is repeated and frozen through overlapping editing and slow motion. Does she clear the hole? Do we *want* her to? These are the questions that haunt us after the film ends—questions central to rethinking discourses of victimization and war responsibility in relation to Hiroshima.

Onibaba's release in 1964 falls within the ten-year period (1955–1965) that James J. Orr defines as "a critical period of common acceptance" of "the mythologies of Japanese war victimhood."[20] Although Orr emphasizes just how polyvalent the discourse of Japanese victim consciousness really is—ranging from left-wing critiques of the militarist wartime government and the postwar U.S.-Japan security alliance to right-wing adoptions of pacifism as a means of evading war responsibility—he also asserts that the 1960s in particular "was an era in which the victim became the hero for Japan not only metaphorically but in monetary terms as well." In this era, government compensation packages "bordered on valorizing . . . victim experiences as service to the state." The government's ability to mobilize victimhood discourse during these years helped forge an ideological connection between Japan's booming economic prosperity and the contributions of the war dead, resulting in a climate of "economic nationalism."[21]

Onibaba both reflects and refutes the status of contemporary notions of victimization. On the one hand, the old woman stands in for precisely those victims "bought" through government gifts of compensation; she is a *hibakusha* figure whose son has died in the war, and she receives a compensatory gift from a government official, the high-ranking masked samurai who asks her to show him the road back to Kyoto. However, this "gift" of his mask is not given freely, but must be stolen through murder. And, of course, the mask's "gift" is actually a curse. In this sense, the exchange between the samurai and the old woman evokes governmental versions of victimhood discourse only to underscore their hollowness. The old woman lays bare government hypocrisy by calling the samurai's use of the mask a failure. "You just lost and ran from a battle," she tells the samurai, "it's useless for a loser to look strong." After the old woman tricks the samurai into plunging to his death in the hole, she removes the mask and discovers not the beautiful visage promised by the samurai, but a hideously scarred, *hibakusha*-like face. "So this is the face of a samurai general?" she laughs. *Onibaba* suggests that in regard to the politics of victimization, things are not nearly as transparent as they might first appear. (See fig. 3.2.)

Still, the presentation of the samurai as a wartime government official whose true identity, beneath the mask, is that of a victimized *hibakusha* rather than a militarist victimizer seems to displace war responsibility even as it questions the governmental politics of victimhood. Or does it? *Onibaba*'s class narrative rests on the fact that the war waged by upper-class samurai has robbed the old peasant woman of both her son and her ability to farm, leaving her no alternative but to scavenge off the class that victimized her. This class narrative echoes contemporaneous views espoused by the Japanese left that attribute blame for the war to Japan's ruling class and military elite. Lisa Yoneyama identifies these views as catalysts for widely embraced memories of the atomic bombings "shaped almost exclusively by the perception that ordinary Japanese people had been the passive victims of historical conditions."[22] But here again, *Onibaba* generates a powerful ambivalence. The disease that evokes atomic burns in the film may have originated with the samurai, but it is clearly a contagious affliction, capable of transcending class and gender distinctions. The film, through its images of repetition and contagion, insists that neither war responsibility nor war victimization can be the exclusive province of "ordinary" Japanese subjects or the "extraordinary" Japanese elite. In fact, the samurai's first words to the old woman, "Don't be afraid. I'm a man, not a demon," return with the old woman's final cry of "I'm not a demon! I'm a human being!" Similarly, the old woman's dismissal of the samurai's pain ("serves you right") recurs later when the young woman is equally contemptuous of the old woman's anguish. In this manner, war responsibility emerges as intertwined between victimizer and victimized, upper class and lower class, male and fe-

FIGURE 3.2 *Onibaba* (Shindo Kaneto, 1964): Victims or victimizers? The masked samurai general (Uno Jukichi) and the old woman (Otowa Nobuko). (Courtesy of Jerry Ohlinger's Movie Material)

male, to complicate the very notion of demarcating "demons" and "human beings" in the face of Hiroshima.[23]

Onibaba's setting reinforces the film's challenge to conventional distributions of war responsibility. Prominent dialogue specifies the film's historical moment as the *nanbokuchō* (or "Warring States") era, a chaotic fifty-year period during the fourteenth century when two different imperial courts, a "northern court" in Kyoto and a "southern court" in the Yoshino Mountains, battled each other for supremacy.[24] Hachi and the old woman's son, Kichi, are first pressed into service by the Ashikaga, supporters of the northern emperor, but are later captured and forced to fight for the Kusunoki, backers of the southern emperor. As Hachi explains, the sides mean nothing to them as peasant soldiers—only survival counts. However, this fourteenth-century period of rival emperors has a suggestive relevance for postwar Japan, particularly in light of John W. Dower's detection of a remarkable continuity, rather than a radical break, between the wartime Japanese militarist regime and the postwar democracy of the American occupation. The two regimes share much at the level of symbolic discourse, including the centrality of Emperor Hirohito. In fact, Dower argues that staunch postwar American support of the emperor, "in whose name all of Asia had been savaged . . . came close to turning the entire issue of 'war responsibility' into a joke."[25] The "joke" stems from an impossible erasure attempted by the American occupation authorities—the "divine" emperor's wartime association with Japanese imperialist aggression was expected to vanish in favor of the "human" emperor's postwar championing of peace and democracy.[26]

In this sense, postwar Japan, not unlike fourteenth-century Japan, was ruled by "two" emperors—in the sense of the divided single person of Hirohito, but also in the sense of the long shadows cast by General Douglas MacArthur and the American occupation, shadows that stretch far beyond the occupation's official end in 1952. If, as Dower argues, postwar Japan must be understood as a hybrid creature constructed by "Americanized" Japanese *and* "Japanized" Americans, then war responsibility must be similarly understood as a shared project between the United States and Japan. Both countries have contributed to "official" narratives of the war and the atomic bombings that simplify or exonerate the roles each nation played in these events. For example, the previously discussed Japanese narrative of victimization that refuses to acknowledge connections between Hiroshima and Japanese wartime aggression, or the American narrative that celebrates the atomic bomb as "the shining example of American decisiveness, moral certitude, and technological ingenuity in the service of the nation."[27] *Onibaba*'s allegorical juxtaposition of the two emperors of the fourteenth century with the double "emperors" of the twentieth century embraces Benjamin's temporality of *Jetztzeit*, when the past and present illuminate each other in such a fashion that the "official" continuum of history explodes. "Has the earth turned upside down?" the old woman asks when Hachi speaks of unnatural war-related occurrences such as the rising of a black sun and the substitution of night for day. These images of solar eclipse are also images of atomic destruction, just as the old woman's question also pronounces the film's allegorical disruption of official narratives of war responsibility.

WOMAN AND GROUND ZERO

Onibaba begins with a precredits sequence that introduces the landscape. A high-angle shot overlooking a field of swaying reeds (susuki grass) tracks until it comes to rest on a large, dark hole. A cut abruptly reverses this frame composition, switching to a low-angle shot that tracks slowly upward from inside the hole. Another cut returns to the previous high-angle shot.

These three shots are accompanied by a brief written narration: "A hole . . . deep and dark . . . a reminder of ages past." One striking effect of this sequence is the animation of a supposedly barren landscape; the alternation between high and low-angle shots lends the hole a kind of living presence, the beginnings of a perspective of its own. The hole is the first "character" we meet in *Onibaba*—it is the film's narrative ground zero.

Of course, the hole might also be imagined as *Onibaba*'s allegorical ground zero. John Whittier Treat notes how common it is for *hibakusha* accounts to begin with an explanation of the narrator's precise distance from ground zero, "as if that place both permits and curbs the words to follow."[28] The hole in *Onibaba* functions similarly—it is the site of trauma in the landscape that both begins and ends the lives of the people surrounding it. *Hibakusha* often divide their lives into preatomic and postatomic selves; the characters of *Onibaba* must also reckon with the hole as a marker of radical life changes—from farmer to killer, from subject of samurai to predator on samurai, from "demon" to "human being." This, however, is not the hole's lone purpose in the film. The hole also represents an important component of *Onibaba*'s overtly sexualized landscape. When Hachi "speaks" to the hole directly and confesses his thwarted desire for a woman, he seems to identify the hole as a sign of "woman." The vaginal opening in the earth mirrors his unrequited sexual desire back to him, just as his words return as echoes from the hole's depths. Once again, the conventional iconography of Japanese victimization presents itself here, with ground zero coded feminine according to the postwar cultural pattern described above by Lisa Yoneyama. Yet in this case, the hole has significant complements in the landscape that invite meanings other than victimization as feminization. The seemingly endless field of reeds also includes an anomalous, bare tree with twisted branches. The old woman "uses" this tree in much the same manner that Hachi "uses" the hole—she clutches the phallic trunk in a fit of sexual frustration, while Hachi and the young woman make love. This parallelism between Hachi and the old woman, drawn along lines of a bisexualized landscape, complicates claims that the film imagines war solely through feminine victimization. Instead, the hole as "woman" rhymes with and matches the tree as "man," just as the tree hosts the crows who feed off corpses dumped into the hole. In addition, the cave belonging to the trader Ushi (Tonoyama Taiji), where the women exchange their stolen spoils for provisions, bears strong graphic and thematic resemblances to the hole. It is also a "deep and dark" space where voices echo, and where the specter of death looms. Hachi meets his demise here, surprised by a looter who has probably killed Ushi as well. The cave is a male-dominated location for economic transactions (whose ultimate collapse seems to critique contemporary "economic nationalism" in Japan), but it suggests more kinship with the hole than difference. In short, *Onibaba's* ground zero exists within a *network* of sites that resists tendencies to define a war-ravaged landscape as either "masculine" or "feminine."

Onibaba also subverts that aforementioned female icon of Hiroshima representation, the "A-bomb maiden." Maya Morioka Todeschini has demonstrated how the "A-bomb maiden" typically embodies qualities associated with an idealized (and desexualized) female youth and beauty, stoic maternal sacrifice, and traditional Japanese cultural values.[29] Although *Onibaba's* old woman evokes the victimized *hibakusha*, she diverges radically from standard conceptions of the "A-bomb maiden." She is neither young nor beautiful, and she retains a fierce sexuality. She struggles tenaciously to maintain ties with the young woman, rather than accepting her departure with silent, sacrificial resignation. The old woman's connection to traditional Japanese culture is similarly unorthodox. As Keiko McDonald explains (and as I will elaborate later in the chapter), her *hannya* mask originates from Noh theater and symbolizes the "jealous fury that transforms a woman into a demon" as well as an "internalized sorrow."[30] The mask's association with the old woman, however, does not celebrate the classical Japanese theatrical tradition; instead, it functions as an affliction. The mask does not safeguard ancient ways, but inflicts modern wounds. If the typical "A-bomb maiden" stands for the enduring beauty and innocence of traditional "Japaneseness" despite the technological onslaught of the atomic bomb, then the old woman of *Onibaba* presents the painful, occluded underside of this image. The harrowing difference between the two speaks to the trauma of Hiroshima, not its wishful redemption via an idealized femininity.

Does this grant *Onibaba*, against all expectation, a feminist inflection on the representation of trauma? The eminent Japanese film critic Sato Tadao includes Shindo, along with Mizoguchi Kenji and Imamura Shohei, among those directors who participate in "the worship of womanhood," a "special Japanese brand of feminism" where "the image of a woman suffering uncomplainingly can imbue us with admiration for a virtuous existence almost beyond our reach, rich in endurance and courage." For Sato, "one can idealize [these women] rather than merely pity [them]."[31] I would argue that *Onibaba's* somewhat paradoxical "feminist" stance derives from its ability to *contest* this "worship of womanhood" rather than inhabit it in any straightforward manner. Sato himself admits that although Shindo's portrayal of women was influenced by his apprenticeship with Mizoguchi, Shindo's own version of womanhood worship "revealed itself to be of a different hue." The difference resides in the movement from suffering to vengeance, a movement that leads Sato to suggest that Shindo's heroines of the 1960s "could have been a reflection of postwar society, since it is commonly said that in Japan women have become stronger because men have lost all confidence in their masculinity due to Japan's defeat."[32] Sato's "reflection" here should not be confused with Benjamin's sense of allegory. *Onibaba* allegorizes Hiroshima in Benjaminian fashion not by "reflecting" dominant narratives about Hiroshima, but by disrupting the desire to map Hiroshima onto the "continuum of history" constituted by these narratives. In other words, allegory poses questions about how the "continuum of history" is constructed, how it attains the authority to explain events such as Hiroshima. In this sense, *Onibaba* is not so much a reflection of postwar Japanese society as an interrogation of how and why the reflections look the way they do. Consequently, *Onibaba* emerges as a "feminist" film not by reflecting the narratives of womanhood worship or an ascendant femininity eclipsing a defeated masculinity, but by questioning the genesis and validity of these narratives.

Even the film's title, "demon hag," gestures toward *Onibaba's* commitment to this work of interrogation. One popular way of understanding the atomic bomb in postwar Japanese culture was as an evil spirit, or a kind of demon. For example, Agawa Hiroyuki's novel *Ma no isan* (*Devil's Heritage*, 1954), which was influential in describing the medical effects of atomic radiation to a mass Japanese audience, represents the bomb as explicitly demonic: "There was nothing to do but to regard the atomic bomb as an evil spirit which had appeared in the world in the form of a scientific creation."[33] Another popular way of understanding the bomb, as we have seen, was as a switch point between Japanese national aggression (coded masculine) and Japanese national victimization (coded feminine). In both its title and its content, *Onibaba* defamiliarizes these two discourses by combining them unexpectedly. Instead of the passive, victimized beauty of a self-sacrificing woman, we see the violent beauty of a resourceful "hag" bent on survival. Instead of an atomic bomb decipherable only as an otherworldly evil spirit, we see the ravages of an all-too-human war. And ultimately, alongside "demons," we see human beings.

NATIONAL IDENTITY AND NATIONAL CINEMA: KUROSAWA AND SHINDO

This chapter began by urging the revision of what it might mean to allegorize Hiroshima. By drawing on Benjamin's sense of allegory as a mode uniquely equipped to engage traumatic history, I interpreted *Onibaba* as a representation of Hiroshima capable of recasting the critical bind between "realist" and "allegorical" treatments of the atomic bomb in Japanese cinema. The stakes of this recasting, as I argued, involve the politics underlying discourses of victimization and war responsibility in postwar Japanese culture, particularly in regard to how those discourses are gendered. These discourses, in turn, generate narratives of Japanese national consensus surrounding Hiroshima and World War II, and I posited *Onibaba*'s allegorical engagement of the war as an interrogation of these narratives. In short, I sought to investigate the place of trauma, of "Hiroshima," in the desire for a national identity called "Japan." But how does this desire for a Japanese national identity intersect with the discursive construction of a Japanese national cinema?

To speak of Japanese national cinema inevitably necessitates turning to Kurosawa Akira. Kurosawa's death in 1998 has only enhanced his standing as Japan's most internationally visible and celebrated director. Indeed, the event of his film *Rashomon* (1950) winning a Grand Prix at the Venice Film Festival in 1951 (and a subsequent Oscar for Best Foreign Language Film) is still conventionally regarded as ushering in a "sudden, and astonished, awareness of Japan's rich heritage of cinematic art."[34] As Mitsuhiro Yoshimoto has recently claimed, "It would not be an exaggeration to say that Kurosawa has been almost singularly responsible for the global recognition of Japanese cinema as a viable national cinema worth paying attention to."[35] Kurosawa himself often embraced this role as the representative of Japanese national cinema. In his 1982 autobiography, he describes *Rashomon*'s success at Venice as "pouring water into the sleeping ears of the Japanese film industry," and responds to the backlash of Japanese critics who belittled his international triumph as little more than a Western orientalist reflex by asking, "Why is it that Japanese people have no confidence in the worth of Japan? Why do they elevate everything foreign and denigrate everything Japanese?"[36]

Given this notion that Kurosawa speaks cinematically for the Japanese nation, it makes sense that no less than three films over the course of the director's career address the subject of the atomic bomb in more or less explicit terms: *Ikimono no kiroku* (*Record of a Living Being*, also known as *I Live in Fear*, 1955), *Yume* (*Dreams*, 1990), and *Hachigatsu no kyoshikoku* (*Rhapsody in August*, 1991). I will focus here on the first and best of these films, *Record of a Living Being*, as it belongs to the same historical moment as *Onibaba*. In addition, the differences between the two films will highlight *Onibaba*'s ability to question the mapping of Hiroshima onto the national image of Japan constructed by Kurosawa, and later deconstructed by Oshima Nagisa as the spearhead of the Japanese New Wave. Shindo provides the allegorical context with which to defamiliarize these two critically established icons of Japanese national cinema.

Record concerns the struggle of elder patriarch Nakajima Kiichi (Mifune Toshiro) to transport his entire family from Japan to South America in the hope of safeguarding them from the fear that consumes him: the possibility of a future atomic apocalypse that will annihilate Japan. The family, which not only includes Nakajima's wife, two sons, two daughters, and various in-laws but also two mistresses and several illegitimate children, resists Nakajima's wishes. They are loath to leave their established lives in Tokyo, which Nakajima's industrial success as a foundry owner has made quite comfortable, and they regard the patriarch's atomic fears as bordering on madness. In fact, his immediate family files suit against him in Tokyo Family Court, claiming that Nakajima must be declared incompetent in order to prevent his emigration plan from proceeding. As tensions between Nakajima and his family rise, he grows increasingly desperate and fearful. After setting fire to his foundry in the delusional hope that the demise of the family business will convince his loved ones to emigrate, Nakajima goes insane and ends up institutionalized. (See fig. 3.3.)

What this brief synopsis of *Record* cannot capture is the film's most powerful suggestion: that Nakajima, living in 1950s Japan and having already faced the facts of Hiroshima, Nagasaki, and the previously mentioned *Lucky Dragon* incident of 1954, is not mad at all but taking the necessary measures to protect his family from an insane world bent on nuclear destruction. Still, how do we evaluate Nakajima's choice to respond *individually* (even when Nakajima believes he acts in the best interests of his family, his decisions are resolutely individual) to what is obviously a social, national, and indeed global problem? This is the question *Record* cannot adequately resolve, and which finally shatters the film into competing thematic and stylistic fragments. Nearly all the major criticism on *Record* comments on the film's troubled, bifurcated nature in some way, ranging from Sato Tadao's sense that the film deals with "the significance of the Bomb . . . as a psychological force devastating human life from within, rather than simply as an outer force of destruction," to Donald Richie's observation that viewers must be "of two minds about [Nakajima's] character and his fears," to Stephen Prince's assertion that "the film is split between its two voices, the social and the psychological, and while wishing to speak in the former, it never fully relinquishes the latter."37

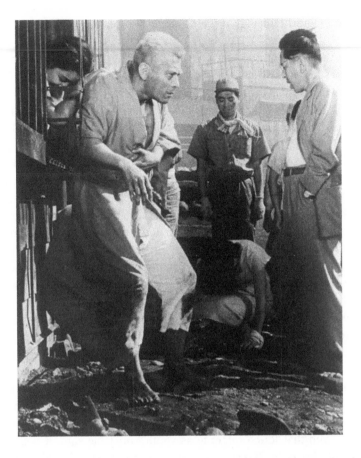

FIGURE 3.3 *Record of a Living Being* (Kurosawa Akira, 1955): The "mad" patriarch Nakajima Kiichi (Mifune Toshiro) after destroying his own foundry. (Courtesy of Jerry Ohlinger's Movie Material)

Record was a box office disappointment in Japan, and Kurosawa himself considered the film at least partially "incoherent" and "chaotic." This sense of confusion seems to begin with the divergent sources of inspiration for the film's production. On the one hand, *Record* sprang from the intensely personal sentiments of one of Kurosawa's closest friends and creative collaborators, the composer Hayasaka Fumio, whose death from tuberculosis during the film's shooting devastated the director: "Truly, at that time, I was like a person half of whom is gone. Hayasaka was indispensable to me." On the other hand, *Record*'s script moved from satire to tragedy based on Kurosawa's growing sense, shared with coscreenwriters Hashimoto Shinobu and Oguni Hideo, that the film must speak in social, national, and even global registers: "We really felt that we were making the kind of picture that, after everything was all over and the last judgment was upon us, we could stand up and account for our past lives by saying proudly: 'We are the men who made *Record of a Living Being.'* "[38]

This tension between the individual and the collective is precisely how Eric Cazdyn characterizes the "historically dominant problem" of Japan's post–World War II moment, particularly in the 1950s and early 1960s when both *Record* and *Onibaba* are released: "A sense of self—of one's capacity and legitimacy to act as an individual and to intervene against the state and collective opinion—was crucial to keep the nation from ever being hijacked again. At the same time . . . the individual must be sacrificed, must give himself or herself over to the collective and to the nation, to rebuild the country. . . . People were forced to exist at the dead center of contradiction."[39] Michael Raine adds an important corollary to the postwar problem of individual/collective contradiction by demonstrating how Japanese cinema from the mid-1950s through the mid-1960s was the "most influential participant" in a cultural debate where " 'youth' in its mental constitution and physical embodiment became an unstable sign, standing for both the future of the country, the producing and consuming generation that would make the economy grow, and for the disaffected and frustrated masses shut out of the Japanese gerontocracy."[40] I will argue that while both *Record* and *Onibaba* are structured by cultural tensions over the nation's definition that Cazdyn articulates in terms of individualism/collectivism and that Raine refers to as youth's unstable sign, it is Shindo's film that interrogates the confused surrender to these contradictions that Kurosawa's film ultimately succumbs to. Comparing the two films along these lines of national identity requires attending to what Raine describes as the "formal obtrusions" apparent in significant Japanese films of this period, those moments when cultural contradictions take shape cinematically through stylistic interruptions of narrative development.[41]

Record and *Onibaba* each conclude with striking instances of formal obtrusion. In *Record*, our final glimpse of Nakajima occurs in his cell on a psychiatric ward. Harada (Shimura Takashi), a sensitive Family Court judge who ruled against Nakajima but has been haunted by the case ever since, visits the old man in the institution. Nakajima, now clearly mad and physically frail, asks Harada if there are many people still living on Earth. Nakajima gestures to his own surroundings and insists that *"this* planet is perfectly safe," that those endangered on Earth must flee. He then looks outside his cell window, where a blazing setting sun overwhelms the view.

"My God!" Nakajima exclaims. "The Earth is burning! It is burning . . . At last the Earth has gone up in flames!" The formal obtrusion in this scene is the camera staring directly into the setting sun through a telephoto lens, generating the visual effect of a blinding atomic blast that envelops Nakajima and Harada in a single spatial plane. But this stylistic obtrusion signifying apocalypse is not the film's final shot. *Record* concludes in the following scene, with another remarkable image captured through a telephoto lens: Harada departs from Nakajima by walking slowly down a ramped stairway, while Nakajima's young mistress and their baby arrive to visit, ascending the same stairway. The flattened space created by the telephoto lens emphasizes the synchronized inversion of their movements, one downwards and one upwards. As Donald Richie observes, "The implications of this scene are inescapable . . . [it] would seem to say there is always room for hope. Perhaps the elders will not be saved, but perhaps the young will be; the experienced are doomed, but the innocent may yet escape."[42]

Richie's observation is bolstered by earlier moments in *Record* that similarly soften the desolation suggested by Nakajima's atomic anxieties (and enacted cinematically by Kurosawa) through redemptive associations with this innocent baby. When a fearful Nakajima mistakes the sound of passing jets for an oncoming atomic attack, Kurosawa presents this hallucination, like the setting sun, as paradoxically substantial—the sound of the planes gives way to blinding lightning, deafening thunder, and a heavy rainfall suggestive of atomic detonation and the "black rain" of nuclear fallout. But just as Nakajima's vision of a burning Earth is redeemed by the hopeful symbol of his infant child coming to visit, the terror of this hallucination is balanced by the simultaneous image of Nakajima's instinctive, protective cradling of this same child. In another scene, Nakajima slips into tranquilized sleep after suffering a nervous breakdown. Kurosawa frames Nakajima's sleeping figure through the meshed cloth surrounding his bed, resulting in a visual approximation of atomic ashes spread over Nakajima's features. Again, this harrowing image is tamed by an analogous connection with the baby; the infant sleeps peacefully in a nearby room, untouched by the "ashes of death."

Where the conclusion of *Record* focuses on formal balance and the redemption of the old by the young in an atomic age, *Onibaba*'s ending insists on stylistic imbalance and youth's abandonment of the old in the (allegorically literalized) face of Hiroshima. The conclusion of *Onibaba*, as noted earlier, features the formal obtrusions of slow motion and overlapping editing in the film's final shots—the old woman leaps over the hole (never landing) not once, but six times, her cry of "I'm a human being!"

uniting this repetitive series of slow-motion shots that call and recall attention to her ravaged face. We never learn if the old woman catches up with the young daughter-in-law who has fled from her in terror. *Record* resolves the "unstable sign" of youth by presenting it as the potential savior of the old, and in the process, it offers a makeshift solution to the tensions between individualism and collectivism splitting the nation's identity. Nakajima's threat to discourses of both individualism (he is a tyrannical individualist, overruling the wishes of others) and collectivism (his insanity doubles as his deep concern for the collective—not only for his family, but for his workers he cannot bear to see disenfranchised by his own act of arson, and finally, for his planet) is ultimately emptied out by removing him from the film's thematic and visual economies. Nakajima himself does not appear in *Record*'s final scene because he is no longer a figure whom the audience must contemplate uncomfortably; his character has been contained through physical confinement and psychological madness, his sense of a catastrophically imbalanced world now balanced through a redemptive association with youth that culminates in Kurosawa's final frame composition.

Onibaba, on the other hand, demands that viewers continue to live with the confrontational presence of the film's old woman, including her searing questions for the nation. The record of the living being named Nakajima Kiichi feels closed by the end of Kurosawa's film, but the record of *Onibaba*'s old woman, still nameless, still existing somewhere in the borderlands between "demon" and "human being," remains horrifyingly open. In her ruined face, projected toward us in the film's final six shots, we must see simultaneously an old witch who is the victimizer of youthful desire, a victim of militarized state violence who bears the scars of a *hibakusha*, a peasant woman desperate to assert her individuality as a human being, and a symbol of collective trauma that crosses boundaries of gender and class. *Onibaba* thus closes with an allegorical moment that leaves viewers *with* the old woman, and *between* the categories she evokes so powerfully—individual/collective, young/old, victim/victimizer, demon/human being.

By contrast, *Record* chooses to leave viewers distanced and isolated from the series of allegorical moments Nakajima has embodied throughout the film—the questions he poses finally seem *outside* of us, put behind us somehow. As Kurosawa comments, "after I had made [*Record of a Living Being*], I felt as if I had put down a heavy load. I felt as though I had gone through a lot of things, had gotten rid of a lot of things."[43] Perhaps not unexpectedly, Kurosawa has also noted that Nakajima is not the character he feels closest to in the film. Instead, it is the minor character of Yamazaki

(Shimizu Masao), an in-law who remarks, as the family exits the institution they have driven Nakajima to exist within, "After all, perhaps it's the happiest state for Father."[44] Shindo, on the other hand, when questioned about his identification with *Onibaba*'s old woman, insists, "she is myself. I am Onibaba."[45]

Another important way in which *Onibaba* questions Japanese national identity on the fronts where *Record* consolidates it is through the deployment of Noh theater conventions. Kurosawa deeply admired Noh as an authentic Japanese national tradition, and its inspiration explicitly marks a number of his films, perhaps most famously *Kumonosu-jo* (*The Throne of Blood*, 1957) and *Ran* (1985).[46] But the influence of Noh can also be felt implicitly in a wider range of Kurosawa's work, including *Record*. Indeed, the aforementioned formal balance that characterizes *Record*'s conclusion could be read as manifesting Noh's common dramatic tendency toward the Buddhist concept of *mujo*, or "the mutability of all earthly things." *Mujo* contrasts human impermanence with the eternal "circularity of time," those natural cycles of destruction and renewal that render human actions fleeting and vain.[47] *Record*'s final image of youthful innocence ascending while elder experience descends harnesses *mujo* to create a sense of closure that affirms time's natural rhythms of death and rebirth. By channeling this affirmation through Noh conventions (not just *mujo* but also Noh's spartan aesthetic of "simplicity-as-complexity" where only two basic character types, protagonist and deuteragonist, are employed),[48] Kurosawa endows *Record*'s ending with an additional form of closure: the comforting permanence of an ancient, authentically "Japanese" national art form to which *Record* ultimately reveals its allegiance. As Kurosawa explains, "Essentially, I am very Japanese. I like Japanese ceramics, Japanese painting—but I like the Noh best of all."[49] The conclusion of *Record* depends, in crucial ways, on Kurosawa's conviction that "the Noh is a truly unique art form that exists nowhere else in the world."[50]

Onibaba also evokes Noh as a sign of Japanese national identity, but the film makes this sign disturbingly strange, not soothingly familiar. Shindo's use of the *hannya* mask and reliance on heavy drumming punctuated by human cries for *Onibaba*'s score (as composed by Hayashi Hikaru) are direct quotations of Noh style.[51] But Shindo subverts the desire to posit Noh as a timeless, authentic national essence by unmasking (both literally and figuratively) the characters of *Onibaba* as allegorical representatives of Hiroshima's traumatic modernity. Any appeal to the sturdy continuity of Noh's national artistic lineage crumbles when the traditional guise of Noh gives way to the nationally disjunctive visage of World War II, when Noh conventions appear only to be turned inside out. For example, nothing could be further from *mujo* (despite the film's origins in a Buddhist folktale) than *Onibaba*'s discontinuous final images, with their insistence on time's frozen paralysis rather than eternal flow.

Onibaba similarly resists Noh's dominant impulse to resolve the struggles of its ghostly, spiritually possessed characters by releasing them from their tortured state (whether through salvation, enlightenment, or defeat in combat).[52] Indeed, one of the most well-known Noh plays to feature the *hannya* mask prominently is Zeami's *Kurozuka* (*Black Mound*), where an old woman's invitation to house a traveling priest and his companion for the night results in a chilling revelation: the old woman is actually a demon who feasts on human flesh and hides a pile of corpses nearby. When the priest and his friend take flight, the old woman pursues them in her demonic form. After engaging her in combat, the priest succeeds in subduing her.[53] Of course, there is no such resolution for the old woman of *Onibaba*, as viewers must wrestle with the ambiguity of her classification as "demon" or "human being." Although this ambiguity is not entirely absent from *Kurozuka*, where the demon has been interpreted as either a "*saidōfūki* (human heart in demon form), a woman whose extreme loneliness has changed her into a man-eating demon," or a "*rikidōfūki* (true demon) who disguises herself as a woman and awaits the arrival of hapless travelers,"[54] Shindo radically recasts the dramatic framework of a Noh play such as *Kurozuka*. Not only is the old woman of *Onibaba* never defeated, but it is unclear whether spectators even wish for her "defeat." In *Onibaba*, the "black mound" becomes an allegorical ground zero—not just a pile of innocent corpses, but the remains of those soldiers at least partially responsible for the old woman's economic plight. Shindo's old woman does not eat her victims, she slays her victims in order to eat. In this sense, the climactic unmasking of the old woman in *Onibaba* also condenses the film's estrangement of Noh conventions, its commitment to interrogating the notion of an authentic national essence rather than appealing to Noh as an artistic crystallization of that essence.

NATIONAL IDENTITY AND NATIONAL CINEMA: SHINDO AND OSHIMA

Of course, this spirit of interrogating Japanese national essences, including the traditional construction of Japanese national cinema, also applies to the critical tone of those contemporary films belonging to the Japanese

New Wave. David Desser, whose *Eros Plus Massacre: An Introduction to the Japanese New Wave Cinema* (1988) remains an invaluable guide to the movement that roughly spans the years between 1960 and 1970, defines the New Wave as "films produced and/or released in the wake of Oshima's *A Town of Love and Hope* [*Ai to kibo no machi*, 1959], films which take an overtly political stance in a general way or toward a specific issue, utilizing a deliberately disjunctive form compared to previous filmic norms in Japan."[55] Although Desser's volume devotes careful attention to social and historical context, its recourse to the organizing frame of an "overtly political" New Wave distinct from contemporary, related, but implicitly less political Japanese films ultimately limits its consideration of what a cinematic "political stance" might look like. While Oshima's films stand as the origin and primary point of interest in the New Wave for Desser (four of the seven chapters in *Eros Plus Massacre* take their titles from Oshima's films), more genre-associated contemporary directors are referred to as "just to the side of the New Wave, trying to deal with its primary issues while being subjugated to genre films" (Suzuki Seijun), "stand[ing] alongside the movement . . . while his films are often thematically appropriate, their style is formally closer to the works of Kobayashi [Masaki] and Ichikawa [Kon] than to Oshima or Yoshida [Yoshishige]" (Masumura Yasuzo), or, at best, "crucial predecessors and contemporaries of the New Wave" (Masumura and Shindo).[56] It is to Desser's credit that these directors are given the brief but meaningful profiles they receive in *Eros Plus Massacre*, but their banishment to the margins of the New Wave has serious implications for how film history interprets the politics of this era of Japanese film, both "inside" and "outside" the New Wave, and, by extension, how film history constructs a certain kind of Japanese national cinema. As Eric Cazdyn reminds us, "film histories do not only analyze their acknowledged objects of study . . . they also, at the same time, symbolically intervene . . . with the politically charged ways in which [the most critical transformations of the nation-state] are thought."[57]

This is not to say that the New Wave never existed or that directors such as Oshima, Yoshida, and Shinoda Masahiro do not represent a significant, identifiable current within 1960s Japanese cinema that distinguishes their work from that of others. What is at stake here is how the New Wave is defined and deployed, how the concept functions to include and exclude certain films as "political" or "apolitical" while constructing a Japanese national cinema for film history. It is important to begin by recognizing that Oshima himself, despite his distaste for the "New Wave" moniker,[58] often contributed to the sense that his films did not (or would not) resemble the body of Japanese cinema—a cinema he often wished to distance himself from.

For example, in an essay published in 1958, shortly before his own debut as a director, Oshima questions whether recent trends in Japanese cinema can be considered meaningful "breakthroughs" toward modernity in a nation and a national cinema he describes as locked in a "premodern system" that stifles "human freedom and human rights."[59] Oshima delineates two groups of filmmakers, the "realists" and the "modernists," whose attempts to rebel against Japanese premodernity are found to be inadequately political in the final analysis. The realists, who include Kinoshita Keisuke, Imai Tadashi, and Kurosawa, are praised for their ability to "maintain a balance between innovation of form and content and audience receptiveness," but critiqued for their failure to undermine the "strong conservatism" that characterizes the "existing relationship between the traditional form of the mainstream Japanese film and the Japanese consciousness and view of life."[60] The modernists, who include Nakahira Ko, Shirasaka Yoshio, and Masumura, are looked on with more promise than the realists. For Oshima, the "newness" of the modernists "probably represents the biggest breakthrough in the wall of the Japanese film," but he also notes their limitations when it comes to "challenging the premodernity of Japanese society": the modernists "decided to shock their audiences, rather than persuade or move them, by filming images of people created on the basis of concepts that had no connection to that social reality and its forms."[61]

Oshima's determination that neither the realists nor the modernists effectively address the social realities of modern Japan opens a space in Japanese cinema that Oshima himself, as the central figure of a Japanese New Wave, will soon step into. But for Oshima to name this space as truly political and, in the process, to denote the work of Japan's realist and modernist filmmakers as apolitical (or at least insufficiently political) obscures what recent scholarship on 1950s and 1960s Japanese cinema has begun to make clear: that directors such as Masumura and Ichikawa, routinely marginalized in film history from the political significance of the New Wave, demand reconsideration as political innovators in their own right. In fact, Michael Raine suggests that once the full import of this reconsideration becomes apparent, the Japanese New Wave will no longer "seem so *nouvelle* after all."[62] I would argue that Shindo's name must be added to this list, that his Hiroshima-centered work challenges the influential definitions of Japanese national identity and national cinema anchored to the figures of Kurosawa, on the one hand, and Oshima, on the other.[63]

These issues of definition arise when David Desser calls Oshima's *Nihon no yoru to kiri* (*Night and Fog in Japan*, 1960) "one of the paradigmatic films of the Japanese New Wave cinema," an "overtly political, stylistically radical film" that marks Oshima's "most complete break with the past."[64] The film concerns the efforts of student radicals in 1960 to protest the U.S.-Japan Security Treaty, a watershed political event in postwar Japan that can be summarized here only briefly.[65] The Security Treaty, a crucial document with regard to shaping military and economic alliances between the United States and Japan, was first passed in 1951; it became a lightning rod for struggles between the left and right before it came due for renewal ten years later. The right, represented by the ruling Liberal Democratic Party (LDP) and Prime Minister Kishi Nobusuke, strongly supported the treaty's renewal but sought certain revisions that would distribute alliances between the two countries more equitably. The left, consisting of a number of organizations representing socialists, communists, trade unions, and student unions, vehemently "opposed the new treaty on the grounds that it permanently subordinated Japan to U.S. strategic interests."[66] Although the left staged mass anti–Security Treaty protests that climaxed during the winter of 1959 through the summer of 1960, the treaty was still ultimately renewed. *Night and Fog in Japan* qualifies (recalling Desser's terms) as "overtly political" because it focuses on a group of students active in the left's anti-treaty struggle, and details the personal and political betrayals that defeat the movement. (See fig. 3.4.) The film is "stylistically radical" not only because of its extensive use of long takes, but because of its juxtaposition of two different time frames, the early 1950s and the year 1960, in order to highlight the conflict and continuity between the Old Left and New Left versions of the student movement.

The problem for film history does not rest with Desser's labels of "overtly political" and "stylistically radical" themselves, but with how these labels come to define *Night and Fog in Japan* through a New Wave national aesthetic—an aesthetic that significantly limits possibilities for imagining Japanese cinema's engagement with historical trauma in the postwar political landscape. These issues come into vivid relief when Desser discusses the film's title, with its explicit reference to Alain Resnais's documentary on the Nazi concentration camps, *Nuit et brouillard* (*Night and Fog*, 1955): "If it strikes the Western observer as extreme to compare the horror of the Nazi extermination camps with the feeling of having been betrayed by the Old Left, it may be that at bottom it is the sense of betrayal that is being highlighted in both films."[67] Indeed, both films offer powerful critiques of how older generations can betray younger ones in the face of social and po-

FIGURE 3.4 *Night and Fog in Japan* (Oshima Nagisa, 1960): Student radicals struggle over ideological divisions from without and within. (Courtesy of Jerry Ohlinger's Movie Material)

litical struggle, whether the point of reference is Resnais's occupied France or Oshima's post-occupation Japan. But to align the films solely through this rather vague "sense of betrayal" minimizes the potential political specificities of their interconnection.[68] The danger implicit in Desser's account becomes explicit in Maureen Turim's impressive major study of Oshima, where she claims that *Night and Fog in Japan* "has entirely different subject matter [than *Night and Fog*]; the link seems to be more in the stylistic daring . . . Resnais brought to the film essay."[69]

What becomes occluded here is the context of historical trauma in the construction of national identity, of the connection between Hiroshima and the Holocaust that disappears when *Night and Fog in Japan* is considered chiefly as a New Wave paradigm but reappears when the film is juxtaposed with *Onibaba*. The allegorical encounter with national discourses of war responsibility and victimization present in *Onibaba* opens up the anti–Security Treaty movement of *Night and Fog in Japan* to World War II and its acts of mass death, rather than closing down the thrust of the film's politics to a depiction of tensions between the Old Left and New Left and the film's style to a merely formal engagement with *Night and Fog*. Yoshikuni Igarashi has argued compellingly for an interpretation of the anti–Security

Treaty protests as anti-Kishi protests, where the prime minister's ties to the pre-1945 militarist regime transformed the demonstrations into (in the provocative words of one of the student participants) "the Japanese people's war criminals trial that came fifteen years late."[70] George R. Packard, III, in an earlier study of the protests, lends additional support to this view when he claims that "the massive participation of the students had as much to do with feelings of inferiority and shame left over from World War II as it did with their proclaimed desire to prevent World War III."[71] The specter of World War II that haunts the anti–Security Treaty movement extends to the atomic legacy of Hiroshima as well. Packard points out how centrally the issue of nuclear arms figures "throughout the whole treaty negotiation period," how "the Socialists kept the issue on the front pages . . . by suggesting Kishi could not be sure that U.S. forces would not import atomic arms."[72] Finally, Oshima's own sense that the core of postwar Japanese protest movements that preceded (and influenced) the anti–Security Treaty struggle originated in a collective "sense of victimization" suggests a striking conjunction between Japanese atomic bomb discourse and *Night and Fog in Japan.* Oshima blames the "sense of victimization" for the failure of the anti–Security Treaty movement, in that the Communist Party, so important for both the Old and New Left, relied upon it rather than seeking a new way to address the masses.[73]

With these factors in mind, the conclusion of *Night and Fog in Japan,* with its devastating portrait of the anti–Security Treaty movement's failure, resonates both with Hiroshima and with the Holocaust context of *Night and Fog.* As the wedding ceremony that has served as the film's primary setting disintegrates, Nakayama (Yoshizawa Takao), the lead organizer of the now older student activists, berates his comrades for sympathizing with radical protestors whom he denigrates as "irresponsible rabble rousers who have lost all contact with reality." Nakayama's position as a sellout is confirmed by the disillusioned expressions of his comrades, as well as by the musical score's engulfment of his words. His calls for unity and responsibility fade into meaninglessness as the music's volume mounts; we become deaf to his words, but the film clearly conveys the fact that it is Nakayama who is deaf to the need for responsibility. This is not the first time the film invokes the term "responsibility," with its inevitable connotations of "war responsibility," a discourse I have shown to be central to the Hiroshima allegories of *Onibaba* as well as at "the heart of cultural considerations" in postwar Japan.[74] Earlier, when certain older activists (including Nakayama) resist what they perceive as the needless probing of the movement's painful past, another student counters, "What do you mean by 'the past'? It's a matter of responsibility."

The conclusion of Resnais's *Night and Fog* places a similar emphasis on a discourse of responsibility. The last of the film's archival footage contrasts harrowing images of the mass graves of concentration camp victims with Nazis testifying, over and over again, to the fact that they are "not responsible." "Who is responsible then?" asks the film's narrator. This question is never answered explicitly in the few remaining moments of the film, but its images of ruin drawn from the present-day sites of the camps generate a powerful answer of their own—an answer that evokes Benjamin's claim for the ruin's significance to allegorical representation. "Allegories are, in the realm of thoughts, what ruins are in the realm of things," writes Benjamin. "In the process of decay, and in it alone, the events of history shrivel up and become absorbed in the setting."[75] The ruin, in other words, has a privileged potential for generating the shock of the allegorical moment. And here, at the conclusion of *Night and Fog*, lies an allegorical moment of ruin that will enter into a constellation with *Night and Fog in Japan*; a constellation encompassing historical trauma made possible, in certain ways, by considering Oshima's film alongside *Onibaba*. As Resnais's camera tracks along the twisted heaps of concrete and metal that once housed the infernal machinery of the camp ("the furnace is no longer in use," says the narrator), one is compelled to recall another iconography of ruins tied to mass destruction, another technology of mass death. Indeed, the narration encourages the connection to Hiroshima suggested by the images when it refers to a newer, more horribly efficient mode of killing: "The skill of the Nazis is child's play today."

The narrator's final words in *Night and Fog* are similarly significant for *Night and Fog in Japan*: "There are those who look at these ruins today as though the monster were dead and buried beneath them. Those who take hope again as the image fades, as though there were a cure for the scourge of these camps. Those who pretend all this happened only once, at a certain time and in a certain place. Those who refuse to look around them, deaf to the endless cry." Just as Oshima's film ends with an evocation of deafness to convey an ideological blindness linked to war responsibility, as Nakayama's words surrender to the score, so too does Resnais's film. I am not arguing that Oshima necessarily intended to echo *Night and Fog* in such a deliberate and subtle manner, but I am claiming that the allegorical moment created through *Night and Fog*'s proximity to *Night and Fog in Japan* is of vital import for film history's construction of a political national cinema during the Japanese New Wave period. In the flash of *Jetztzeit* that Benjamin admonishes us to guide our writing of history, the deafness to the Holocaust critiqued in *Night and Fog* illuminates the deafness to Hiroshima critiqued in *Night and*

Fog in Japan.[76] The spark for this flash was made possible by yet another "endless cry": the old woman calling out, "I'm not a demon! I'm a human being!" at the conclusion of *Onibaba.* To attend to such illuminations is to honor the spirit of Shindo's own dream of *Jetztzeit,* a two-hour depiction of one second in Hiroshima, whether the film is ever made or not.

"ONLY A MOVIE"

Specters of Vietnam in Wes Craven's *Last House on the Left*

"Can a movie go *too far?*"

The question appears as the banner above an advertisement for Wes Craven's notorious independent American horror film, *Last House on the Left* (1972). (See fig. 4.1.) The ad's disclaimer supplies an answer: "The movie makes a plea for an end to all the senseless violence and inhuman cruelty that has become so much a part of the times in which we live. WE DON'T THINK ANY MOVIE CAN GO *TOO FAR* IN MAKING THIS MESSAGE HEARD AND FELT!" According to the ad, the film's ability to force viewers into "feeling" its "message" is so potent that audiences are instructed: "To avoid fainting, keep repeating, it's only a movie . . . only a movie . . . "

Rather than dismissing this remarkable (and remarkably successful)[1] ad as a meaningless publicity stunt, I wish to use it as a point of entry into the allegorical moments that lend *Last House* a powerful cinematic and cultural significance for America's traumatic Vietnam era. What the ad refers

FIGURE 4.1 Advertisement for *Last House on the Left* (Wes Craven, 1972). (From Richard Meyers, *For One Week Only: The World of Exploitation Films*, 96)

to as "the times in which we live" are times of extraordinary national crisis in the late 1960s and early 1970s, when the definition of "America" is subject to such fiercely opposed forces that the nation often verges on tearing itself in half. The two halves show themselves in a number of interrelated, polarized guises, which of course only begin to suggest the deeper political complexities beneath the generalized labels: right/left, old/young, prowar/antiwar, bourgeois culture/counterculture, white/black, middle class/working class, straight/gay, and patriarchy/feminism, among others. The Vietnam era did not invent these cultural oppositions, but the remarkable degrees of polarization they reached during the height of the Vietnam War centrally characterizes the national and historical trauma of these years. In this sense, the Vietnam era depends on particularly strong manifestations of what Michael Rogin calls "political demonology," a "tradition at the heart of American politics" consisting of "the creation of monsters . . . by the inflation, stigmatization, and dehumanization of political foes." Rogin notes that political demonology functions through "replacing history by visionary myth,"[2] and it is precisely this realm of fantasy that *Last House* both collaborates with and rages against. The allegorical shocks of the film unquestionably mobilize the monstrous, mythical figures of political demonology, but they also interrogate the validity of contemporary political discourses that rely on demonization to narrate history.

In short, this chapter argues that what the *Last House* ad offers as a dare—that this film will force viewers to reassure themselves that what they are watching is "only a movie"—also offers an indirect glimpse of the film's allegorical promise: that "only a movie" as extreme, confused, and courageous as *Last House* can confront the divisive historical trauma of the Vietnam era along the axes of political demonology that constitute it. *Last House* plays what Siegfried Kracauer describes as "the *go-for-broke game* of history," a risky venture where "the emancipation of consciousness" and "the eradication of consciousness" circle each other so relentlessly that one often overlaps the other in the arena of mass-mediated representation. Kracauer, writing in Germany in 1927, was attempting to articulate how a cultural "turn to photography" was reshaping conventional notions of history and memory.[3] In certain important ways, this "turn to photography" that Kracauer captured so brilliantly during its early stages in Weimar Germany would come to fruition in Vietnam-era America.

KENT STATE, *JOE*, AND THE VIOLATION OF THE NATION

Craven refers to *Last House*, his debut as a writer and director, as "the primal scream of my cinema."[4] The description still seems apt today, even after such subsequent Craven efforts as *The Hills Have Eyes* (1977), *A Nightmare on Elm Street* (1984), and *Scream* (1996). All these films bear thematic resemblances to *Last House*, but none duplicates the first film's savage intensity or stark depiction of violence and vengeance. *Last House* begins with two teenage girls leaving an affluent suburb for a rock concert in New York City, where they are abducted by a gang of escaped convicts. The convicts torture, rape, and murder the young women, then unwittingly seek shelter at the home of one of the girl's parents after their car breaks down. The parents eventually discover the true identity of their guests and exact a bloody retribution that mirrors the violence visited on their daughter.

The aforementioned disclaimer attached to *Last House*'s newspaper ad reveals that the film's story is a "retelling of Ingmar Bergman's Academy Award Winner *The Virgin Spring* [1960] in 1972 terms" (a comparison I will return to later in the chapter) and states that the film "relates to a problem and a situation every teenage girl is vulnerable to and every parent lives in dread of." Furthermore, a "number of parents . . . have taken their daughters to see the film. These parents regard this movie as a perfect deterrent to this type of behavior." Although the "type of behavior" is never specified by the disclaimer, the "problem" seems to be the threat of rape and murder faced by innocent, vulnerable young women: "A young girl savagely brutalized, killed by a wanton band of degenerates." The next sentence suggests another dimension to this threat: "Revenge of the most horrible kind exacted by the parents of the dead girl—the killers are themselves killed." Spectators are assured that they *should* "hate the people who perpetrate these outrages," but suddenly troubling questions arise. Toward which perpetrators and which outrages should the audience direct their hatred? The "degenerates" who brutalize the young girl? Or the parents, the older generation who retaliate with "revenge of the most horrible kind"? The disclaimer does not provide a clear answer, and the ad's accompanying still from the film only heightens the political urgency of this disturbing ambiguity. The still recalls one of the Vietnam era's most famous photographs, an unforgettable document of "a decade of simmering conflict between the younger and older generations [that] had finally come to a boil":[5] John Filo's Pulitzer Prize–winning depiction of the tragedy incurred when Ohio National Guardsmen opened fire on student demonstrators at Kent State University on May 4, 1970.[6] (See fig. 4.2.)

The affinities between the young women featured in the two images (similar kneeling positions, outstretched arms, long dark hair, and open-mouthed expressions of horror) extend to a coincidence of names. The *Last House* advertisement misidentifies the pictured Phyllis Stone (Lucy Grantham) as Mari Collingwood (Sandra Cassell), her friend and fellow victim; Filo's photograph features Mary Vecchio, a fourteen-year-old runaway from Florida who acquired national attention through the wide dissemination of Filo's photo.[7] By calling to mind Mary Vecchio in the same context as *Last House*'s Mari Collingwood, the advertisement underlines the film's connection to the traumatic national event James Miller characterizes as the day "the New Left collapsed, plummeting into cultural oblivion as if it had been some kind of political Hula-Hoop."[8] Indeed, *Last House*'s publicist attributes part of the "evocative" appeal of the title "Last House on the Left" (which has no direct relation to the film) to the fact that

FIGURE 4.2 Kent State University on May 4, 1970. (Photograph by John Filo; courtesy of Getty Images)

"the use of the word 'left' had a certain significance, because that was back in the hippie days, when so many young people thought of themselves as 'leftists.'"9 The *Last House* ad's evocation of Kent State suggests the film's ability to tap into various fears and frustrations surrounding the disintegration of the New Left, as the antiwar movement came up against the shattering realizations that not only was President Nixon willing to escalate the Vietnam War abroad by invading Cambodia, but that at home, "the government was willing to shoot you."10 The film locates the grim consequences of these profound social upheavals—what the ad's disclaimer refers to as "the senseless violence and inhuman cruelty that has become so much a part of the times in which we live"—on the body of a teenage girl. It is this body, imagined as innocent and exposed to the risk of rape, which serves as the locus for anxieties concerning the nation as feminized and susceptible to violation in the Vietnam era.11

Kent State marked a crisis point for contemporary fears that America, divided against itself over the Vietnam War, might be in danger of losing its disembodied, masculine integrity and succumbing to an overly embodied, feminine vulnerability. James A. Michener frames his *Kent State: What Happened and Why* (1971) with a vivid illustration of precisely this fear. The book begins with a description of Kent State student Bob Hillegas, a "representative of that enormous group of stable, solid young people who form the reliable central core of our great universities." Hillegas is earning a degree in aerospace technology, volunteers for ROTC, and plans to enter the air force after graduation. Michener emphasizes the fact that the "quietly patriotic" Hillegas is "a most attractive young man," with a tall frame, "intelligent-looking face" and a carefully groomed appearance—he "wears his hair short and his trousers pressed."[12] This description contrasts sharply with the character sketch of Mary Vecchio that closes the book. Michener depicts the fourteen-year-old Vecchio as "a large child . . . no less than immense at five-feet-ten and 190 pounds, most of it in her legs." She strikes Michener as a "big lumbering girl" who "frequently gazes off into space, at nothing in particular, and ignores the words around her."[13] By juxtaposing Hillegas and Vecchio as the poles representing "what happened and why" at Kent State, Michener symbolically suggests that the answer resides in the decline from the intelligent Hillegas's lean, impeccably maintained male body to the dull Vecchio's fleshy, clumsy female body. This transformation aligns the source of national disgrace and decadence with the grotesquely embodied feminine and attacks that body through a contemptuous characterization.

Michener's scapegoating of the female body for Vietnam-related social unrest resonates with representations of violence in a number of popular, influential, and roughly contemporaneous American films. *Joe* (John G. Avildsen, 1970), *Dirty Harry* (Don Siegel, 1971), and *Death Wish* (Michael Winner, 1974) all feature vigilantes who resort to brutal violence directed against a perceived corruption of American culture resulting from "the radicalism and permissiveness of the 1960s."[14] In all three films, the body that must suffer most spectacularly as the originary "cause" for the retaliatory violence that follows is a violated female body. In the case of *Joe*, a film cited explicitly by the *Last House* ad to encourage intertextual comparisons, the female body is doubly punished. First Melissa Compton (Susan Sarandon) must endure humiliation at the hands of her drug-dealing hippie boyfriend, Frank (Patrick McDermott), who ignores her sexual advances and criticizes her "fat ass." Melissa's father, Bill Compton (Dennis Patrick), inadvertently "avenges" Frank's mistreatment of his daughter (which has resulted in Melissa's hospitalization for an overdose) by killing him during a beating that spins out of control. At the end of the film, her father and his working-class "buddy" Joe Curran (Peter Boyle) kill a houseful of hippies

FIGURE 4.3 *Joe* (John G. Avildsen, 1970): Joe Curran (Peter Boyle) introduces Bill Compton (Dennis Patrick) to his working-class friends at the bowling alley. (Courtesy of Jerry Ohlinger's Movie Material)

during an ill-conceived search for the missing Melissa—a massacre whose death toll finally includes Melissa herself. (See fig. 4.3.) In this manner, *Joe* posits Melissa as the victim whose suffering is intended to underline the tragic consequences of the violent national climate. But in order for her to fulfill this role, she must undergo extreme physical punishment as her body is first sexually humiliated, then hospitalized, and finally torn apart by bullets. The need to enact bodily violence against the "innocent" victim becomes just as central to the film's "message," and perhaps more so, than the subsequent acts of vengeance.

In certain ways, *Last House* repeats and intensifies the violent dynamics that characterize *Joe*. Mari Collingwood and Phyllis Stone pay a brutal physical price to establish the motive for Mari's parents, the bourgeois Collingwoods, to avenge themselves on the criminal Stillo clan—a price that far exceeds any purely plot-driven function. Psychopathic ringleader Krug Stillo (David Hess), his bisexual girlfriend Sadie (Jeramie Rain), and his child-molesting partner Weasel (Fred Lincoln) subject the two young women to a series of physical humiliations for their pleasure while Krug's heroin-addicted son, Junior (Marc Sheffler), looks on uneasily. The ordeal begins with Phyllis's offscreen rape, and continues with the graphic depiction of Phyllis forced to urinate on herself, Mari and Phyllis coerced to make love to each other, Mari scarred by Krug's carving of his name in her skin, Phyllis stabbed and disemboweled, and finally Mari raped and shot to death.[15] But the violence depicted in *Last House* differs from what appears in *Joe* in more aspects than just sheer, harrowing intensity. *Joe*'s two key murders, the deaths of Frank and Melissa, employ technical devices such as freeze frames, superimposed images, and distorted sound to set them apart stylistically from the rest of the film. In addition, these acts are committed exclusively by older males supporting conservative, bourgeois values in opposition to the younger counterculture. In this manner, the film contains its violence both formally and thematically by designating it as an extraordinary event tied to a specific character type, if not social class.[16]

Last House, on the other hand, emphasizes the *continuity* between its depictions of brutality and the ordinariness of everyday life. Everything is filmed with the same gritty, unadorned newsreel style (reflecting Craven's own previous experience working on documentary productions), where men and women, rich and poor, and young and old alike are captured participating in ferocious violence. Even the Stillos, the film's "ghouls" (a role underlined iconically by their assault on Phyllis in a graveyard), cannot be pigeonholed simply as representatives of an older generation that victimizes the younger. The Stillos complicate the bourgeois culture/counterculture dichotomy by displaying and contesting traits of both the youth counterculture and the bourgeois nuclear family. Like hippies, the Stillos mock bourgeois values, defy conventional notions of sexual morality, and use drugs. They hide out in downtown New York City, an area (especially the East Village and Lower East Side neighborhoods) synonymous with the counterculture in both *Joe* and another notable film mentioned in some ads for *Last House*, Paul Morrissey and Andy Warhol's *Trash* (1970). (See fig. 4.4.) When their getaway car breaks down, the Stillos are en route to Canada—the standard destination for young draft dodgers. The Stillos expose the bleak underside of certain countercultural impulses taken to their limit, where the outcome is not progressive social change and self-awakening but addiction, rape, and murder.[17] In this sense, the Stillos also stand in for the era's most terrifying countercultural "family," the Mansons (indeed, Sadie's name duplicates that of Manson Family member Susan "Sadie Mae Glutz" Atkins), and anticipate the horror genre's dissection of conventional family values during the 1970s in films such as *The Texas Chain Saw Massacre* (Tobe Hooper, 1974) and *It's Alive* (Larry Cohen, 1974).[18]

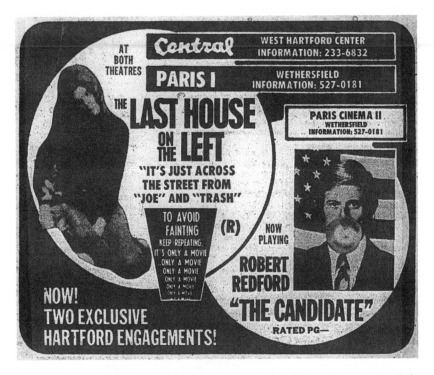

FIGURE 4.4 Newspaper advertisement for *Last House on the Left* (Wes Craven, 1972) and *The Candidate* (Michael Ritchie, 1972). (*Hartford Courant*, August 23, 1972)

Even so, the Stillos' performance of "respectable" family manners during a dinner scene with the as-yet-unsuspecting Collingwoods foregrounds the Stillos' ability to simulate bourgeois civility. During the meal, the Stillos act like the Collingwoods, doing their best to mimic their manners, conversational tone, and familial structure. The fact that they fail in this performance through displays of excess (they eat too much, drink too much, talk too much) does not prevent viewers from recognizing bourgeois traits in the Stillos—the convicts just literalize these traits and unmask their hollow pretensions, taking John Collingwood (Gaylord St. James) at his word when he says, "Our home is your home." Indeed, the dinner scene recalls an earlier sequence in the film where the Stillo and Collingwood "homes" are strikingly juxtaposed. Craven intercuts the Stillos' imprisonment of Mari and Phyllis in their ramshackle apartment with shots of the Collingwoods at home preparing a surprise seventeenth birthday celebration for Mari. The first signs of deadly threat to the young women clash with trivial rituals of affluent suburban family life, as John samples the cake icing while his wife Estelle (Cynthia Carr) dutifully reads the cookbook; after she puts the final touches on the cake, John asks his wife to come with him to the living room because he wants "to attack" her. The film's bloody conclusion enacts what this sequence and the dinner scene intimate, as the Collingwoods shed their "civilized" exteriors and reveal the bourgeois capacity to participate in murderous violence with the same brutal and unforgiving abandon as the Stillos. The "living" room—the site of the suggested lovemaking between the Collingwoods and thus the space marked by the film for the literal and symbolic reproduction of the bourgeois family—instead becomes the resting place for Mari's corpse and the setting for John's chainsaw mutilation of Krug by the film's end.

Last House's blurring of distinctions between the counterculture and the bourgeois family results in a complex and disturbing depiction of violence's relation to the social. Craven claims that the film grew out of his desire to demythologize abstracted Hollywood-style violence, to capture the kind of raw documentary footage from Vietnam that he suspected was being censored in film and on television.[19] For certain brutal scenes in *Last House*, Craven opts for what he describes as "a very high-speed film I'd used before in documentaries. The darks tend to cloud up and the whites burn out. You get a terrible World War II super-grainy footage, almost like those Auschwitz films which were embedded in my memory as a kid."[20] Craven's commitment to bringing Vietnam "home," to transposing the war's traumatic violence to the domestic realm stripped of political demonology's reassuring polarizations, ultimately complicates the claims of kinship with *Joe* asserted by *Last House*'s ad. In the ad, the "last house on the left" is located "just across the street from *Joe*." But in the film, the violence that *Joe* explains away via political demonology refuses to fade so easily. Nowhere is this dissonance more pronounced than in the scene of Mari's death.

Mari's rape and murder are the final acts in the Stillos' protracted torture of their young victims. (See figs. 4.5 and 4.6.) The confrontational horror of the rape itself, which includes an excruciating shot of Krug slobbering on Mari's cheek, is matched by its aftermath. Krug, Sadie, and Weasel, exhausted and bloodied, suddenly fall silent and can only glance at each other furtively. They busy themselves by nervously removing blades of grass from their blood-caked hands. Their shame is intensified by Mari's disbelieving look toward them as she pulls on her clothes, vomits, and whispers a fragment of the Lord's Prayer. A melancholy acoustic folk song plays on the sound track, commenting on the desolation felt by all parties

FIGURE 4.5 *Last House on the Left* (Wes Craven, 1972): The abducted Phyllis Stone (Lucy Grantham) and Mari Collingwood (Sandra Cassell) before they are brutally murdered. (Courtesy of Jerry Ohlinger's Movie Material)

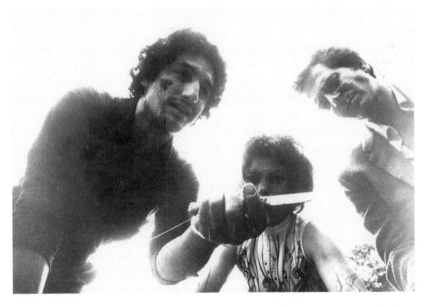

FIGURE 4.6 *Last House on the Left* (Wes Craven, 1972): Krug Stillo (David Hess), Sadie (Jeramie Rain), and Weasel (Fred Lincoln), awash in the blood of their victims. (Courtesy of Jerry Ohlinger's Movie Material)

involved: "Now you're all alone / Now you're by yourself . . . " Mari walks unhurriedly toward the nearby pond, with the Stillos in slow, reluctant pursuit. Mari wades waist-deep into the water and then waits for what she and Krug both seem to understand as inevitable: the bullet in her back from Krug's pistol.

Mari's death restages the demise of *Joe*'s Melissa Compton, who is murdered by a gunshot wound to her back fired by her father. Released only two months after Kent State, *Joe* functions as a virtual "explanation" of Kent State reducible to the narrative of an older, monstrous generation victimizing a younger, innocent generation. The helpless representatives of the youth counterculture are killed by the older, conservative, and aggressive generation embodied by World War II veterans Joe Curran and Bill Compton. Curran, a factory worker, draws on their shared experience as veterans to forge a friendship with advertising executive Compton that bridges their class differences—he applauds Compton's murder of Melissa's boyfriend as a patriotic act and compares killing hippies to killing enemy soldiers. In this manner, the film ultimately subordinates class concerns in order to essentialize the older generation as pro-war veterans and the younger generation as innocent, pacifist victims. Contemporary reviews of *Joe* noted its timely topicality, its ability to appeal to "the mass of blue collar workers whose feelings are here given full expression"[21]—feelings, of course, assumed to be hawkish, especially given the heavily publicized riots of "Bloody Friday" (May 8, 1970) in New York. Four days after Kent State, construction workers attacked and wounded a number of antiwar demonstrators before marching to City Hall, where they demanded that the flag, which flew at half-mast in recognition of the slain students at Kent State, be fully raised. The construction workers then moved on to nearby Pace College, where they assaulted more students before dispersing. Less conspicuously reported in the mass media coverage of Bloody Friday were the complicating factors of its orchestration by the publisher of a right-wing newspaper, its tacit support from the police (who apparently ignored warnings about the march), and earlier statistics that strongly suggest "antiwar sentiment was stronger in the working class than in the middle class."[22] *Joe* substantiates the reductive image of a predatory, pro-war working class as the "real" force behind the Kent State violence; even as Compton fires at Melissa, it is Curran's goading voice that floods the sound track, just as it is Curran's identity as a "working-class Joe" that provides the film with its title.

Mari's death, unlike Melissa's, resists being categorized as evidence of a hawkish working class victimizing an antiwar youth counterculture. Cer-

tain elements present in *Last House*'s original script, such as the specifi-
cation of Krug and Weasel as Vietnam veterans and a concluding shot of
Phyllis's severed hand frozen in the "V" sign associated with the counterculture, are notably absent from the finished film.[23] The inclusion of these
elements would have made *Last House* more similar to *Joe*, more instantly
recognizable as a simplified reproduction of political demonologies routinely used to narrate Kent State. Instead, *Last House* stages an allegorical
challenge to entrenched viewer affect underpinning such demonizing narratives and strives to fulfill the hype of its ad by pushing its viewers "too
far"—shocking them into a recognition of their own private complicity in
the violence they have projected onto a monstrous public other.

PUBLIC AND PRIVATE FACES OF HISTORY

Last House's blending of private and public affect acknowledges precisely
the kind of allegorical shock in Filo's Kent State photograph that Roland
Barthes disavows in *Camera Lucida* (1980). Barthes does not discuss Filo's
photo explicitly, but he does refer to a certain inert quality he finds characteristic of photographs depicting war-related trauma. In a passage framed
by his reaction to photographs documenting savage guerilla warfare in Ni-
caragua during the late 1970s, Barthes refers to the *studium* as those aspects of the photograph that arouse in him "a kind of general, enthusiastic
commitment . . . but without special acuity." The *studium* encompasses a
"general interest" in the historical, political, and cultural implications of
the photograph, but the viewer remains locked at the level of what Barthes
calls "*average* affect." Barthes designates the *punctum* of a photograph as
that rare quality which breaks the *studium*, that "element which rises from
the scene, shoots out of it like an arrow, and pierces me." The *punctum*
wounds the viewer and allows "the detail to rise of its own accord into affective consciousness."[24] Barthes steadfastly resists the notion that this "affective consciousness" generated by a photograph's *punctum* might escape
the personal realm or intersect with social and political consciousness, but
the concept of the *punctum* nonetheless evokes Kracauer's assertion that
"in order for history to present itself, the mere surface coherence offered
by photography must be destroyed."[25]

Filo's photograph presents a version of the *punctum* that Barthes distances himself from—one that penetrates the affective consciousness of a
collective public and inflicts the kind of wound that bleeds history, rather
than effacing history at the level of "average affect" or "surface coherence."
The photo played a key role in the short-lived but explosive resurgence

of the antiwar student movement that followed the Cambodian invasion and Kent State, a moment which has been called "the greatest display of campus discontent in American history."[26] Five hundred campuses and four million students participated in protests and strike actions across the country,[27] with "hundreds of thousands of students leafleting in the surrounding communities, working for peace candidates, and . . . 'reconstituting' their courses to address the international crisis."[28] Filo's photograph became an emblem for the revitalized antiwar movement, appearing "on posters and broadsides; students carried blowups of the picture with the word AVENGE written across it in dripping letters."[29] Here, then, is a photograph in which history is made visible and available for collective action, whose *punctum* exceeds the bounds of private affect.

As Michener's demonization of Mary Vecchio suggests, however, Filo's photograph also invites the emergence of a reprivatized version of "what happened and why" at Kent State that simplifies the systemic social factors underpinning the event. Michener made Vecchio monstrous by describing her body as grotesque and unnatural. This physical description reflected her "improper" status as a teen runaway, which excluded her from "that enormous group of stable, solid young people who form the reliable central core of our great universities" and made Kent State explicable as a crisis instigated by a few deviants responsible for the reprehensible "radicalization of the young."[30] Similarly, an article in the conservative *National Review* coinciding with the one-year anniversary of Kent State and Filo's reception of the Pulitzer Prize begins by reasserting that the photograph's "kneeling girl was not in fact a student at all, but a runaway drifter inhabiting the hippie-radical fringes of the campus, and an excellent symbol therefore of the pathology of Kent State and many other campuses as well."[31] Claude Kirk, governor of Vecchio's home state of Florida, went so far as to imply that Vecchio was part of a Communist conspiracy. In the three years following Kent State, Vecchio received over 50,000 pieces of hate mail, including notes like this one: "You hippie Communist bitch! Did you enjoy sleeping with all those dope fiends and Negroes while you were in Ohio? The deaths of the Kent State Four lies on the conscience of yourself and other subhuman rabble-rousers like you."[32]

The demonizing attribution of blame to Vecchio and those fringe radicals imagined as her manipulators has its seeds in the national press coverage of Kent State. Although many different photographs from Kent State appeared in newspapers and magazines, it was Filo's portrait of Vecchio that figured consistently as the highlighted image accompanying the news stories. Photographs depicting more collective scenes of student

protestors and National Guardsmen almost always appeared less prominently than the Vecchio picture, and often on subsequent pages; *Newsweek*, for example, featured a cropped version of Filo's photo on its cover
that excised all but the screaming Vecchio and the lower half of slain
student Jeff Miller's body.[33] Lauren Berlant points out that this media
tendency to portray mass protest by putting a "'face' on an otherwise
abstract issue" often results in a "facialization of U.S. injustice . . . [that]
enables further deferral of considerations that might force structural
transformations of public life." According to Berlant, this privatization
or "facialization" of public, systemic crisis "can only symbolize (but never
meet) the need for the radical transformation of national culture."[34] Kent
State's aftermath bears out Berlant's observation—despite the momentary electricity provided by Filo's photograph for the antiwar movement,
Kent State marked the end of the New Left rather than a new beginning.
Todd Gitlin admits that "activism never recovered from the summer vaca-
tion of 1970";[35] another historian comments that "as an era when masses
of people, most of them young, regularly took to the streets to challenge
the practices of society, the 1960s ended with a thirteen-second fusillade
in a small Ohio town."[36]

Did the privatizing "facialization" of Kent State contribute to the defus-
ing of the New Left that *Last House* evokes with its title? Gitlin argues
that the movement, and particularly its core organization Students for a
Democratic Society (SDS), had begun self-destructing before Kent State.
But he acknowledges that Kent State effectively "dead-ended" the logic of
the movement by forcing the question of whether demonstrators were
"supposed to buy guns in turn"—"it was double or nothing, and to many
old movement hands the answer was nothing."[37] In Gitlin's reading of
the contemporary political climate, the very perception of a "dead-ended"
movement—as reflected in the formulation of the New Left's position as
an impossible "double or nothing" bind—is underwritten by the facializing
logic tied to the dissemination of Vecchio's image. Gitlin's analysis supports Lesley Wischmann's claim that the message ultimately conveyed to
students by Filo's photograph was "one of fear—'look what can happen to
you'—rather than one of moral outrage—'this should never have happened
to anyone.'"[38] In short, a privatized reaction finally supersedes a collective
one in response to the mass media's facialization of the crisis; and if facializing mechanisms aid in allowing private fear to overwhelm collective
outrage, then facialization also enables the figures of political demonology
to flourish. Facialization shares with political demonology the tendency
to reduce "discrete individuals and groups . . . [to] members of a single

political body directed by its head."³⁹ As Gilles Deleuze and Félix Guattari argue, the construction of "faciality" mirrors the binarizing mechanisms of demonization, where a face appears in a "biunivocal relation with another: it is a man *or* a woman, a rich person or a poor one . . . "⁴⁰ In the end, Filo's Mary Vecchio becomes either the anguished voice of a victimized generation *or* a "hippie Communist bitch"; the processes of facialization leave room for precious little else.

Now we can turn to the matter of how *Last House*'s echoes of Mary Vecchio duplicate or complicate these facializing strategies. The advertisement's own "Mari" puts a familiar "face" on the disclaimer's reference to "the inhuman cruelty that has become so much a part of the times in which we live," but already there are dissonances. As noted earlier, the ad's image of "Mari" is actually her friend Phyllis; the facialization is undermined by its own caption. Walter Benjamin claims that the caption may be "the most important component of the shot" in a modern age when photography captures "transitory and secret pictures which are able to shock the associative mechanism of the observer to a standstill." For Benjamin, the caption is related to the photographer's mission to "uncover guilt and name the guilty in his pictures."⁴¹ In the arresting Kent State photograph, captions seem superfluous because guilt seems to rest so unquestionably with those forces responsible for provoking Vecchio's horror, whether they are imagined as the guardsmen, the government, or the president himself. But where does guilt lie in an image whose direct caption betrays it, and whose extended caption (the disclaimer) fails to distinguish clearly between the "outrages" committed by a "wanton band of degenerates" and "revenge of the most horrible kind exacted by the parents of the dead girl"? The representational logic of facialization has become unsettled.

Last House's ad both suggests and recoils from an allusion to Kent State, just as the film paradoxically disrupts a wholesale facializing and demonizing of Kent State by participating obsessively in the processes of facialization and demonization. *Last House* invites, but then undermines, the impulse to distinguish the Collingwood "face" of bourgeois normality from the Stillo "face" of the counterculture by embracing the ad's confusing solicitation of both the bourgeoisie ("parents who have taken their daughters to see the film") and the counterculture ("Warning! Not Recommended for Persons Over 30!"). Viewers identifying with either group are encouraged to recognize *themselves* as implicated in the historical trauma accessed by *Last House*, especially the repetition of Kent State staged through the interwoven text constituted by the film and its advertising.

Freud understood that repeating a traumatic event involves components of both mastery and revenge. As I argued in chapter 1, Freud's famous example of the *fort/da* game illustrates just how interdependent the mastery of trauma through repetition and the experience of revenge on the perceived agent of that trauma really are. But in order to feel vengeful, one must first feel implicated in the trauma itself—an implication that viewers of *Last House* are confronted with when they encounter the film's allegorical repetition of Kent State. Revenge is not merely *Last House*'s narrative theme; vengeful affect is exactly what the film brutally and repeatedly arouses in the viewer. The Stillos enact viewer desire for vengeance against the Collingwoods and their smug, privileged insularity. The Collingwoods, in turn, enact audience wishes for a reciprocal vengeance against the murderous Stillos. In both cases, the acts of revenge are unflinchingly cruel and graphically extreme; the disturbing dimensions of viewer *participation* in the desire for vengeance are laid bare through their realization as sickening bloodshed. In this way, *Last House*'s promise of mastering historical trauma through repetition cannot be divorced from a painful investment of affect in that trauma and the vengeful rage it engenders.

Last House's insistence on the risky collision of public and private identifications as part of the audience's allegorical engagement with historical trauma concurs with Benjamin's claim that "to articulate the past historically does not mean to recognize it 'the way it really was.' . . . It means to seize hold of a memory as it flashes up, at a moment of danger."[42] But in its own way, *Last House* also contends to portray "the way things really are." The very first seconds of the film feature a title that announces, "The events you are about to witness are true. Names and locations have been changed to protect those individuals still living." This bit of unfounded information was probably dismissed by most viewers as empty hyperbole typical of exploitation film sales tactics.[43] Indeed, Eric Schaefer has demonstrated that at least since the founding of the Hays Office in 1922, exploitation films have sold themselves routinely as "true" or "educational" in order to secure viable space in an American market haunted by censorship and dominated by Hollywood product oppositionally defined as wholesome, education-free "entertainment."[44] Of course, over time the often inflated guarantees of "truth" touted by exploitation films have become a source of entertainment in themselves. But when the *Last House* ad conjures the famous Kent State photograph, exploitation's well-worn "truth" claims incorporate an iconic document of news reporting that consequently allows modes of viewer reception designated for photographic "news" or cinematic "entertainment" to lose their distinctiveness. Christian Metz admits that to define film as "collective entertainment" while associating photography with the domain of "the presumed real, of life" is reductive (even more so in the age of video and digital technologies), but argues that these designations remain "alive and strong as a social myth, half true like all myths; it influences each of us, and most of all the stamp, the look of photography and cinema themselves." Metz emphasizes the importance of acknowledging differences in the two modes of viewer reception, of recognizing the variance in audience expectations pertaining to the "principal legitimated use[s]" of film and photography in the social arena.[45] *Last House*'s invocation of "the presumed real" of photography under the sign of exploitation cinema's fantastic claims to "truth" obtains the space necessary to penetrate viewer defenses that tend to anesthetize historical trauma when it is presented as photographic news.[46] In its simultaneous suggestion and evasion of expectations associated with "news," *Last House* gains the opportunity to confront viewers with historical trauma allegorically as they engage with the film as "entertainment."

By the time *Last House* concludes with the frozen still of a blood-stained John and Estelle Collingwood collapsed in their living room after murdering the entire Stillo clan, the line between true events captured in news photos and fictional cinematic events has faded—now the final still image seems somehow more akin to a news photograph than a film sequence. As Garrett Stewart points out, such "photo finish" endings were common in films of the late 1960s and early 1970s such as *Butch Cassidy and the Sundance Kid* (George Roy Hill, 1969).[47] *Last House*'s conclusion resembles these other photo finishes in terms of connoting death, but its evocation of news photography is more specific and problematic. The final shot mirrors the film's introduction of the Collingwoods, where John sits in the living room reading a newspaper and ignores Estelle's attempts at conversation. When she asks him disinterestedly about what is going on "in the outside world," he responds, "Same old stuff. Murder and mayhem. What's for dinner?" In the still that ends the film, the Collingwoods *become* the public news they had so easily dismissed from the private isolation of their suburban home. In this context, *Last House*'s closing credits—which capture each character in poses from the film over which the actor's name is then superimposed—now exceed their conventional function and appear as uncanny snapshots. There is an unusual slow-motion shot appended to the end of these credits which features Mari during an early moment in the film, laughing and gesturing joyfully with her arms and then falling down, out of the frame, as the image fades to black. In the darkness of the empty screen, it is possible to imagine Mari Collingwood's fall culminating in a replication of Mary Vecchio's kneeling image.

CIVILIZED SELVES, SAVAGE OTHERS: *DELIVERANCE* AND THE MAPPING OF THE NATION

Given the common perception of Vietnam as the "living room war," a war ultimately lost "at home" through unprecedentedly shocking television coverage, one might ask just how confrontational *Last House*'s representations of Vietnam-related violence could have been while appearing alongside these televised images. In a carefully documented study, Daniel C. Hallin demystifies the conventional wisdom concerning the "oppositional" role supposedly played by national television news coverage of Vietnam, pointing out that even in the later years of the war, "the Nixon administration retained a good deal of power to 'manage' the news" and "journalists continued to be patriots in the sense that they portrayed the Americans as the 'good guys' in Vietnam." As a result, "the public came to see the war as a 'mistake' or 'tragedy,' rather than the crime the more radical opposition believed it to be." Television's contribution toward containing public disillusionment with the war can be attributed partly to two important trends Hallin detects in the news coverage: the relative lack of aired footage depicting actual combat or casualties, "despite the emphasis on military 'action,'" and the "almost perfectly one-dimensional image of the North Vietnamese and Vietcong as cruel, ruthless, and fanatical."[48]

In other words, television's portrayal of the Vietcong supports the processes of political demonology—a portrayal that finds its analogues in Vietnam-era films that transpose the inhuman "savagery" so often attributed to the Vietcong to a monstrous Southern other. For example, the motorcycling adventures of Wyatt (Peter Fonda) and Billy (Dennis Hopper) in *Easy Rider* (Dennis Hopper, 1969) are cut short by the shotgun blasts of Southerners, while the whitewater rafting expedition of *Deliverance* (John Boorman, 1972) also takes a violent turn during an encounter with Southern "mountain men." As Margie Burns points out, these two films each pose the question of what happened to the "spirit of the sixties" in America, and they seem to offer a remarkably similar answer: "It died, done in by evil rednecks, in the South."[49] This reductive cinematic logic makes a certain amount of symbolic "sense," given that the civil rights movement—the movement that facilitated the birth of the student-driven New Left and therefore was perhaps most constitutive of the "spirit of the sixties"—faced violent resistance in the South.

But *Easy Rider* and *Deliverance* are not directly concerned with the civil rights movement. They are far more invested in evoking the American national myth of the frontier that Richard Slotkin (writing in the early 1970s with an eye toward "the murderous violence that has characterized recent political life") has defined so influentially as "the conception of America as a wide-open land of unlimited opportunity for the strong, ambitious, self-reliant individual to thrust his way to the top."[50] Of course, this myth of the frontier is at the center of that film genre so closely associated with American national identity, the western; both *Easy Rider* and *Deliverance* can be seen as variations, sometimes critical and other times not, on the classic western. In fact, the traditional icons and narrative structures of the western occupy a significant place not only in these two films, but in a striking number of other key American films released during the late 1960s and early 1970s.[51] Placed beside films such as *Bonnie and Clyde* (Arthur Penn, 1967), *The Green Berets* (John Wayne and Ray Kellogg, 1968), *The Wild Bunch* (Sam Peckinpah, 1969), *Little Big Man* (Arthur Penn, 1970), *Patton* (Franklin Schaffner, 1970), and *Billy Jack* (Tom Laughlin, 1971), *Easy Rider* and *Deliverance* emerge as two cinematic attempts among many others during the Vietnam era to map and remap the nation through the frontier myth, with its violent conflicts between "civilization" and "savagery," "city" and "country." But what do these maps reveal and conceal about the nation as it struggles to imagine itself in a moment of disrupted confidence, when "the true nature of the larger story of America itself became the subject of intense cultural dispute"?[52] To answer this question, this section examines *Last House* alongside *Deliverance*. Both films were released in 1972, but what makes their comparison most compelling is how each channels its encounter with a Vietnam-inflected frontier myth through the related networks of rape-revenge and vigilantism, themselves conspicuous motifs in popular American cinema throughout the 1970s.[53]

Deliverance's link to Vietnam may appear tenuous at first. James Dickey, author of the novel *Deliverance* (1970) and screenwriter of the film, was criticized by Robert Bly in 1967 for the lack of responsible political engagement with the Vietnam War in his poetry.[54] Bly's criticism was echoed in at least one acidic review of the *Deliverance* novel, which charged that "the world that lies outside [the novel] might as well not exist for all the notice that is taken of it. That a real and bloody war is going on . . . nowhere intrudes."[55] The film, which follows four Atlanta businessmen during their deadly weekend rafting trip down what their survivalist leader Lewis (Burt Reynolds) calls "the last wild, untamed, unpolluted, unfucked-up river in the South," makes no explicit mention of Vietnam. However, Ed's (Jon

Voight) words at a crucial transitional point in the film, when the group's "good" day on the river comes to a close and the nightmarish events of the next day loom ahead, allude provocatively to a larger contemporary social context: "No matter what disaster may occur in other parts of the world, or what petty little problems arise in Atlanta, no one can find us up here."[56]

The prophetic implication of Ed's statement, that to indulge in the naïve fantasy of flight from foreign and domestic realities can result only in the horrifying materialization of Vietnam around you, is borne out by the film. *Deliverance*'s depiction of the four men, clad in fatigue-like green life jackets, at war with an elusive indigenous enemy indistinguishable from the threatening landscape, mirrors recurring narrative representations of American soldiers "in country" during the Vietnam War. In turn, such representations of Vietnam point to the frequency with which narrating the war invites a revisiting of the frontier myth. The slippage between the Vietcong and Native Americans is equally apparent in military slang denoting enemy territory as "Indian country" and the tendency of the counterculture to identify with the demonized other by fetishizing "the American Indian as revolutionary figure."[57] For example, a number of students participating in the Kent State demonstrations dressed as Daniel Boone and Davy Crockett, historical figures famous for their mythic adoption of Native American ways.[58] But the substitution in *Deliverance* of Appalachian "mountain men" for Native Americans and/or the Vietcong indicates an important departure in signification: class supplants race as a white "internal" other replaces a nonwhite "external" other.[59]

Kathleen Stewart has shown how the space of Appalachia can function in relation to the frontier myth, as an " 'Other' America" where "the anxieties and desires that motivate the master narratives of center and margin, self and other, and naturalize an order of things 'in here' and a space of culture 'out there' " may be questioned and reexamined. *Deliverance* responds to this opportunity by defensively constructing what Stewart calls "an encompassing symbolic order written through with the spin of idyllic and horrific otherings."[60] In this sense, the idyllic "dueling banjos" sequence near the beginning of the film, where Drew (Ronny Cox) strikes up a magical musical "dialogue" with a mentally retarded Appalachian boy, matches the later horrific assault on Ed and Bobby (Ned Beatty) by two mountain men in terms of reasserting the absolute otherness of Appalachian culture in both its utopian and its dystopian guises. (See fig. 4.7.) The repulsiveness of the mountain men is emphasized by inflecting the representation of their class difference with markers of physical and sexual "degeneracy": they have rotting teeth and wild eyes; one sodomizes Bobby and the other

FIGURE 4.7   *Deliverance* (John Boorman, 1972): Ed (Jon Voight) suffers at the hands of the "mountain men." (Courtesy of Jerry Ohlinger's Movie Material)

is poised to force Ed to fellate him (before Lewis rescues his comrades by killing one of the attackers with an arrow). The film guarantees that by the time the mountain men are brought down like wild game, they have already explicitly announced their subhuman, animalistic relation to their environment—they urge Bobby to "squeal like a pig" during his rape, and they refer to Ed as an "ape."

Why is *Deliverance* so insistent on keeping Appalachian "country" culture at such a dramatic and tightly controlled remove from the norms embodied by the "city" businessmen? Carol J. Clover argues that "the real motor of the city-revenge or urbanoia film" of which *Deliverance* is an example "is economic guilt." In these films, "the city . . . could hardly be richer and the country could hardly be poorer; and the job of the narrative is to acknowledge in order to override that fact, to engage the spectator in the project of destroying the country despite—or, rightly, because of—that guilt-inducing difference."[61] Bobby's rape both answers and rationalizes the "rape" of the impoverished country landscape (particularly its "unfucked-up" river) by urban development depicted in construction sequences that frame the film. The result is that *Deliverance* becomes "an object lesson on just how the demonizing mechanism of the urbanoia or white settler plot enables the telling of a rape-revenge story, and at the same time how a rape-revenge story enables the rehearsal of the old story whereby the have-nots are exterminated with impunity by the haves."[62] In other words, the narrative arc of rape-revenge in *Deliverance* legitimizes the glaringly uneven resolution of the film's class conflict, where the "civilized" city men kill the "savage" country men without ever positively identifying them as their true attackers or facing legal consequences for their actions.[63] Although this narrative enables the "regeneration through violence" that Slotkin finds symptomatic of the frontier myth's persistence, the film concludes by intimating that Ed has been forever "contaminated" by his grueling encounter with the country. He dreams of a ghostly hand rising from the depths of the river where he has helped bury three bodies, including Drew's, but he wakes up in the safety of his own bed, with his wife beside him. That the hand emerging from the grave is an image associated most strongly with the horror genre suggests that it is in the horror film where the nightmares indivisible from Vietnam cannot simply be awoken from, where the dead cannot be so easily buried.[64]

Last House substantiates this suggestion by complicating the demonizations offered by the rape-revenge and frontier myth narratives in *Deliverance*. Just as the Stillos resist identification as representatives of either the counterculture or the bourgeoisie, they also defy convenient categorization as "country" or "city" forces. They spring from the city's "urban jungle," but they perform the majority of their acts of violence in the country setting of an isolated forest. The "civilized," suburban Collingwoods and the "savage," urban/country Stillos are most sharply contrasted during their shared dinner, a previously mentioned scene where the Collingwoods look on in thinly veiled disgust as the Stillos wolf down their meal and attempt "polite" conversation with the same awkwardness in which they inhabit their ill-fitting middle-class costume clothing. But rather than use this scene as additional evidence of the Stillos' pure animality as they further desecrate the "respectable" Collingwood home, Craven does just the opposite. After the dinner ends and the Stillos retire to Mari's empty bedroom, Krug comments indignantly to his comrades, "Goddamn high-class tight-ass freakos. All that goddamn silverware. Who do they think they are, anyway? People in China eating with sticks and these creeps got sixteen utensils for every pea on the plate."

Unlike the mountain men in *Deliverance*, Krug is here given a rough but legitimate voice for his class rage that frustrates the audience's ability to dismiss him unthinkingly as Mari's inhuman rapist. Craven highlights this dissonance through the mise-en-scène, by placing Krug on Mari's bed beneath her "Peace" poster while he makes his speech. This frame composition, like other moments in *Last House*, applies pressure to the rape-revenge narrative by highlighting contradictions in the class narrative unfolding alongside it. The rape can no longer stand so easily as the act that somehow exceeds class yet simultaneously justifies the extermination of "savage" have-nots by "civilized" haves acting in righteous self-defense. Even the demonization of Krug as the heartless violator of Mari, the most innocent flower of the counterculture, loses its apparent simplicity when he raises the issue of class under the countercultural sign of "Peace" and posits a kind of countercultural politics that Mari never does.[65] Indeed, Krug's distrust of class privilege is confirmed later in the film when John Collingwood uses a piece of fine silverware as a weapon to trap and murder the Stillos.

Yet another crucial way in which *Last House* complicates the demonizing of the country characteristic of *Deliverance* is by including active women on both sides of the savage/civilized divide. *Deliverance* resembles Joseph Conrad's *Heart of Darkness* (1899) in many ways, including the shared conceit of a life-shattering journey along a river leading into a "savage" darkness. But perhaps the most striking affinity between the two works is the creation of an emphatically male world within the fiction where women function only as abstract symbols of the civilization left behind. In *Deliverance*, Ed must "lose" his wife by dropping her photograph before he can accomplish the task of killing his mountain man foe. And just as Marlow must lie to the Intended about what he has seen and experienced in the jungle, so Ed seems poised to live out a lie with his wife after his return, unable to communicate with her after all that has occurred on the river. In both cases, the encounter with the "savage" country forecloses the possibility of the men reentering relationships with women, who must stand outside "male" experience (though often within "civilization" and imperialism) as bearers of what Marlow calls "that great and saving illusion that shone with an unearthly glow in the darkness."[66]

The exclusion of women from the world of *Deliverance* results in a narrative logic whereby the worst crime imaginable in the film is to be forcibly feminized. In this manner, "woman" and "country" blur as feminized categories opposed to a properly masculine "city" identity. Bobby is stripped of his "city" masculinity as an accomplished salesman when he is raped by the "country" mountain man, while Ed finally sheds his soft "city" femininity (he lacks the nerve to shoot a deer) by killing a mountain man and severing emotional ties with his wife. In each instance, "women" are reduced to the status of placeholders signifying a weakness within "city" masculinity that either overwhelms (in Bobby's case) or is "overcome" (in Ed's case).

Last House, on the other hand, locates women firmly within the processes of history and national trauma. Although Mari and Phyllis certainly serve as the symbolic stakes over which the "civilized" and "savage" masculinities of Krug and John Collingwood compete, the role of the young women is supplemented by the characters of Sadie and Estelle Collingwood. Neither of these two women is reducible to a simple extension of her male part-ner or a footnote to issues of masculinity. They force an acknowledgment of the impact that a lived and embodied femininity makes in representing class conflict according to savage/civilized difference. Sadie's bisexuality is coded as an excessive, monstrous desire similar to the "homosexuality" of *Deliverance*'s mountain men, but her proto-feminist consciousness (she re-fers to Freud and calls Krug and Weasel "male chauvinist dogs") disrupts a wholesale demonization of the Stillos as lower-class villains capable only of primitive "country" beliefs. She is also allowed to express emotions besides pure savagery, including moments of compassion for both Phyllis and Ju-nior. Estelle's more traditional role as the female guardian of middle-class propriety (she criticizes Mari for associating with the working-class Phyllis) and "civilized" sexual values (she scolds Mari for not wearing a bra) is com-plicated when she wreaks an intensely sexual vengeance on Weasel. She seduces him, goads him into tying his hands behind his back, and then per-forms fellatio. She verbally encourages him to orgasm, and then bites off his penis. Estelle's castration of Weasel, like Sadie's disemboweling of Phyllis (which is coded as lesbian sex), supports misogynist fears concerning active, devouring female desire. But these deeds also disturb empty characteriza-tions of women as the passive victims or abstract symbols of "male" national trauma. Instead, the women become vital agents in the shaping and living of that trauma. When Estelle slits Sadie's throat in the Collingwood pool near the end of the film, the imagery of Mari's death in the pond is recalled and a specifically *female* network of violation and revenge is established (not un-like the one described in chapter 1 with *Eyes Without a Face*). This network of violence locates women at the center of traumatic history, actively participat-ing and suffering in all its social and political dimensions. Nothing could be further from the marginal presence of Ed's wife in *Deliverance*.

Although *Last House* often troubles the demonologies structuring class conflict in the rape-revenge and frontier myth narratives of films like *Deliverance*, Craven's use of "comic relief" demonstrates the limitations of *Last House*'s engagement with contemporary national trauma. The film's comic subplot involves two inept police officers and their pathetic attempts to come to the aid of the Collingwoods. In a spectacular show of incompetence, the cops must hitch a ride after their own car runs out of gas. First they are ridiculed by a carload of teens, and then they flag down Ada (Ada Washington), a black woman driving a truck carrying crates of live chickens. Ada refuses to unload any of the chickens, so the cops must ride on the roof of the cab; naturally, they fall off. As the humorous counterpoint to the harrowing ordeal endured by Mari and Phyllis, this sequence speaks volumes about what the film considers painful and what seems merely "funny." The portrayal of two innocuous, bumbling white cops squaring off in a silly war of wits against a toothless, cackling black woman (the truly other face of "country," complete with chickens in tow) beckons but immediately closes down audience encounters with questions of racism and police brutality just as thoroughly as the torture of Mari and Phyllis opens a space for the reevaluation of Kent State. In the case of *Last House*, energizing the representation of class conflict, intergenerational tension, and sexual violence demands a minimizing of racial injustice.

In this sense, of course, the film has many analogues in contemporary social history. Ten days after the Kent State shootings, police opened fire on a women's dormitory at Jackson State College in Mississippi, killing two students and wounding nine, all of whom were black. In comparison with Kent State, the event "inspired far fewer headlines, or demonstrations."[67] As one sophomore at Kent State commented bitterly on the similarly indifferent reception given to an even deadlier face-off between National Guardsmen and black civil rights protestors in Augusta, Georgia: "Draw your own conclusions."[68]

ART, EXPLOITATION, AND *THE VIRGIN SPRING*

This chapter concludes by returning to where it began, with the extraordinary advertising campaign for *Last House*. I want to focus specifically on the ad's assertion that *Last House* is "in fact, a retelling of Ingmar Bergman's Academy Award Winner *The Virgin Spring* in 1972 terms." This claim foregrounds the collision of art and exploitation so central to the allegorical moment, and its implications for the reception of *Last House* in terms of historical trauma and national identity demand further exploration.

Robin Wood has thoughtfully discussed the significance of "art" and "exploitation" discourses in relation to *Last House*, pointing out that the cultural perception of *The Virgin Spring* as "Art" and *Last House* as "Exploitation" establishes two very different kinds of "audience-film relationship[s]," both of which nonetheless "permit the spectator a form of insulation from the work and its implications—Art by defining seriousness in aesthetic terms implying class superiority . . . Exploitation by denying seriousness altogether."[69] Critics, according to Wood, impede the productive transgression of these forms of viewer insulation by engaging seriously only films that can be defined as Art while ignoring (or, at best, condescending to) those that seem to qualify as Exploitation.[70]

While Wood's call for an earnest critical reappraisal of *Last House* is courageous and valuable, his method of situating the film between the discourses of "art" and "exploitation" ultimately stops short of refiguring the boundaries assumed to divide those discourses. In the cause of defending Craven's film against accusations of being a Bergman "rip-off," Wood argues that "the relationship of *Last House* to *The Virgin Spring* is not, in fact, close enough to repay any detailed scrutiny."[71] What is lost here is a full consideration of the *interconnections* between art and exploitation that simultaneously produce and destabilize their distinctiveness. These interconnections contribute to the shock of the allegorical moment by implicating the spectator within and between the discourses of art and exploitation.

Contrary to Wood's downplaying of any meaningful connection between *Last House* and *The Virgin Spring* (itself an adaptation of a medieval ballad, written for the screen by Swedish novelist Ulla Isaksson), Craven's film draws upon and revises Bergman's in a number of provocative, sometimes remarkably explicit ways.[72] For example, Mari's rape both refers directly to and comments critically upon Bergman's rape scene. The chilling two-shot of Krug's face over Mari's nearly reproduces a similar shot from *The Virgin Spring*, and Mari's utterance of the Lord's Prayer underscores her kinship with Bergman's heroine Karin (Birgitta Pettersson), who is assaulted on her way to church. (See fig. 4.8.) Even Mari's baptismal death in the pond recalls the religious imagery of *The Virgin Spring*'s climactic miracle, where a freshwater spring bursts forth from the site of Karin's rape and murder.

But *Last House* does not allude to Bergman's film simply for the sake of legitimation through imitation. Instead, Craven's film reminds us that its "legitimate" art film counterpart, despite its Academy Award for Best Foreign Film in 1960, received a somewhat mixed critical reception due to its shocking violence. Indeed, the specter of exploitation arises when reviewer Bosley Crowther complains that *The Virgin Spring*'s violent sequences "tend to disturb the senses out of proportion to the dramatic good they do,"[73] especially in light of the fact that the rape scene was slightly

FIGURE 4.8 *The Virgin Spring* (Ingmar Bergman, 1960): Karin (Birgitta Pettersson) does not yet realize the danger that has befallen her. (Courtesy of Jerry Ohlinger's Movie Material)

trimmed for the film's American release.[74] Craven also brings Bergman to mind in order to present, but then explode, the possibility of recuperating *Last House's* violence through the redemptive mechanisms present in *The Virgin Spring*. In Bergman's film, Karin's death results in the appearance of a miraculous spring in which her father can literally wash his hands of the blood he has shed to avenge her. Mari's death inverts Karin's—instead of creating the spring that will soothe her parents, Mari's body is swallowed by the pond in which her killers then bathe (although her parents later recover her body). Mari's parents are not redeemed at the end of the film, but instead sit dazed and blood-spattered in their living room, surrounded by the dead bodies of Krug, Junior, and Mari. This is the "miracle" Mari's suffering has produced.

Of course, this kind of confrontational dissonance between Craven's film and Bergman's would be lost on those unfamiliar with *The Virgin Spring*. But a closer inspection of *Last House's* distribution and exhibition strategies suggests a remarkable (albeit often accidental) attempt to address precisely those viewers who might embrace a Bergman film, especially one with an

Academy Award to its name, but who would never dream of watching a film like *Last House*. After several test screenings under a number of titles, *Last House* opened officially in two theaters near Hartford, Connecticut, on August 23, 1972.[75] The Paris Cinema in Wethersfield was an unusual choice for the premiere of a graphic, low-budget horror film, since the suburban theater catered to a mainstream, middle-class clientele quite distinct from urban grindhouse or drive-in crowds. While *Last House* played on one Paris Cinema screen, the other featured the acclaimed Robert Redford star vehicle *The Candidate* (Michael Ritchie, 1972). Advertisements for the Paris Cinema appearing in the *Hartford Courant* went so far as to place special emphasis on the *combination* of *Last House* and *The Candidate* by overlapping illustrations from the films and referring to them together as "two exclusive Hartford engagements." (See fig. 4.4.) This unorthodox exhibition strategy was made possible by the fact that Hallmark Releasing Corporation, the small Boston-based production company that financed and distributed *Last House*, also operated the Paris Cinema. Hallmark's decision to thrust *Last House* on an audience of unprepared middle-class spectators was a momentous one—the film went on to accomplish the rare feat of recognition from these viewers, although this acknowledgment was not earned without resistance.

According to an editorial in the *Hartford Courant*, appalled viewers walked out of *Last House* screenings at the Paris Cinema and "gather[ed] in the parking lot petition-bound to stop the manager from showing the movie." The editorial defends the disgruntled protestors as "unsuspecting witnesses" to the "lingering gore, senseless cruelty, sadism and fetishism" of a "horrible, 'sick' film."[76] Hallmark responded with an "open letter" in the same newspaper several days later that acknowledged (and perhaps exaggerated) the public hostility toward the film while supporting the management's decision to continue *Last House*'s Paris Cinema engagement, given that the film is ultimately "morally redeeming and does deliver an important social message."[77] The main content of this letter was subsequently incorporated into Hallmark's general publicity campaign for *Last House* as the aforementioned disclaimer above future newspaper advertisements. While it is tempting to regard the disclaimer as nothing more than another exploitation trick in an established Hallmark tradition—they had already achieved great success by dispensing "vomit bags" to viewers at screenings of *Mark of the Devil* (Michael Armstrong, 1970)—the disclaimer's references to *The Virgin Spring* and "parents who have taken their daughters to see the film" can be read as attempts to reassure and reclaim precisely the kind of middle-class viewers who protested at the Paris Cinema.[78]

Another major breakthrough in *Last House*'s acquisition of a wider audience came with Roger Ebert's glowing review in the *Chicago Sun-Times*. Advertisements for the film in Chicago newspapers did not include the disclaimer, but Ebert's review made its use unnecessary. He pointed out *Last House*'s resemblance to *The Virgin Spring* and placed the film in the same company with such "artful" exploitation films (or "exploitive" art films) as *Hell's Angels on Wheels* (Richard Rush, 1967), *The Honeymoon Killers* (Leonard Kastle, 1970), *Straw Dogs* (Sam Peckinpah, 1971), and *Boxcar Bertha* (Martin Scorsese, 1972). Ebert even defended the veracity of the film's sensational marketing campaign: "I've got to admit that I did not expect much after its advertising campaign ("Keep repeating—It's only a movie, it's only a movie . . . "). But you know something weird? At one point I actually did find myself repeating that."[79] Chicago newspaper advertisements for the film began to include quotes from Ebert's review: "A tough, bitter little sleeper of a movie that's about four times as good as you'd expect . . . sheer and unexpected terror . . . a powerful narrative . . . the audience was rocked back on its psychic heels. . . . It's a find, one of those rare, unheralded movies." These ads appeared in both the *Sun-Times* and the *Chicago Tribune*, where film reviewer Gene Siskel expressed his revulsion for the film in terms that echoed the sentiments of the Paris Cinema protestors: "I am surprised any theater owner would want to make a living by playing it. Theater owners who do not control themselves invite others to do so."[80] Siskel's grave words did not prevent *Last House* from continuing its exclusive engagement at the downtown Woods Theater, and after a solid month of successful business, the film opened in the Chicago suburbs as well.

Last House's arrival in New York in December 1972 (another step in Hallmark's platform, or regional release strategy) was met with a scathing notice in the *New York Times*. Howard Thompson's review confirmed that the reactions of Gene Siskel and the *Hartford Courant* would be representative, with Roger Ebert's praise remaining an isolated exception. Thompson refers to *Last House* as "a thing (as opposed to a film)" that he freely admits walking out of. For Thompson, this "sickening tripe" featuring "inept actors" is fit only for those "interested in paying to see repulsive people and human agony."[81]

Ironically, the audience of horror genre diehards that Thompson imagines enjoying the film often reproduces his own reaction to *Last House*, even years after its original release. Chas. Balun, editor of the splatter movie fanzine *Deep Red*, only reluctantly includes *Last House* in his self-published *Connoisseur's Guide to the Contemporary Horror Film* (1983). Balun defends the film's inclusion on the grounds of its impact on the genre, as it marked

a turning point in the depiction of graphic violence and launched the careers of director Craven and producer Sean Cunningham (who went on to
produce and direct *Friday the 13th* [1980]). But Balun nevertheless labels
the film "very repulsive," "criminally manipulative," and "disgraceful." His
review concludes: "Supposedly based on Ingmar Bergman's classic, *The
Virgin Spring*, [*Last House*]'s unceasing sadism makes it one of the most
repugnant 'horror' films ever made."[82]

The reviews by Balun and by Thompson both convey an unmistakable sense of disgust that blurs the line between art and exploitation. In
his reading of Kantian aesthetics, Pierre Bourdieu describes disgust as a
vexed pleasure: "disgust is the paradoxical experience of enjoyment ex-
torted by violence, an enjoyment which arouses horror." The shock implicit in disgust is "the ambivalent experience of the horrible seduction
of the disgusting and of enjoyment, which performs a sort of reduction
to animality, corporeality, the belly and sex . . . removing any difference
between those who resist with all their might and those who wallow in
pleasure, who enjoy enjoyment."[83] Thompson's disgust seems characteristic of one accustomed to what Bourdieu calls the "pure pleasure" of
contemplation and distance (Kant's "taste of reflection"), who resists with
"all their might" the "horrible seduction" of sensation that Bourdieu refers
to as "facile pleasure" (Kant's "taste of sense").[84] Thompson's participation
in the facile pleasures of *Last House* (he admits to staying for fifty minutes
before walking out) demands a disgusted repudiation designed to reestab-
lish him within the bounds of respectable taste while banishing the film
to the realm of exploitation aficionados, those with a taste for "repulsive
people and human agony."

Balun's disgust, on the other hand, involves a different kind of repudiation. His open enthusiasm for the disreputable horror genre indicates a
willingness to "wallow" in facile pleasure, yet his revulsion at *Last House*
elicits an attempt to dissociate the film from the generic pleasures it embodies so threateningly (he calls it a "horror" film only in quotation marks).
In a later essay, Balun includes *Last House* in a survey of extreme horror
films that he classifies as "films that bite," characterized by their trigger-
ing of the "Why-Am-I-Watching-This Syndrome." Balun claims that "these
nihilistic nasties have forced even the most adamant genre aficionado to
reexamine his moral universe. Perhaps the most notable contribution of
such films . . . is that they provoke an examination of conscience and force
you to reveal your hand . . . and then they cut it off."[85] No matter how
strong his desire to reappropriate these "films that bite" into the playfully
gory terms of horror fandom, Balun's language of "reexamination," "mo-

rality," and "conscience" inevitably calls to mind (like Hallmark's own disclaimer) the traditional critical discourses of the art film.

What is at risk in exposing, as *Last House* does, the affinities between "tasteful" art and "tasteless" exploitation? Bourdieu underlines the political significance of taste, its kinship with the dynamics of political demonology, by observing that taste "fulfill[s] a social function of legitimating social differences."[86] Taste defines and divides classes by virtue of its negative essence, wherein taste takes shape in contradistinction to other tastes. In this sense, "tastes are perhaps first and foremost distastes, disgust provoked by horror of visceral intolerance ('sick-making') of the tastes of others."[87] Bourdieu's formulation of taste as distaste allows for a reading of *Last House* that acknowledges its status as a "disgusting" experience for a variety of audiences across the "art" and "exploitation" spectrum. In this reading, the reactions of disgust generated by the film overwhelm viewer defenses geared to realign taste boundaries after "the sacrilegious reuniting of tastes which taste dictates shall be separated." In other words, disgust has the potential to conjoin artful taste and low tastelessness in a shocking allegorical moment, to expose "with horror the common animality on which and against which moral distinction is constructed."[88]

It is significant that *Last House* stages its unsettling encounter between artful "good" taste and exploitive "bad" taste at exactly the time when Hollywood is experimenting with what has now become a nearly legendary foray into artistic rather than corporate accomplishment. I am referring, of course, to the so-called Hollywood Renaissance, that period between (roughly) the late 1960s and mid-1970s when a combination of cultural and industrial factors enables the production of an unusual number of risky, unconventional films in Hollywood.[89] Some have suggested that the Hollywood Renaissance may be seen as a belated "American New Wave," comparable to the earlier New Waves of Italy, France, Britain, and other countries. One factor in making this case for an "American New Wave" is the tendency of Hollywood films such as *Bonnie and Clyde*, *Five Easy Pieces* (Bob Rafelson, 1970), *McCabe and Mrs. Miller* (Robert Altman, 1971), and *Taxi Driver* (Martin Scorsese, 1976) to borrow stylistic flourishes from the European New Waves, particularly the French *nouvelle vague*.[90] Another factor is the internalizing of *auteurism* to some degree in Hollywood during this period, the notion (again, originating in France) of directors as the genuine "authors" of their films.[91] However, the Hollywood Renaissance also overlaps with what Stephen Prince has called "the genesis of ultraviolence," a massive escalation of graphic violence in Hollywood cinema whose origins are traced conventionally to *Bonnie and Clyde*[92] and whose influence certainly extends to contemporaneous films such as *Deliverance* and *Joe*. So the Hollywood Renaissance ultimately depends upon a sense of "having it both ways"—weaving together artistic ambition ("good" taste) and visceral provocation ("bad" taste).

Last House, an independent American film produced far from Hollywood but alongside the films of the Hollywood Renaissance, does not refer to *The Virgin Spring* the same way the "American New Wave" tends to refer to the French *nouvelle vague*, with the knowing wink of artistic self-legitimation. Nor does *Last House* bracket ultraviolence as mere stylistic grandstanding, the way the Hollywood Renaissance sometimes does. Instead, Craven's film allegorically uncovers how the workings of taste shield us from recognizing, amid the national trauma of Vietnam, the other half of political demonology's tortured oppositions: right/left, old/young, prowar/antiwar, bourgeois culture/counterculture, middle class/working class, and finally, art/exploitation.

TRAUMA AND NATION MADE FLESH

David Cronenberg and the Foundations of the Allegorical Moment

David Cronenberg once described the purpose of his films as "to show the unshowable, to speak the unspeakable."[1] Cronenberg's words capture the confrontational essence of the allegorical moment, just as his films—with their shocking images, blurring of horror film–art film boundaries, and thematic preoccupations with physical and psychological trauma—constitute the most powerful, sustained manifestation of the allegorical cinematic mode analyzed in previous chapters. But if each of the preceding chapters examined the allegorical moment as the collision of film, spectator, and history where the representation of historical trauma was at stake, then what exactly is at stake in Cronenberg's cinema? Where can we locate the presence of historical trauma in his films?

At first glance, nowhere. In fact, one of the reasons *The Dead Zone* (1983) and *M. Butterfly* (1993) stand out as exceptional in Cronenberg's oeuvre is precisely because they include significant references to traumatic historical events such as the Holocaust and China's Cultural Revolution—events notably absent in Cronenberg's other films.[2] But if we recall Walter Benjamin's claim that "the heart of the allegorical way of seeing" can be found in the image of the death's head, an image that not only captures "everything about history that, from the very beginning, has been untimely, sorrowful, unsuccessful" but also questions "the biographical historicity of the individual," then the relation of Cronenberg's films to the allegorical moment begins to come into focus.[3] For Benjamin, the image of the death's head, or the corpse, reveals the sorrow behind a falsely redemptive face of history, just as it reveals the fragments behind a mirage of unified individual identity. Benjamin designates this mode of revelation as allegorical, where "meaning" is glimpsed between the dead corpse and the living body, between individual interiority and historical exteriority. Cronenberg, like Benjamin, conceptualizes "meaning" as a state of transformation, where the body must be defined in terms of the corpse, and private subjectivity in terms of public objecthood. "And if it is in death that the spirit [or reason, or the mind] becomes free, in the manner of spirits, it is not until then that the body too comes properly into its own. For this much is self-evident: the allegorization of the physis can only be carried through in all its vigor in respect of the corpse."[4] Although Benjamin refers here to the seventeenth-century German *Trauerspiel*, his words could also describe the late-twentieth-century Canadian films of Cronenberg.

Rather than describe Cronenberg's cinema as responding to a particular event of historical trauma in the manner of this book's previous cases, I want to show how his films interrogate the constructions of the body that ground conventional narratives of trauma and national identity—narratives that underlie all the films analyzed in preceding chapters. Trauma, for instance, is narrated traditionally as enacting a shocking rupture between private self and public community, a rupture that must be healed by reintegrating the self with the community.[5] National identity is narrated traditionally as offering citizens the promise of connecting their private selves with a collective, invulnerable national body as well as an eternal, immemorial national time.[6] Cronenberg's cinema crystallizes the fraught translation of a private, embodied self into a public, abstracted social body that structures both of these narratives. His films insist that the traumatized body cannot be explained simply as a diseased self in need of reintegration with a healthy social public. Instead, the films maintain that mythologies of the self and the nation have *never* been natural, that trauma unmasks the alienation, exclusion, and violence that were always part of the everyday exchanges between private and public that the self and the nation depend upon. Cronenberg muddies distinctions between private and public, disease and health, in order to critique the very conception of the self as split into discrete components of mind and body—a split that enables conventional understandings of identity, and by extension, of national identity, to persist in the face of traumatic experience that threatens their coherence.

All the horror films examined in *Shocking Representation* uphold the challenge trauma presents to discourses of national identity and national cinema in each of their separate cases. These films pose the question, "How does one represent historical trauma without taking refuge in the comforting myths of national identity?" Cronenberg's films ask instead, "How does one reveal the structural tensions between body and mind, private and public, and self and object upon which narratives of trauma and identity are built?" In this final chapter, Cronenberg's cinema will be addressed as a meditation on the fundamental elements of the allegorical moment—as an exploration of allegory's challenge to foundational conceptions of self and nation.

ALLEGORIZING SELF AND NATION

Cronenberg's career in commercial features began in 1975 with *Shivers* (also known as *They Came from Within* and *The Parasite Murders*), a horror film greeted by the prominent Canadian cultural critic Robert Fulford (writing as "Marshall Delaney") with the infamous proclamation, "If using public money to produce films like [*Shivers*] is the only way English Canada can have a film industry, then perhaps English Canada should not have a film industry." It is important to recall that Fulford not only damns *Shivers* as "an atrocity" and "the most repulsive movie I've ever seen," but grounds this judgment in an attack on the film's irresponsible governmental co-sponsor, the Canadian Film Development Corporation (CFDC)—in fact, the title of Fulford's review is "You Should Know How Bad This Film Is. After All, You Paid For It."[7] In this sense, *Shivers* repulses Fulford not just because it is a horror film, but because it delivers an unacceptable image of Canadian national cinema.

Although Fulford aligns *Shivers* with other films produced by the CFDC as "so imbued with the Hollywood ethos that they seemed like pale imitations of something from Los Angeles," I believe that one reason the film strikes him as so reprehensible is its sense of Canadianness, rather than just its Americanness.[8] Cronenberg, like the CFDC itself, came to filmmaking during a cultural moment in the mid-1960s and early 1970s characterized by a surge in English Canadian nationalism.[9] The spirit of that moment is captured in Margaret Atwood's *Survival: A Thematic Guide to Canadian Literature* (1972), a particularly influential volume of literary criticism. Atwood sets out to provide a founding symbol for the unique character of Canadian literature, and by extension, of Canadian national culture. She selects "Survival" as the symbol, as distinct from "The Frontier" for America or "The Island" for England. Atwood explains, "Our stories are likely to be tales not of those who made it but of those who made it back, from the awful experience—the North, the snowstorm, the sinking ship—that killed everyone else." For Atwood, "Survival" is a symbol not only rooted in the beginnings of Canadian national literature and cultural history but also indicative of its current state of sickness, its lack of national self-awareness in the face of dominant American influences: "Canadians are forever taking the national pulse like doctors at a sickbed: the aim is not to see whether the patient will live well but simply whether he will live at all."[10]

This diagnosis of Canadian national identity as diseased surfaces in another contemporaneous and influential critical document of Canadian culture, Robert Fothergill's essay "Coward, Bully, or Clown: The Dream-Life of a Younger Brother" (1973). Fothergill argues that Canadian cinema suffers from a "younger brother syndrome," an inferiority complex caused by an uneasy proximity with its dominant American older brother. The syndrome manifests itself through the predominance of Canadian cinematic representations of men as impotent, as cowards, bullies, or clowns. For Fothergill, Canadian cinema's "psychic debilities" must be subjected to a psychotherapy of self-awareness in order to achieve "self-realization."[11]

What Cronenberg does in *Shivers*, and continues to do in various ways throughout his career, is literalize, defamiliarize, and subvert this discourse of Canadian identity as diseased. In Cronenberg's cinema, disease is not just the enemy of identity, it is also the source of identity. Parasites, plagues, and mutations in Cronenberg's films surely bring pain and death, but they simultaneously endow his "diseased" characters with a savage life, an undeniable power and fascination that also structures the films themselves. By embodying the discourse of diseased Canadian identity in such a spectacularly literal and confrontational fashion, his films open a space for reimagining "Canada" in tension with (rather than unreflective acceptance of) these desires for a foundational national identity. In effect, Cronenberg asks what it means for Atwood and Fothergill to cast Canadian national culture as a diseased body and to call for self-awareness as the solution to the problem of Canadian national selfhood. By interrogating what counts as "self" or "awareness," "problem" or "solution," Cronenberg's cinema questions what the conjunction of selfhood and nationalism finally signifies.

In an oft-quoted formulation, Benedict Anderson defines the nation as "an imagined political community—and imagined as both inherently limited and sovereign."[12] But in the case of Canada, as Michael Dorland argues, the nation has *not* been imagined as sovereign: "Whereas nationalism elsewhere has usually been conceived, like the nation itself, as one and indivisible, Canadian nationalism is, like the nation itself, infinitely divisible."[13] According to Tony Wilden, many Canadians "go so far as to say that Canadians, of whatever sort, do not exist; others make it plain that whatever 'Canadian' means, they want nothing to do with it."[14] Canada's imagination of itself as illusory and divisible complicates what Lauren Berlant describes as the nation's utopian promise "to provide a passage for the individual subject to the abstract identity of 'citizen,'" because this promise of abstraction rests on the nation's hypothetical ability to ensure that the citizen will reach "another plane of existence, a whole, unassailable body, whose translation into totality mimics the nation's permeable yet impervious spaces."[15] In Canada, the utopian promise of an abstracted, indivisible national body resists being imagined in its comforting wholeness; instead, the national body is imagined as fragmented, fragile, even colonized. Cronenberg's films give shape to this phantasmatic, fractured national body through stunning images of the unstable, metamorphosing bodies of individuals. The "body," for Cronenberg, is neither entirely private nor entirely public; it is both an individual body and a national body, where the competing claims between these two bodies that are always actually one manifest themselves in shockingly literal forms. As Cronenberg explains, "I tend to view chaos as a private rather than social endeavor. That's undoubtedly because I was born and raised in Canada. The chaos that most appeals to me is very private and very personal. You have these little pockets of private and personal chaos brewing in the interstices in the structure of society, which likes to stress its order and control, and that's the collision you see."[16]

When Cronenberg insists, "I'm sure if had I been born and raised in some other country I would not think of chaos strictly in terms of private chaos," he suggests how the Canadian imagination of a wholly public, fully national body tends to remain something of an impossibility.[17] The question of Quebec's contested relation to the rest of Canada is of course important to consider here; indeed, Cronenberg (himself a native of Toronto, where he continues to live and base his production headquarters)[18] connects his experience filming *Shivers* and *Rabid* (1977) in Montreal for a small French Canadian production company to his "introduction to the fierce nationalism of Quebec, and how well it worked in terms of a very enclosed culture that could excite itself. It was very hard for English-Canadian culture to excite English Canadians. They were excited by Americana."[19] Atwood and Fothergill, as we have seen, diagnose this Canadian reliance on America for its sense of national identity as a disease that must be "cured" through a healthier sense of autonomous national selfhood. But Cronenberg chooses another path. He articulates "Canada" not as an authentic national essence to be uncovered or realized, but as a constructed process of narration. Cronenberg's films capture what Homi K. Bhabha refers to as "the ambivalent, antagonistic perspective of nation as narration," a perspective that promises to "establish the cultural boundaries of the nation so that they may be acknowledged as 'containing' thresholds of meaning that must be crossed, erased, and translated in the process of cultural production."[20] Cronenberg channels this translation of "Canada" *through* (rather than simply with or against) "American" genres and cultural icons, forging images of the "body" that become a powerful interrogation of how Canadian national identity and Canadian national cinema have been imagined traditionally.

Andrew Higson writes that "the concept of a national cinema has almost invariably been mobilized as a strategy of cultural (and economic) resistance; a means of asserting national autonomy in the face of (usually) Hollywood's domination."[21] Central to this strategy of resistance is the development of some aspect of national cinematic specificity that stands in marked contrast to Hollywood films. In Canada, the origin of this "authentic" national cinema has been traced conventionally to John Grierson and the organization he helped establish in 1939, the National Film Board of Canada (NFB).[22] Grierson, the Scot most famous for his role in founding the British documentary film movement of the 1920s and 1930s (as discussed in chapter 2), successfully institutionalized documentary realism as Canada's "official" national mode of film expression; as recently as 1991, Gary Evans could refer to the NFB as "one of the few cultural life-savers Canada may point to as genuine and home-grown, a buoy that has helped prevent the nation from becoming either the largest Balkan hinterland in the world or the fifty-first member of the United States."[23] But this idealization of Grierson as the visionary responsible for a truly Canadian national cinema that wards off internal disintegration and external colonization is ultimately more of an anxious wish than an invincible legend. As Michael Dorland argues, "If Grierson was the founder of a distinct Canadian cinematic realism (and not merely just another colonial administrator) how does one account for the fact that the debate as to the nature of that realism rages on?"[24] Peter Morris suggests that the NFB's assumed popular success in Canada may be significantly exaggerated, and that Grierson may have to be recognized not only as the architect of a misleadingly "popular" NFB, but as the agent of "the moribund state of the [Canadian] commercial film industry for more than two decades." Morris claims that the extremely de-layed development of Canadian feature-length fiction films (usually dated to 1964, with Don Owen's *Nobody Waved Goodbye* and Gilles Groulx's *Le Chat dans le sac*) can be traced partly to Grierson's influential essay "A Film Policy for Canada" (1944), which anticipates the principles of the Canadian Cooperation Project so precisely that "it is difficult not to believe that it was used by the Motion Picture Association of America in drafting the Project."[25] The Canadian Cooperation Project, which lasted between 1948 and 1958, was the notorious agreement in which the Canadian government pledged not to promote the growth of a Canadian commercial film industry in exchange for Hollywood's promise to mention Canada in as many of its films as possible (in the hope of boosting tourism).[26]

I have gone to some length in order to underline an important point: the Canadian case presents a national cinema whose very "authenticity" exists inside, not outside, the realm of American domination; whose establish-ment of national specificity colludes with, rather than combats, "Canada's marginalization in the film world."[27] Cronenberg's films enact, acknowl-edge, and analyze this tension, rather than portraying the matter as a sim-ple face-off between authentic Canadian identity and the forces of Ameri-can imperialism. It is not surprising, therefore, to learn that Cronenberg (perhaps not unlike Michael Powell during the production of *Peeping Tom*) felt "the heavy hand of John Grierson" and the NFB as a "suffocating" influ-ence on him during his early years as a filmmaker. In fact, Cronenberg had to campaign for three long years before even the CFDC (which, unlike the NFB, had a mandate to produce commercial feature films) would agree to contribute toward the financing of *Shivers*.[28]

Cronenberg's project was also at odds with the contemporary renaissance in Canadian narrative cinema, a modest seventies "new wave"[29] spearhead-ed in English Canada by *Goin' Down the Road* (Don Shebib, 1970)—a film greeted immediately by many Canadian critics as a model for a genuine national cinema.[30] *Goin' Down the Road* chronicles the adventures of two working-class men from depressed Nova Scotia who travel to the metropo-lis of Toronto seeking a "good life" that proves hopelessly beyond their grasp. Shebib films his subjects in a gritty documentary realist style clearly indebted to the aesthetics of the NFB as well as the "kitchen sink realism" of the British New Wave in the 1960s. The considerable success of *Goin' Down the Road*, which has helped canonize the film as "the foundational text for Canadian cinema in English,"[31] ensured that the English Canadian "new wave" would be characterized by a social realist style that dutifully pays its respects to the NFB, rather than opens up radically new vistas for Canadian cinema. So for Cronenberg at the outset of his career, the concept of Canadian national cinema, with its aversion to "filmmaking of the imagination" as a synonym for Hollywood, was a point of alienation rather than identification.[32]

This is not to deny the existence of very real social and economic factors that have informed the deployment of a "Canada vs. Hollywood" and/or a "Canada vs. America" oppositional logic at the levels of Canadian film policy and film criticism. The title of Manjunath Pendakur's study of the Canadian film industry's political economy speaks volumes: *Canadian Dreams and American Control*. Pendakur cites a Canadian government report which estimates that 90 percent of annual revenues from Canadian film and video markets are controlled by U.S. interests, and notes that since 1974, Canada has had "the dubious distinction of being the number one [foreign] market for American feature films."[33] Even the CFDC, the federal institution that helped make *Shivers* possible, cannot be regarded as an overall success.[34] After all, the "principal legacy" of films produced during the mid-1970s and early 1980s under the CFDC's sponsorship, especially after the supplement of the Capital Cost Allowance of 1974 (a 100 percent federal tax shelter used to stimulate private investment), has been aptly described as a "gaping, self-inflicted national wound."[35] Many films produced during this period were approached primarily as tax write-offs, with a significant number never even reaching the theaters; the ones that did were often weak imitations of Hollywood genre fare, resulting in "the anonymous films of Hollywood North."[36] It is no wonder that Barry Keith Grant (paraphrasing Peter Harcourt) goes so far as to conclude "it is nothing less than the Canadian imagination that has been colonized by American culture."[37]

Given these factors, it is not surprising that Canadian film criticism has continually anchored its engagement with Cronenberg in sharply opposed poles defined by America and Canada. For example, William Beard describes the "violent dualism of Cronenberg's films" in terms of a "Canadian drama of restraint, internalized violence and stasis" (corresponding to the paradigms of national literary character constructed by Margaret Atwood and Northrop Frye) and a competing "American drama of freedom, externalized violence and progress" represented cinematically by "the blood and guts and disease" derived from "low-budget American horror movies" and the "gaudy plebeian traditions of Hollywood in general." For Beard, the

"Canadian" ultimately triumphs over the "American" in Cronenberg's cinema: "at narrative's end . . . the dominant attitude in Cronenberg's world is one of stasis and repression. . . . Cronenberg seems very much an *Ur*-Canadian."[38] Gaile McGregor also argues for the "profound unAmericanness" of Cronenberg's films by demonstrating how "Cronenberg's oeuvre is 'out of sync' with the American pattern" of cinematic horror.[39] For Bart Testa, even the most apparently "American" element of Cronenberg's films, their graphic horror, is best understood in terms of a "discourse on technology springing from the Canadian ethos" and exemplified by such seminal Canadian philosophers as George Grant, Harold Innis, and Marshall McLuhan.[40] Testa's conclusion, that Cronenberg's films are an extension of Canadian discourses on technology and are thus closer to science fiction than horror, again suggests neat boundaries between Cronenberg's philosophical "Canadianness" and visceral "Americanness." Finally, Jim Leach claims that "attempts to situate Cronenberg's films in a national rather than generic context often seem to obscure the ways in which they are constructed and received," intimating that the "Canadian" national context and "American" generic context may finally have to be treated as mutually exclusive in Cronenberg's case.[41]

In each of these essays, the "Canadian" Cronenberg is distinguished from the "American" Cronenberg and the troubling convergence of "national" cinema and "generic" horror safely evaded. I would argue instead that Cronenberg's films generate precisely this convergence—they insist on imagining Canadian national cinema as an ambivalent dialogue with American genre cinema, and maintain that "self" and "nation" must resist (rather than sustain) naturalized definitions. I have chosen to focus on *Shivers* and *Crash* (1996) in the analyses that follow partly because of their location at opposite ends of Cronenberg's career, but also because they represent two of the most provocative instances of Cronenberg's engagement with American genre cinema, on the one hand, and discourses of anti-Hollywood art cinema, on the other. The two films also share an oddly intimate kinship; Cronenberg has suggested, perhaps only half-jokingly, that *Crash*'s characters might actually be the parasite-infected condominium dwellers of *Shivers*.[42]

SHIVERS AND *NIGHT OF THE LIVING DEAD*: FOREGROUNDING THE CANADIAN/AMERICAN NIGHTMARE

Cronenberg has characterized his early contributions to the horror film as "be[ing] part of bringing horror into the twentieth century. At the time

I started to make *Shivers*, there was already *Night of the Living Dead*. But for the most part horror was gothic, distant, not here. . . . I was certainly influenced, in the style of what I was doing, by the tenor of those particular times."[43] Of course, Cronenberg is not alone when he cites *Night of the Living Dead* (1968), George A. Romero's American independent first feature, as a crucial benchmark in the development of the modern horror film and its engagement with social history. What is less common is the designation of *Shivers*, Cronenberg's own feature-length debut—after the experimental mini-features *Stereo* (1969) and *Crimes of the Future* (1970)—as a kindred genre effort similarly influenced by contemporary social crisis. But *Shivers* does not simply mimic *Night*'s allegorical moments; instead, it implicitly critiques the limitations of Romero's film on precisely those issues concerning the self and the nation in relation to historical trauma. In this sense, *Shivers* foregrounds the mapping of the "Canada vs. America" opposition as it challenges the conceptual underpinnings of the allegorical moment.

Like *Shivers*, *Night* opened to critical outrage and condemnation. *Variety* proclaimed that "until the Supreme Court establishes clearcut guidelines for the pornography of violence, *Night of the Living Dead* will serve nicely as an outer-limit definition by example . . . [the film] casts serious aspersions on the integrity and social responsibility of its Pittsburgh-based makers, distrib Walter Reade, the film industry as a whole and exhibs who book the pic, as well as raising doubts about . . . the moral health of filmgoers who cheerfully opt for this unrelieved orgy of sadism."[44] Seven years later, of course, Robert Fulford would describe *Shivers* in similar terms, as "sadistic pornography" beyond redemption.[45] *Night* would soon overcome its initial critical drubbing by doing phenomenal box office business and attracting defenders who highlighted the film's value as social commentary: Elliott Stein compared the film's zombies to the " 'silent majority,' "[46] while Joseph Lewis claimed that Lyndon Johnson might never "have permitted the napalming of the Vietnamese" had he seen *Night*.[47] The critical tide turned so radically that by June 1970, Romero was appearing at New York's Museum of Modern Art to host a screening of his film—a prestigious honor that attests to *Night*'s critical redemption in America. By contrast, *Shivers* never really escaped the shadow cast by Fulford's review in Canada; although the film was a financial success, Cronenberg's critical standing in Canada would not improve significantly until the release of *Videodrome* in 1983.[48]

Why was *Night*'s "orgy of sadism" ultimately amenable to redemptive interpretations as social commentary while *Shivers*'s "sadistic pornography" was not? Examining Robin Wood's influential distinction between *Night*'s "progressive" horror and the "reactionary" horror of *Shivers* begins to provide an answer. In "An Introduction to the American Horror Film" (1979), Wood assigns to *Night* the qualities of an "'apocalyptic'" horror film that expresses "despair and negativity, yet its very negation can be claimed as progressive: the 'apocalypse,' even when presented in metaphysical terms (the end of the world), is generally reinterpretable in social/political ones (the end of the highly specific world of patriarchal capitalism)." Wood adds that apocalyptic horror films such as *Night* are "progressive in so far as their negativity is not recuperable into the dominant ideology, but constitutes (on the contrary) the recognition of that ideology's disintegration, its untenability, as all it has repressed explodes and blows it apart." *Shivers*, on the other hand, is singled out by Wood for its "unremitting ugliness and crudity" and its rare "achievement of *total* negation," where "the idea of releasing what has been repressed" can only be expressed as "unqualified horror" and "sexual disgust."[49] Wood returns to this formula of apocalyptic, "progressive" negativity versus "reactionary" negation in a later essay, where he explains that "Romero's ghouls are the embodiment of established values/dominant norms . . . they are linked specifically to the tensions and conflicts within the bourgeois patriarchal family. The problem for the survivors, then . . . is to extricate themselves from these values and create new ones, new forms of relating." Wood rejects Cronenberg's own claim that infection by the parasites in *Shivers* can be interpreted precisely as a new and even liberatory "form of relating"; at the end of his analytic rope, Wood asks, "And what, in any case, could we possibly make of a film that dramatized liberation like *that*?"[50]

What could *not* be made of *Shivers*, by Wood or less perceptive critics, was an interrogation of "liberation" itself at a moment when the utopian promise held out by the sexual revolution in the late 1960s had already given way to the commodified excesses of the "me" generation.[51] Wood reads *Shivers*'s disturbing sexual imagery as an indication that the film regards the prospect of sexual liberation with "unmitigated horror" and "sexuality in general as the object of loathing."[52] This reading suggests that the film's horror is organized solely by sexual disgust, and does not account for so much else in the film that is treated with a profound sense of horror—including the loss of community in a sterile environment structured by the commodification of the sexual revolution. Starliner Towers, the luxury condominium setting of *Shivers*, is clearly modeled on the "youth-oriented apartment complexes" constructed in the 1970s to capitalize on the economic boom surrounding "a new singles culture" that "glamoriz[ed] the lifestyle of the unmarried."[53] *Shivers* opens, appropriately, with a commercial for Starliner Towers, featuring slide photographs of the complex

accompanied by a voice-over which promises that Starliner Towers transforms "day-to-day living into a luxury cruise" by providing every possible
amenity, including "the most modern, name-brand electrical appliances."
Even before the voice-over ends (with the ominous corporate sign-off "from
Star Co., a division of General Structures, Incorporated"), the commercial
slides give way to shots of a young heterosexual couple driving up to Starliner Towers to inquire about an apartment. The slippage between commercial and narrative continues as the couple meets with building agent
Ronald Merrick (Ronald Mlodzik), the smarmy man who is already familiar as the commercial's announcer. But by the time Merrick seduces the
couple with an apartment blueprint featuring what he calls "the big view,
the panoramic view," the audience's own "view" of Starliner Towers has
been subjected to intercut images utterly at odds with the placid commercial's consumer attractions: an older man breaking into an apartment and
violently assaulting a young girl in a school uniform. The man, Dr. Emil
Hobbes (Fred Doederlein), is the creator of a strain of phallic/fecal-look-
ing parasites that cause sexual dementia in their human hosts, promoting
uninhibited, sometimes violent sexual activity that allows the parasites to
access new bodies. The girl, Annabelle Brown (Cathy Graham), is Hobbes's
experimental subject, a test host for the parasites; he kills her and himself
when he realizes the parasites have exceeded his control.

Wood describes Annabelle as "the film's Pandora whose released eroticism precipitates general cataclysm"; for Wood, she is one of the film's
several "sexually aroused preying women" who are "presented with a particular intensity of horror and disgust."[54] This interpretation overlooks
the carefully constructed cinematic framework Cronenberg builds around
Annabelle, which situates the "cataclysm" of her "released eroticism" in
a specific social and historical context. She is not Hobbes's sole experimental subject—in a very real sense, Starliner Towers itself is portrayed as
Hobbes's "patient," a living organism that is suggested to have been in need
of "treatment" long before Hobbes's unorthodox intervention.[55] Hobbes's
introduction of Annabelle's infected presence into the building environment (he pays her rent) facilitates the spread of the parasites through her
affairs with at least two male residents. But the infection of these men is
hardly tragic or "cataclysmic"—both men are depicted negatively, as symptoms of a living environment in which unfeeling male narcissists are allowed to manipulate sexual "liberation" for their own selfish ends. One is
an abusive husband who cheats on his kind, sensitive wife, and the other is
a "swinging" older man who spouts rehearsed lines regarding the wonders
of megavitamins (the intimated source of his sexual prowess) to young

women unfortunate enough to be seated beside him in a doctor's waiting room. Hobbes himself is revealed as a corrupt teacher and doctor (he is caught examining Annabelle for "breast cancer" at age twelve in the faculty lounge) with only one true source of genius: winning research grants from medical corporations. His colleague, Rollo Linsky (Joe Silver), initially describes Hobbes's parasite research as a business scam, where funds from an organ transplant corporation are utilized by Hobbes to develop parasites that will make organ transplants obsolete and thus bankrupt the corporation. Linsky later decides that what Hobbes was *really* after was the means of turning the world into "one beautiful, mindless orgy." The film suggests that the truth is a combination of Linsky's two theories—Hobbes's real project is to replace the hollow, disembodied commercialization of the sexual revolution with an "authentically" physical sexual revolution that is realized nonetheless through cutthroat capitalist business practice.

In this manner, *Shivers* presents both the "problem" of the sterile, suffocatingly commodified Starliner Towers environment and the "solution" of the sexually liberating parasites as similarly troubling and, perhaps, after all, more intimately connected than radically opposed. (See fig. 5.1.) The film confronts viewers with the realization that the sexual revolution, which is usually traced to the late 1960s and is often equated reductively with the progressive political movements of that era, was actually largely the work of "entrepreneurs who extended the logic of consumer capitalism to the realm of sex." As John D'Emilio and Estelle B. Freedman point out, "The consumer society of the sixties helps explain how the singles culture could emerge from a period seemingly rooted in a marital sexual ethic and why it won such ready acceptance."[56] Starliner Towers sells itself on the promise of an intertwined sexual and consumerist bliss, where every day is a "luxury cruise" and sexual partners (whom the opening commercial suggestively invokes as "your fellow passengers") as well as consumer goods can be acquired effortlessly, without ever leaving the building. But the promise is literally empty—the hallways and public spaces of the complex are eerily underpopulated during the beginning of the film, and interaction between residents (even those living in the same apartment) is uniformly cold and disappointing. It is only with the onset of the parasite epidemic that the hallways come alive and residents are able to express a delirious passion for each other. Yet as Wood reminds us, the imagery of infection that accompanies this parasitic "liberation" is undeniably disturbing and extremely visceral: parasites undulate visibly beneath skin, wriggle out of mouths covered in blood, and even invade a bathing woman vaginally.[57] On the basis of such imagery, Wood concludes that "Cronenberg's movies tell us that we shouldn't want to change society because we would only make it even worse."[58] I would contend that *Shivers* imbricates the notion of self-transformation, which the popular version of the sexual revolution had distilled as "sex as the source of personal meaning,"[59] with discourses of social regulation and exclusion that often masquerade as personal liberation and empowerment. *Shivers* understands, in a way Wood finally does not, Michel Foucault's assertion that sexuality is not simply "repressed" by social networks of power, but produced by them. For Foucault, "relations of power are not in a position of exteriority with respect to other types of relationships (economic processes, knowledge relationships, sexual relations) but are immanent in the latter."[60] Therefore "progressiveness" itself is not as simple as the project Wood ascribes to the "progressive" horror film, of exposing the untenability of the dominant ideology, because even the utopian imagination of "new values" and "new forms of relating" must be seen as bound up in existing power relations—relations that *produce* the regulating concept of the self, rather than simply prevent the self from attaining its "natural" privacy and interiority. *Shivers* acknowledges this painful inextricability of public and private, and demands that spectators inhabit it as a complex, endless moment of ambivalent transformation.

During the climax of *Shivers*, the "hero" Roger St. Luc (Paul Hampton) is forcibly "baptized" into the new sexual order by succumbing to a parasitic kiss from his long-denied nurse Forsythe (Lynn Lowry) while struggling against other infected residents in the swimming pool of Starliner Towers.[61] Cronenberg shoots the kiss in agonizing slow motion, giving viewers time to experience both the frightening violence and the exhilarating energy of self-transformation. The attack on St. Luc is certainly unsettling, but it is also a welcome release from the stifling disconnection from desire he has exhibited throughout the film. This ambivalence also structures the film's denouement, when St. Luc and the other infected residents calmly exit Starliner Towers as contented (unmarried) couples who drive off happily to infect nearby Montreal. Their appearances are picture-perfect, and Forsythe's lighting of St. Luc's postcoital cigarette completes the artificial conventionality of the scene. In this sense, the film ends as it began, inside a commercial. Only now the movement is outward, toward the city, rather than inward; Merrick's saccharine voice-over has been replaced by the harsh voice of a news radio announcer reporting a series of "violent sexual assaults" in Montreal. Has the sexual "revolution" finally come to its fruition, with the political literally infecting the personal? After all, Emil Hobbes's famous namesake, Thomas, was unusual among classical political philosophers for insisting on the political nature of sexual relations,

FIGURE 5.1 *Shivers* (David Cronenberg, 1975): Roger St. Luc (Paul Hampton) examines one of the parasites that have transformed the population of Starliner Towers. (Courtesy of Jerry Ohlinger's Movie Material)

an insistence which contradicts the "fundamental assumption of modern political theory . . . that sexual relations are not political."[62] Perhaps, to paraphrase Wood, we cannot possibly know what to make of a film that dramatizes politics like *that*—and "that" is precisely its power.

Like *Shivers*, *Night of the Living Dead* concludes with its protagonist falling victim to the forces of mass chaos he had been struggling against. Ben (Duane Jones), *Night*'s African American hero, survives the onslaught of flesh-eating zombies only to be shot by his "rescuers," a redneck posse of trigger-happy militiamen. Ben's murder closes the film on a bleak, disturbing note. *Night*'s final moments, which depict Ben's body being dragged outside and hoisted onto a bonfire of zombie corpses, are presented as a series of grainy, newspaper-quality photographs that produce inescapable connotations of lynchings and contemporary civil rights–related violence. Yet Ben's transformation from survivor to casualty, unlike St. Luc's transformation from uninfected and frigid to infected and passionate, is finally relatively unambiguous. Viewers are clearly meant to feel sorrow and anger at Ben's senseless death, to criticize the society that murders him, and to recognize that his supposed saviors are no less deadly than the ravenous zombies—in short, problem and solution are indistinguishable, so no real future can be imagined as emerging from the disintegration of the present. This message, for all its nihilism and its stunning divergence from 1950s science fiction and horror "disaster" film conventions,[63] is still instantly readable; *Night* allows viewers to channel its horror through signposted value judgments that, however boldly pessimistic, work to absorb any further challenge to the audience's complicity in that horror. To be sure, *Night*'s conclusion certainly qualifies as a brilliant allegorical moment, but the film erects a critical barrier that *Shivers* ultimately goes beyond. (See fig. 5.2.) Both films attack the evils of the existing social order, but *Shivers* then extends its critique to show how the very future that *Night* leaves unimagined *must* be imagined, although this future cannot be divorced from the crises of the present. This crucial difference permits *Shivers* to allude to *Night* while contesting Romero's construction of the allegorical moment.

The issue of allusion is foregrounded during a short but pivotal scene midway through *Shivers*, where an uninfected St. Luc rifles through trash in the basement of Starliner Towers to locate a dead parasite for examination. Just as he finds the parasite and holds it up to the light to inspect it, an infected black maintenance man attacks him.[64] The ensuing fight is brief but disturbingly violent; St. Luc responds to the punches of the maintenance man by splitting his head open with a crowbar. The brutality of St. Luc's "self-defense" is doubly shocking because it is the first of only a few rare moments during the film in which he reacts to situations with anything other than impassive restraint—so spectators are initially thrilled to see him finally take action, but are then horrified by what that action entails (the same tension is revisited during St. Luc's parasitic kiss with Forsythe during the film's climax). In this manner, St. Luc's status as the film's "hero" is questioned, along with the positive or negative valuation of the "threat" represented by self-transformation through infection. An allusion to *Night* (one of several in the film) also informs the impact of this scene—not only is this maintenance man, like Ben, the only significant black male character in the film, but he is killed in exactly the same way that Ben kills his first zombies in *Night*: through blows to the head with a metal rod. In addition, the form of the maintenance man's demise (obliteration of the skull) echoes Ben's death (bullet in the head). This allusive equation of Ben and the maintenance man in *Shivers* heightens audience ambivalence toward St. Luc, who is consequently aligned with the posse that shoots Ben. The critical difference between the two films, which the allusion underlines, is that *Night*'s posse never accrues much substance for the viewer beyond a comic-book-like "search and destroy" simplicity, while

FIGURE 5.2 *Night of the Living Dead* (George A. Romero, 1968): The protagonist Ben (Duane Jones), treated as just another corpse for the bonfire by the militiamen. (Courtesy of Jerry Ohlinger's Movie Material)

St. Luc's complicated behavior occupies the center of *Shivers*. It is one thing for *Night* to invite audiences to identify with Ben as the sympathetic victim of violence;[65] it is quite another for *Shivers* to posit St. Luc as the focus of viewer identification, with his simultaneously sympathetic and unsympathetic roles as both violator and victim, "alive" (after infection) and "dead" (before infection).

In drawing these distinctions between the two films, I do not want to diminish the significance of *Night*'s daring representation of racial conflict. Indeed, the fact that Romero's film only began to attract substantial positive attention from critics and non-drive-in audiences after it had been re-

released in 1969 on a double-bill with a slavery drama (Herbert Biberman's *Slaves* [1969])[66] suggests that the presence of the film's racial subtext may have proved crucial to its appeal. But Romero himself has noted the disparity between the film's unintended function as racial commentary and the extremes to which some critics pushed that function; the director reports bemusedly that *Night* "caused one critic in his exuberance to write that he heard the strains of 'Ole Man River' in the music score when Ben meets his fate." Romero explains that Ben's role was not written for a black actor, but that they cast Jones "because we liked Duane's audition better than others we had seen."[67] The film bears out Romero's claim—not once is Ben's race explicitly acknowledged or referred to. This lack of overt recognition does not prevent Ben's blackness from charging the film's events,[68] but it does signal a certain boundary of frankness and conventionality regarding racial representation that *Night* does not cross. Instead, the film takes certain measures to contain Ben's blackness. Sumiko Higashi notes that the traditional "supermasculine" sexual threat of the black male is tamed in *Night* through Ben's "desexualized" portrayal as a "technician" associated with "machinery, gadgets, and hardware" rather than sexuality.[69] In this sense, Ben resembles the white occupants of the besieged farmhouse, because they too are remarkably desexualized: Barbara (Judith O'Dea), catatonic after the death of her brother; Harry and Helen Cooper (Karl Hardman and Marilyn Eastman), a loveless, resentful married couple with a wounded daughter, Karen (Kyra Schon); even Tom (Keith Wayne) and Judy (Judith Ridley), the film's young lovers, are barely permitted a single fleeting kiss before Tom reminds Judy that they have "work to do." Indeed, teamwork and survivalist efficiency take such precedence in *Night* that Barry Keith Grant rightly detects a "striking similarity to the adventure films of Howard Hawks" and the Hawksian "code of professionalism." Grant continues, "As with, say, the cowboys on the Chisholm Trail in *Red River* [1948] or the men in the Arctic in *The Thing* [produced by Hawks, directed by Christian Nyby, 1951], the characters in the living dead films are cut off from established codes and ethics, forced to survive on an existential precipice even steeper than the mountains surrounding the flyers in *Only Angels Have Wings* [1939]."[70] *Night* ends with the failure of one Hawksian system (the farmhouse group) and the success of another: the all-male militia who efficiently dispose of every zombie in their path, clearing the way for a return to order. Romero presents the militia's "success" with profound ambivalence—one aerial shot deliberately confuses them with the zombies—but their mastery of the zombie menace is unquestioned. Near the end of the film, a news reporter traveling with the militia sums up the current situation as "everything appears to be under control."⁷¹ Even in the grim scenario offered by *Night*, one of the last things that continues to "work"—long after sex has become outmoded—is professional masculine might.

Shivers reverses and critiques *Night*'s masculine desexualization of human relations by presenting non-heteronormative sex as the force capable of undermining patriarchal order. While *Night* stifles sexual relations in favor of showcasing the spectacle of masculine teamwork, *Shivers* multiplies sexual possibilities in a graphic overturning of normative sexual regimes—by the film's end, gay, lesbian, and even child sexuality achieve vivid expression. It is with *Shivers*'s depiction of child sexuality that *Night* is most directly invoked and critiqued. In one of *Night*'s most notorious scenes, the young girl Karen Cooper returns from the dead to feast on her mortally wounded father and then murder her mother with a trowel. William Paul has noted this scene's importance for the film's escalating economy of "grossness" through its addition of "incestuous desire" to previous displays of cannibalism; in this sense, it may be the film's closest approximation of transgressive sex. But as Paul points out, this eruption of child sexuality necessitates "two striking departures from the rest of the film—one a shift in narrative logic, the other a break in visual continuity."⁷² The shift in narrative logic involves the substitution of Karen's violent *murder* of her mother for the expected zombie behavior of *eating* her mother. The continuity break occurs when the undead Karen attacks Ben: instead of shooting her, his rifle momentarily "disappears" in an apparent continuity glitch, allowing Ben to use both his hands while shoving Karen away. These divergences from the film's narrative and spatial logic tame the threat of a fully sexualized child "monster." Karen does not consummate her incestuous desire by consuming her mother, nor does Ben recognize her as a true zombie and kill her with a rifle blast.

By contrast, *Shivers* includes a harrowing scene in which an infected Karen look-alike (right down to a similar dress and corresponding bloodstains on her mouth) joins forces with her mother and another man to overpower an uninfected security guard. The assault concludes with a slow-motion shot showing the young girl kissing the guard on the mouth, transmitting the parasite orally. This scene confronts the viewer with everything that *Night*'s depiction of Karen shrank from—a fully sexualized "monster" child who cannot simply be put aside by masculine authority, but who sexually violates the very authority (a security guard, no less) that would deny non-heteronormative sexuality. The girl's kiss is one of three slow-motion parasitic kisses in the film—the other two involve the lesbian coupling of Janine (Susan Petrie) and Betts (Barbara Steele) and the aforementioned climactic coupling of St. Luc and Forsythe—that cinematically establish a chiefly non-heteronormative sexual *community* which presents a confrontational alternative to the sexual revolution's safely commodified belief in sex as the source of personal, rather than collective meaning.

With its shocking images of a radically sexualized community, *Shivers* implicitly challenges one of the most influential modern American horror films on what it regards as "horrifying." Although both films were condemned as "pornography" at one point, only *Night* attained critical redemption as social metaphor. Now we can see that one possible factor contributing to this disparity in reception is *Shivers*'s portrayal of a sexualized, non-heteronormative community in place of *Night*'s desexualized, masculinist one. In the American film, the apocalypse is now; in the Canadian film, the apocalypse is always and ongoing. It is somehow fitting that Cronenberg believes *Shivers* has a "happy ending,"[73] while Martin Scorsese, an avowed Cronenberg enthusiast as well as a quintessentially American director, regards the ending as "genuinely shocking, subversive, surrealistic and probably something we all deserve."[74] Perhaps not surprisingly, Scorsese has also claimed that Cronenberg doesn't know what his own films are about.[75]

CRASH: THE WRECKAGE OF GENRE, ART, AND AUTHORSHIP

Patricia Pearson's 1996 article on *Crash*, like Robert Fulford's review of *Shivers* twenty years earlier, appeared in *Saturday Night*, one of Canada's leading cultural magazines. But that is where the similarities between the two pieces seem to end. Pearson introduces Cronenberg as "Canada's preeminent filmmaker" and describes what must have been Fulford's nightmare in 1975: Cronenberg given permission by the city government to close sections of major Toronto freeways in order to film car crashes and actors "[making] explicit, moaning love amidst the wreckage."[76] Despite the striking difference in tone, Pearson, like Fulford, still carefully situates Cronenberg between Canada and Hollywood. Her Cronenberg is not just a director but a "radical philosopher" because his films feature provocatively graphic sex rather than mindless Hollywood violence; she focuses special attention on Cronenberg's casting difficulties with Hollywood stars because "Hollywood actors seem to have an easier time being shot than being made love to."[77]

Whether testifying to Cronenberg's poisonous proximity to Hollywood as a genre film hack or his immaculate distance from Hollywood as Canada's own "radical philosopher" of cinema, Fulford and Pearson both read the director's films through a critical matrix that opposes genre films and art films. (See fig. 5.3.) Previous chapters have already shown how the allegorical moment disturbs the tendency to polarize these two categories, but how does Cronenberg's cinema, with its capacity to question the foundations of the allegorical moment, reframe distinctions between genre films and art films along the axis of authorship? If film, spectator, and history collide during the allegorical moment, then authorship must be understood as a key variable in the allegorical equation. Indeed, recent scholarly accounts posit film authorship as an invitation, issued to the spectator, to engage in a certain mode of cinematic interpretation. Dudley Andrew, for example, describes the author's existence as precisely those elements connecting spectator and film that "can thicken a text with duration, with the past of its coming into being and with the future of our being with it."[78] Andrew's formulation suggests that the mode of identification offered to audiences by the figure of an author thus includes connections that span time, such as intertextual associations between a number of the director's films. Tom Gunning boldly enacts this type of proposition in his recent book on Fritz Lang, where the author emerges as a crucial aspect of interpretive practice for the viewer. For Gunning, the author functions as "an invitation to reading . . . precisely poised on the threshold of the work, evident in the film itself, but also standing outside it, absent except in the imprint left behind." What anchors Gunning's study is the firm belief that reading this imprint constitutes a valuable act of interpretation, one that allows audiences to engage authorship as an encounter not with the biographical author, but with "the language of cinema" as negotiated between viewer and director.[79]

A crucial ingredient in the marketing and criticism of art cinema is its identity as an author's cinema, associated with the names of certain recognizable *auteurs*. The art film, according to David Bordwell, often "uses a concept of authorship to unify the text." The effect is that "the competent viewer watches the film expecting not order in the narrative but stylistic signatures in the narration."[80] Cronenberg's *Crash*, an adaptation of J. G. Ballard's 1973 novel about eroticizing car crashes in order to blur the boundaries between affect and automatism, directly preserves Ballard's literary imprint of authorship by retaining the name of the novel's protagonist, "James Ballard." But where are the cinematic "stylistic signatures" of Cronenberg in the film? Certainly the broad thematic components (bodies, technology, agonized metamorphosis) match his oeuvre,[81] but where are the fantastic images, the grisly metaphors made flesh that earned him his cult status as the "Baron of Blood"? The scars and prosthetics of *Crash* can-

FIGURE 5.3   Genre cinema "hack" or art cinema "philosopher"? Director David Cronenberg (*left*) on the set of *Crash* (1996) with actor James Spader. (Courtesy of Jerry Ohlinger's Movie Material)

not begin to approach the visceral convergence of human, housefly, and telepod in *The Fly* (1986). The spectacle of James Ballard's (James Spader) metallically restructured leg barely registers next to the flamboyance of the exploding head sequence in *Scanners* (1980). Even when James sexually penetrates Gabrielle (Rosanna Arquette) through the wound in her thigh, we are only given the *suggestion* of an image made graphically explicit by Max Renn's (James Woods) slit stomach in *Videodrome* (1983).

The fact is that Cronenberg's cinema has always experimented with juxtaposing and recombining genre film vocabularies of spectacle and violence with art film vocabularies of psychological depth and enigmatic, self-reflexive narration. *Shivers*, along with Cronenberg's subsequent films through *The Fly*, might be described as genre films that utilize art film devices to complicate their generic structures. Beginning with *Dead Ringers* (1988), the equation may appear to work primarily in reverse: art films whose structures are challenged by the injection of genre elements. But what unites all these films is not just a common thematic focus developed with a distinctive cinematic style, but the presence of deliberate friction between genre and art elements geared to strain viewer expectations and frustrate genre/art categorizations.

This friction is apparent even in *Crash*'s advertising, which trumpets the Special Jury Prize (for "originality, daring, and audacity") awarded the film at the 1996 Cannes Film Festival alongside the film's preoccupation with "sex and car crashes." Additional publicity came from the film's struggles with censors and distributors, most notably in Britain (where it was banned by Westminster City Council)[82] and the United States (where media mogul Ted Turner's "appalled" reaction to the film delayed its release).[83] A number of critics dismissed *Crash* on the basis of a perceived failure to live up to the "genre" end of its bargain, promising "sex and car crashes" aplenty but delivering unerotic sex and unthrilling car crashes.[84] For Anthony Lane, the film's problem was obvious: "*Crash* could have been thrilling, nasty, and horribly alive; what threw it off the road and stopped it dead was the desire—the deep, ridiculous desperation—to be a work of art."[85] What these critics miss is how *Crash* purposely resists such schematic "breakdowns" into categories of failed genre exercise or unrealized art film. James's first car crash staggers us in its jagged, real-time violence, while Vaughan's (Elias Koteas) climactic suicide wreck stuns us for the opposite reason—it forgoes dynamic violence in favor of a brief aftermath shot. Likewise, the stagy emptiness of the opening three sexual encounters lulls us into unreadiness for the intensity and erotic danger of scenes like the car wash sequence, which establishes an electric relay of threat and desire between Catherine Ballard (Deborah Kara Unger), Vaughan, and James. Cronenberg's staccato rhythm of engagement and estrangement of audience expectations persistently questions just what these wishes are, and how our desperation to fulfill them may access the very subjectivity of desperation embodied by the film's characters. Murray Pomerance eloquently distills the philosophy propelling these characters, as well as the film itself: "Action is nothing in the face of the desire for action, and the desire for action is exhausting."[86] *Crash*'s ever-receding address of audience desire for sex and violence, the primary components of generic "action," ensures that its level of viewer confrontation remains both challenging *and* exhausting. The film paradoxically maintains its affective power by querying the very desire for affective arousal.

Crash, like *Shivers*, resists conforming to the goal-oriented patterns of narrative progression that organize viewer expectations of classical Hollywood cinema. Instead, *Crash* invests the moment of self-transformation, the crash itself, with deep ambiguity. Cronenberg refuses to assure audiences that Catherine and James are a "normal" couple who are then perverted by entering Vaughan's twisted world of violent car crash eroticism, only to reemerge as an intact couple following Vaughan's death. The director insists on tweaking such standard and often implicitly moralistic narrative structures: "Some potential distributors said, 'You should make [Catherine and James] more normal at the beginning so that we can see where they go wrong.' In other words, it would be like a *Fatal Attraction* [Adrian Lyne, 1987] thing . . . I said, 'That isn't right, because there's something wrong with them right *now*.' "[87] As in *Shivers*, it is made deliberately unclear whether the violence aimed at transforming the self is destructive or beneficial—only the terrifying *need* for self-transformation cannot be denied. Although J. G. Ballard originally described the "ultimate role" of his novel as "cautionary," he also posed the questions regarding the narration of the self that Cronenberg's film takes to their confrontational limits: "Will modern technology provide us with hitherto undreamed-of means for tapping our own psychopathologies? Is this harnessing of our innate perversity conceivably of benefit to us?"[88] In the spirit of such questions, Jean Baudrillard's recognition of the special impact of Ballard's novel applies equally well to Cronenberg's film: "This mutating and commutating world of simulation and death . . .—is it good or bad? We will never know. It is simply fascinating, though this fascination does not imply a value judgment. There lies the miracle of *Crash*."[89]

During the film's opening three scenes, sex is indistinguishable from the lifeless daily grind of work—Catherine has sex with a man in an aircraft hangar, James has sex with a woman in the camera room of the film studio where he works as a producer, and then Catherine and James have sex with each other at home while they compare notes about the day's sexual labor. All three encounters are remarkably impersonal, with rear entry alleviating the need for any face-to-face contact. James and Catherine live in a high-rise not unlike Starliner Towers, and the world of *Crash*, like that of *Shivers*, is characterized by an "automatic emptying of the liberation of sex into the free-floating realms of consumer capitalism"[90]—James's studio is producing (what else?) an automobile commercial. At first glance, *Crash* seems even less hopeful than *Shivers* about the ramifications of a new social order supplanting the status quo. The last lines of the film, spoken by James to Catherine after she survives her own crash, are "Maybe the next one . . . maybe the next one." (See fig. 5.4.) This doubled phrase is itself a duplication of lines spoken by Catherine to James during their first sexual encounter; the sense of an inescapable standstill is highlighted by the camera movement in the last scene, which effectively cancels the roving, inward motion of the film's opening shot as it tracks toward Catherine inside an airplane hangar by concluding with an ascending crane shot that moves upward and outward, withdrawing from the Ballards. James and Catherine in this final scene, like Catherine and her lover in the film's first

FIGURE 5.4 *Crash* (David Cronenberg, 1996): Catherine Ballard (Deborah Kara Unger) and James Ballard (James Spader) after Catherine's car crash—"Maybe the next one . . . maybe the next one." (Courtesy of Jerry Ohlinger's Movie Material)

scene, are again having sex—but this time they are receding from view, not growing closer, dwarfed by the overturned car and the vast expanse of empty grass beside the highway.

Yet the ascending movement of this last shot also comes closest to achieving the potentially liberating but finally untapped possibility of flight—a possibility foregrounded in the setting of the opening scene and revisited throughout the film by repeated trips to the airport and its immediate environs.[91] In the same vein, the film's crashes are horrifying in their violent destructiveness but somehow also affirming in their furious determination to connect with a sense of lived experience—at any cost. Cronenberg has called *Crash* "an existentialist romance,"[92] and the label rings true in terms of the film's ability to convey the affect at stake in the desperate desire for experience. The disarming long take of James gently retracing and caressing the bruises inflicted by Vaughan on Catherine's body reveals the need to heal as intertwined with the drive to alienate and destroy. Similarly, Catherine's tears at the end of the film disclose the powerful emotion motivating an increasingly mechanical series of forced, disengaged simulations of crashes and sex. *Crash* insists that these tears cannot be fully explained as an empty gesture of mourning practiced by a culture that Walter Benjamin foresaw in "The Storyteller" (1936) as peopled by those consumed with "the hope of warming his shivering life with a death he reads about."[93] Instead, Catherine's tears also signify the anguished vulnerability of groping for experiential meaning in a deeply threatening world. Benjamin's description of such a world, which bears a somewhat spiritual resemblance to the final shot of *Crash*, vividly captures this dimension of pain: "A generation . . . now stood under the open sky in a countryside in which nothing remained unchanged but the clouds, and beneath these clouds, in a field of force of destructive torrents and explosions, was the tiny, fragile human body."[94]

Benjamin's countryside belongs to a Europe irrevocably altered by the destruction of World War I. Where does the landscape of *Crash* finally belong? In a certain geographic sense, it belongs to Canada; rarely before in Cronenberg's work has such extensive and strategic use been made of Toronto locations. Jim Leach goes so far as to claim that *Crash* "works best as a documentary . . . it is a film about Toronto, a slightly skewed account of the experience of living and, especially, driving there (it would work for any urban centre but the film really does draw attention to and use its Toronto setting)."[95] In this manner, *Crash* seems to fulfill art cinema's penchant for using indigenous locations as a method of asserting (and selling) national specificity in the face of Hollywood domination.[96] But in sequences such as the aftermath of the Jayne Mansfield crash reenactment, where a Toronto freeway is completely denaturalized by heavy stillness and the absence of diegetic sound, *Crash*'s status as a location-showcasing art film is reduced to a mirage.

Cronenberg's own "appearance" in *Crash* is also best discussed as a mirage, and as a further complication of the art cinema's conventional deployment of authorship. Near the end of the film, James and Catherine visit the auto pound to claim Vaughan's wrecked Lincoln. The pound officer, invisible behind his post, tells the couple he cannot fathom their attachment to the car, aside from its value as "a total write-off," and informs them that they will have to return during regular business hours to file the correct form. The disembodied voice of the pound officer belongs unmistakably to Cronenberg himself. This unusual, spectral cameo (Cronenberg has guested notably only once before in his own feature films, as a gynecologist in *The Fly*) appears at a point in Cronenberg's career when his status as a cult celebrity had reached a level of significant visibility. In addition to playing himself on Canadian television programs like *Maniac Mansion* (1991), Cronenberg had landed starring roles in Clive Barker's horror film *Nightbreed* (1989) and Don McKellar's Canadian short *Blue* (1992), along with smaller parts in *Trial by Jury* (Heywood Gould, 1994), *To Die For* (Gus Van Sant, 1995), and the Canadian vampire film *Blood and Donuts* (Holly Dale, 1995), among others. So why has Cronenberg, whose chief authorial sign would have to be depictions of the body in all its painful corporeality, chosen to present his own now-recognizable person in such a flagrantly disembodied manner in *Crash*?

Cronenberg's appearance as a faceless voice (upholding the tidy order of Canadian bureaucracy, no less!) satirizes the mystique surrounding notions of the author as individual genius that lends the art film its coherence—both as an industry and as a mode of viewing practice. When Vaughan refers to "the reshaping of the human body by modern technology"—the standard critical interpretation of Cronenberg's films—as a "crude sci-fi concept that floats on the surface and doesn't threaten anybody," employed only to "test the resilience of my potential partners in psychopathology," he might as well be speaking directly to the audience. Vaughan's challenge underlines the fact that there is no truly comfortable position offered to spectators of *Crash*, whether they appeal to the familiarity of genre conventions or to the art film's trademarks of authorial expressivity. Cronenberg's cameo ultimately questions the nature of his own identity as an icon of the horror film, on the one hand, and of Canadian national cinema, on the other. Cronenberg's (dis)appearance in *Crash* mirrors the film itself as it frustrates attempts to compartmentalize identity under art film banners of the author and national essence or through genre film economies of spectacle. Rather than display a celebrity visibility in the style of Hitchcock, Cronenberg's cameo emphasizes the unseen, suggesting that capturing authorial identity or national character is as tantalizing (and as improbable) as placing an invisible face to an ethereal voice. But the *desire* to capture such definable identities brings viewers to the heart of *Crash*—the imagination of self and nation across the divide of public and private in the mass media age.

Crash's characters are obsessed with the pleasure and pain drawn from the crashes of American public icons such as James Dean, Jayne Mansfield, and John F. Kennedy. For Vaughan, who literally lives in a replica of the car Kennedy died in, the president's assassination is a "special kind of car crash." Vaughan and his circle reflect the audience's own participation in "the public fascination with torn and opened bodies and torn and opened persons" described by Mark Seltzer as a "wound culture." The phenomenon of Princess Diana's 1997 death in a car crash is yet another instance of the "collective gathering around shock, trauma, and the wound" characteristic of wound culture, with its ability to function as a "switch point between individual and collective, public and private orders of things."[97] The characters of *Crash* also worship the violent and erotic moment of impact, but participate physically in crashes in order to bring themselves ever closer to the fulfillment the crash appears to offer: a flashing instant, however brutal or fleeting, which could truly bind a private self and public icon, along with the networks of fantasy and desire traversing them. For the relation between private selfhood and public star iconicity is volatile, fluid, and resolutely ambivalent. According to Michael Warner, public star bodies are at once "prostheses for our own mutant desirability" as well as humiliated objects "reminding us that they do not possess the phallic power of their images: we do."[98] Or, as Hal Foster characterizes this fraught dynamic, "the star is too far from us, or too close . . . the star has too little, or too much, over us."[99] By painstakingly restaging James Dean's crash down to the smallest "authentic" detail, Vaughan and his comrades (including, by proxy, ourselves, represented by the onscreen audience of witnesses) attempt to capture a moment when the shifting private relation to the public star body—identification and abstraction, longing and hatred, sympathy and revenge—crystallizes and coheres. There is no longer a private self existing in tension with a famous public other, but a perfect fusion, an integrated embodiment of all the psychic energy that has attracted and repelled them.

Because the utopian moment of private/public fusion always proves beyond realization, compulsive repetition ensues. Vaughan plans the Jayne Mansfield reenactment as blood still trickles down his temple from the Dean crash. Vaughan's group feverishly pursues activities that strive to surmount the impossibility of fusion by testing the divisions between public spectacle and private act: studying crash-test videos with the rapt (and erotic) attention of devoted movie fans, posing in photographs designed to evoke the documents of famous crashes, having sex in cars and public spaces with interchangeable partners to erode the intimacy of the act. But eventually and inevitably, there is only repetition, and then the simulation of repeated events. Vaughan dies with a cry of frustration, not triumph, as he abandons yet another attempt (whether using cars or sex) to collide with James and Catherine. The doomed cycle continues even after Vaughan's death, as James assumes Vaughan's role by driving his car and stalking Catherine on the highway. However, the film's other surviving couple, Gabrielle and Helen Remington (Holly Hunter), suggests the possibility of modifying the endless loop of destructive repetition that James and Catherine cannot extricate themselves from. While the Ballards file a claim for Vaughan's wrecked car, Gabrielle and Helen begin to make love in Vaughan's backseat. But after a few seconds of contact, they stop and simply hold each other. Barbara Creed reads this moment as a "completely tokenistic" representation of a "coy and awkward" lesbian desire,[100] yet this brief scene is remarkable for its rare substitution of shared loss for the desperation of compulsive repetition.

In J. G. Ballard's *Crash*, Vaughan dies in an attempt to fulfill his obsession of crashing into a famous film actress intimated to be Elizabeth Taylor. In Cronenberg's *Crash*, there is no mention of this; in fact, *living* stars do not exist in the universe of Cronenberg's film. Instead, emphasis is placed solely on "performing" dead celebrities. It is significant that the two celebrities Cronenberg focuses on, Dean and Mansfield, represent a particular kind of Hollywood stardom that is inseparable from careers whose ends coincide with the waning of the classical Hollywood studio system. Dean's demise in 1955 and Mansfield's in 1967 may be seen as roughly marking the beginning and the bitter end of a slow death visited upon what Kenneth Anger calls "Old Hollywood."[101] *Crash*'s investment in two stars whose deaths mirror the passing of a once-healthy Old Hollywood points to the film's fascination with Hollywood itself not as a living legend, but a dying one.

As Cronenberg himself points out, *Crash*'s episodic narrative self-consciously contradicts the standard narrative structures of classical Hollywood cinema: "I'm questioning a lot of the things that are, certainly in Hollywood terms, considered the immutables of film narrative ... all those 'well-made play' kind of things that Hollywood has been so successful selling over the years."[102] In a similar fashion, *Crash*'s discourse on stardom critiques the conventional function of the classical Hollywood star system. While the star system has been described as one method utilized by classical Hollywood cinema to reinforce "the tendency toward strongly profiled and unified characterization,"[103] others have posited the star as a site of potential excess that can puncture the fabric of normative classical Hollywood spectatorship.[104] For example, Miriam Hansen claims "the star performance weakens the diegetic spell in favor of a string of spectacular moments that display the 'essence' of the star" and demonstrates that Rudolph Valentino's female fans "assailed the barriers that classical cinema was engaged in reaffirming, taking the star system more literally than the institution might have intended." The desire of these female viewers to literally touch Valentino "provoked a fetishistic run for buttons from his suit or at least candles and flowers from the funeral home" when Valentino's corpse was displayed for the public in 1926, and even this was not enough for the fans who committed suicide when Valentino died.[105] In *Crash*, this form of suicidal star worship is not the extreme case, but the baseline. The star system has become an engine for death, its ability to bind viewers to classical Hollywood narratives now so completely disintegrated that fans no longer want to experience the cinematic "lives" of stars but to suffer their extra-cinematic deaths.

Cronenberg's own use of casting in *Crash* underlines this critique of the classical star system by parodying its ideal function. The established stars of *Crash* perform such grotesquely exaggerated versions of the star system's desired match between an actor's accrued intertextual connotations and the actor's current role that the system collapses beneath the weight of its literalization. James Spader, best known for his portrayal of a sexual obsessive in *sex, lies, and videotape* (Steven Soderbergh, 1989), plays James, an even more obsessed sexual obsessive. Elias Koteas, seen previously as a guru-like insurance adjuster (*The Adjuster* [Atom Egoyan, 1991]) and a guru-like strip club disc jockey (*Exotica* [Atom Egoyan, 1994]), plays Vaughan, the supreme guru and ultimate "adjuster" of car crash eroticism. Rosanna Arquette, perhaps most memorable in her role as a bizarre woman who may or may not be hiding hideous burn scars in *After Hours* (Martin Scorsese, 1985), plays Gabrielle, a crippled crash victim whose scars are externalized and accentuated by an elaborate body cast made of metal and leather. Even Holly Hunter, who at first seems miscast, engineers a brilliantly awkward synthesis between her schizophrenic screen personae as motormouth (*Broadcast News* [James L. Brooks, 1987]) and mute sensual body (*The Piano* [Jane Campion, 1993]) through her portrayal of Helen Remington, a doctor and crash victim whose sharp verbal explanations are juxtaposed with scenes in which she "speaks" only through her body (she does not talk at all until her third scene in the film, and remains silent during her final scene as well).

Crash's constantly shifting movement between invocation and deconstruction of both the art cinema and the genre cinema associated with classical Hollywood climaxes with the Jayne Mansfield crash sequence. The scene begins with Vaughan, James, and Catherine driving together toward the wreckage of a massive highway accident. As Vaughan sees the destruction stretching out before him, he begins snapping photographs and says, "This is a work of art. Absolutely a work of art." And so it is—and isn't—on a dizzying number of levels. The seemingly endless row of mangled cars inevitably recalls Jean-Luc Godard's *Weekend* (1967), and this scene displays one of the best-known "stylistic signatures" of Godard's art cinema: ruthless self-reflexivity. Vaughan acts not only as cameraman but as director—he treats the car as a dolly, instructing James to slow down as they drive alongside the accident. He also has Catherine pose for photographs inside one of the wrecked cars, creating his own staged imagery out of the event's "reality." During these moments, it is impossible not to imagine Cronenberg and Vaughan mirroring each other; the self-conscious artifice of the scene only increases as Howard Shore's eerie score replaces virtually all diegetic sound besides the clicking of Vaughan's camera and the clanking of rescue machinery.

There is a supplement to this self-reflexivity, however, where the art film's distantiation surrenders to the genre film's economy of spectacle. Vaughan, like Cronenberg, refuses to remain completely outside the spectacle he is documenting—at one point, Vaughan lowers his camera and attempts to *touch* one of the twisted cars that James drives past. And at the end of the scene, when Vaughan discovers that this massive accident was caused by his accomplice Colin Seagrave (Peter MacNeil) during a suicidal reenactment of Mansfield's crash, he responds first as an exasperated director ("you did the Jayne Mansfield crash *without* me?!") and then as an enraptured fan ("the dog is *brilliant!*"). Similarly, for all the alienating strangeness that Cronenberg cloaks this sequence in, it also has an undeniable attraction as breathtaking spectacle. The loving visual detail lavished on Seagrave's bloodied blonde wig and cross-dressed corpse, not to mention the dead Chihuahua in the backseat, are characteristic of the disturbing but spectacular splendor of a scene whose images are meticulously composed but never enervated. As Vaughan says, the crash is a work of art—but as the images attest, it is also a work of genre.

Seagrave's body is perhaps the most emblematic "national" body in Cronenberg's cinema. It is a body that impersonates an iconic Hollywood body and a body whose visual impact depends on genre spectacle; it is also a body whose horrific representation reflects back an image so fractured with ambivalence that any uncritical association with American mythology crumbles. In short, Seagrave provides the flesh for the concept of "Canada" constructed in Cronenberg's films—a nation imagined not as an invulnerable national body, but as an entangled network of contested relations traversing "America" and "Canada." In the space of simultaneously intimate resemblance to and shocking difference from American cinematic iconography, Seagrave's body, like Cronenberg's films, registers both horrific self-erasure and the potential to think beyond the categories of "the self" and "the nation" that structure the allegorical moment. Paradoxically, Cronenberg has helped pioneer a "Canadian" framework for the sometimes fantastic and often unnerving recent contributions to Canadian cinema by directors such as Atom Egoyan, Don McKellar, and Guy Maddin.[106] The fact that Cronenberg has provided a recognizable "national" context for these visions precisely by challenging both "American" genre conventions and definitions of "Canadian" national art cinema is an appropriately ironic tribute to a career that continues to expand the horizons of both the modern horror film and the Canadian cinema—by never truly finding a home in either.

AFTERWORD

9/11/01, 8/6/45, Ground Zero

This book began by asking how cinematic horror relates to the horrors of history, and it has now addressed that question by describing particular instances of allegorical collision between filmic texts and traumatic historical contexts—collisions that challenge the power of national narratives to regulate the meaning of collective trauma. In the book's previous cases, the allegorical confrontation between past and present focused on traumatic events lodged in the past but whose echoes resonate in the present. But what of traumatic events located not in the past, but in the present? What happens when the allegorical moment's "past" and "present" become compressed in the "immediate," in the desire to figure the now not only as "history," but as "national" history? I wish to conclude by sketching a few preliminary responses to these questions—questions anchored to a still-unfolding series of events commonly designated by the originary shorthand "9/11."

Barely two months after the attacks of September 11, 2001, the *New York Times* ran a feature story concerning the emergence of museum exhibitions across New York City devoted to representing 9/11. The story's headline is "History Is Impatient to Embrace Sept. 11."[1] Today, this impatience to periodize 9/11, to construct it as "history," is more powerful than ever. Even if those devastating early days after the attacks, when "cultural prognosticators" announced an end to "the age of irony,"[2] may now seem somewhat distant and alien, the desire to posit 9/11 as the end or the beginning of an era does not. The theoretical and political stakes of history's impatience to embrace 9/11 are still very volatile, but glancing at two films released in the immediate shadow of 9/11 allows us to speculate on the workings of the allegorical moment in the present, and perhaps in the future as well.

We Were Soldiers (Randall Wallace, 2002) offers one provocative test case for cinema's role in generating allegorical moments attached to 9/11. The film, released in the United States in March 2002, is one of several Hollywood war films, including Behind Enemy Lines (John Moore, 2001) and Black Hawk Down (Ridley Scott, 2001), that were rushed into theaters ahead of schedule once studio executives decided that the post-9/11 national mood would be receptive to war films, rather than averse to them.[3] This, of course, was not the initial verdict, when the Arnold Schwarzenegger terrorist action vehicle Collateral Damage (Andrew Davis, 2002) was pulled from its October 2001 release slot and delayed until February 2002, and John Woo's World War II film Windtalkers saw its 2001 opening postponed until summer 2002. So although We Were Soldiers and the other war films of this cycle were conceived before 9/11, their reception in the public sphere is intimately linked to 9/11 and its aftermath; in fact, none of these films reached theaters until after the U.S. war on Afghanistan began on October 7, 2001. The cover of Newsweek magazine, dated March 18, 2002, testifies to the power of this connection by borrowing the title of We Were Soldiers to tell the story of U.S. military casualties in Afghanistan. (See fig. B.1.)

The film, which writer-director Randall Wallace adapted from the book We Were Soldiers Once . . . and Young (1992) by Lt. Gen. Harold G. Moore and Joseph L. Galloway, focuses on the story of a disastrous American defeat during the Vietnam War, the battle of the Ia Drang Valley in 1965. Yet We Were Soldiers, which stars Mel Gibson as Moore, has little interest in the fact or even the possibility of American defeat—at Ia Drang, in Vietnam, or, by extension, in the post-9/11 "war on terrorism." Over and over again, the film chooses American heroism and exceptionalism as its "truth," rather than pursuing surrounding questions of destructive political policy. In this sense, We Were Soldiers resembles a conventional World War II–era war film much more closely than most Vietnam-themed war films, despite its attention to graphic battlefield mayhem. In fact, one of the film's most tell-

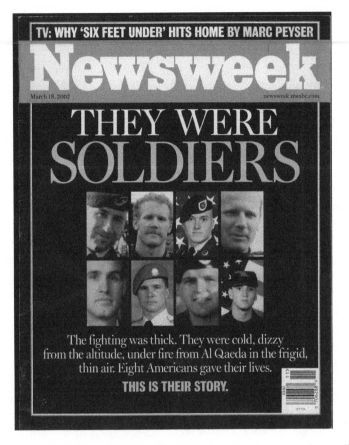

TV: WHY 'SIX FEET UNDER' HITS HOME BY MARC PEYSER

Newsweek

March 18, 2002

newsweek.msnbc.com

THEY WERE
SOLDIERS

The fighting was thick. They were cold, dizzy
from the altitude, under fire from Al Qaeda in the frigid,
thin air. Eight Americans gave their lives.
THIS IS THEIR STORY.

FIGURE B.1   Cover of *Newsweek* magazine, March 18, 2002. (© 2002 *Newsweek*, Inc. All rights reserved. Reprinted by permission.)

ing moments deploys brutally explicit imagery not to conjure Vietnam, but to recall World War II. One of Moore's young soldiers whom we meet on the battlefield at Ia Drang is named Jimmy Nakayama (Brian Tee). Nakayama, whose name ostentatiously codes him as Japanese American, suffers horrible burns during the fighting when American warplanes accidentally bomb their own troops with napalm. When Joe Galloway (Barry Pepper), an intrepid American journalist, attempts to move the wounded soldier from harm's way by grabbing his legs, Nakayama's scalded skin peels away in bloody pieces.[4]

One might be tempted to identify this shocking moment as the "blasting open of the continuum of history," in Walter Benjamin's sense. After all, the eruption of visceral images unmistakably reminiscent of Hiroshima and Nagasaki within a Vietnam setting brings 1945 and 1965 into an arresting conjunction that might suggest implications for the post-9/11 context. However, as Benjamin warns, every allegorical representation of history, every moment of *Jetztzeit*, is also a "moment of danger." And the oppressive appropriation that occurs here in *We Were Soldiers* is that in the very instant Nakayama embodies an American wartime atrocity against Japan, he becomes an American casualty, not a Japanese one. Nakayama's heroism and cries of selfless concern for his wife and newborn child, qualities that the film presents as uniquely and fundamentally American as recovering all American dead from the battlefield at any cost, transforms him from a typical, immigrant-derived American soldier into a model, universal American soldier. The very wounds that could have marked him as visual evidence of American brutality and racism now transport him to the racially unmarked realm of upstanding "Americanness."[5] The iconography of the atomic bomb is invoked only to conclude with Galloway dropping his rifle in favor of his camera, as the specter of Hiroshima gives way to a gesture of American pacifism and memorialization, and as Nakayama joins Galloway's photographic pantheon of American soldier heroes. Of course, this transformation has profound repercussions for the 9/11 context as well; rather than point out the disturbing continuities between Hiroshima, Vietnam, and Afghanistan, *We Were Soldiers* subsumes their sameness into a matter of American heroism. This is not blasting open the continuum of history—it is sealing the cracks.

But to judge *We Were Soldiers* solely on the basis of the film's formal elements would be to ignore the arena of reception so important to Benjamin in his studies of mass culture as social force.[6] If the film could have somehow inspired reactions in the public sphere that questioned the narrative of American exceptionalism as political policy, then the potential for "brushing history against the grain" could have been preserved. Unfortunately, as the previously mentioned *Newsweek* cover helps to indicate, *We Were Soldiers* seems to function culturally in the opposite direction. The film solidifies, rather than interrogates, one of the most troubling aspects of public discourse surrounding 9/11—its apparent parallels to World War II, and particularly to Pearl Harbor.[7] Consider, for example, the powerful juxtaposition of two formally similar images widely circulated in the wake of 9/11: the American flag at Iwo Jima in 1945, and at the World Trade Center's "Ground Zero" in 2001. (See fig. B.2.) Both images are drawn from iconic historical photographs that convey the undeniably moving courage of the soldiers and firefighters depicted within them. However, the status

FIGURE B.2   A segment of a makeshift 9/11 memorial inside New York's Pennsylvania Station that combines iconic images of the American flag at Iwo Jima in 1945 and at the World Trade Center in 2001. (Photograph by Adam Lowenstein, December 2001)

of these images as icons, as visuals that supposedly speak for history, lends their juxtaposition the quality of a "moment of danger." If America's role in the Pacific during World War II becomes crystallized by heroism at Iwo Jima rather than atrocity at Hiroshima, then we run the risk of "explaining" Hiroshima as a justified "solution" to Pearl Harbor. The pairing of Iwo Jima with the World Trade Center's Ground Zero compounds this risk by effectively occluding Hiroshima's own Ground Zero. In the space between the juxtaposition of Iwo Jima and the World Trade Center, 9/11/01 eclipses 8/6/45 as the location of Ground Zero—an eclipse *We Were Soldiers* encourages and enacts.

A very different version of the conjuncture between Hiroshima and 9/11 appears in director Imamura Shohei's contribution to *11'09"01—September 11* (2002), an anthology film consisting of eleven responses to 9/11 by directors from eleven different countries. *11'09"01* was organized by French producer Alain Brigand, who commissioned each director to create a short film with a running time of exactly eleven minutes, nine seconds, and one frame (to translate the film's title into cinematic duration). Before each episode, Brigand inserts a digital map of the globe identifying the episode's country of origin as well as the director's name. In this sense, *11'09"01* presents itself explicitly as a work of art cinema and of national cinema—categories the allegorical moment has been shown to rely upon as reference points but to contest as authoritative. It is fascinating to note that Imamura, representing Japan, is alone among his fellow directors when choosing to set his episode entirely in the pre-9/11 past and to utilize iconography reminiscent of the horror film to relate his story.[8]

In Imamura's episode, written by his son Daisuke Tengan from a poem by Tou Fou, a rural Japanese village must deal with a local crisis during the last days of World War II—a time when the atomic bomb has already devastated Hiroshima, but when news of this event circulates in the village only as ominous rumor in this period before the Emperor's surrender. One of the village's residents, the soldier Yukichi (Taguchi Tomorowo), has returned home from the war so deeply traumatized that he no longer acts as a human being, but as a snake. Yukichi's family is disturbed by his bizarre behavior, but they tolerate and even respect him for sacrificing himself "for the Emperor." Their patience runs out, however, when Yukichi bites a family member and devours a rat (interpreted as an act of disrespect toward his grandfather, born in the Year of the Rat). After his family drives him out, a village meeting is convened to discuss the matter of Yukichi. Some villagers accuse him of eating their fish and livestock, and there is a general consensus that Yukichi must be captured to preserve the reputation of the village. During the hunt, Yukichi is granted a flashback that seems to provide the origin of his trauma: cowering amid the corpses of his fellow soldiers on all sides, a terrified Yukichi surrenders to an officer he assumes is the enemy, but who turns out to be Japanese. The enraged officer berates him for his cowardice and screams, "What does the Holy War mean to you?" When we return to the present, a young woman discovers Yukichi during the torch-lit search of the jungle. She asks him whether living as a man disgusts him. He looks at her but does not reply; instead, he slithers into the water of the surrounding river and his body disappears beneath the surface. The episode's final shot presents a talking snake, who says, "There is no such thing as a Holy War."

Imamura's decisions to set his 9/11 story in the shadow of Hiroshima and to foreground the horrific images of a human being transformed into a snake point toward the allegorical significance of this episode. Imamura understands intuitively Benjamin's claim that "every image of the past that is not recognized by the present as one of its own concerns threatens to disappear irretrievably."[9] While *We Were Soldiers* evokes Hiroshima only to neutralize its relevance for a critique of America's post-9/11 war on terror,

Imamura insists that the concept of "Holy War" must ricochet between its varied historical coordinates: the imperialistic Japanese violence of World War II; the American obliteration of Hiroshima and Nagasaki; the 9/11 attacks on America perpetrated by Al Qaeda; and the American war on terror. Imamura also demands that the nationalistic and/or religious fervor animating the "righteousness" of any and all of these "Holy Wars" receive precisely the kind of critical scrutiny that *We Were Soldiers* refuses to supply. When asked what "personal echo" he wanted to bring to his episode in *11'09"01*, Imamura said, "[George W.] Bush appealed to national solidarity and proclaimed his love of his country against the backdrop of the national flag. This image seemed somewhat excessive to me."[10] This discomfort with nationalist "excess," whether displayed by America or Japan, propels Imamura to situate the allegorical moments of his episode *between* 1945 and 2001, rather than having one era justify the other (or having one nation emerge as more justified than the other).

Indeed, the representation of 9/11 through the allegorical lens of Hiroshima and World War II deployed by Imamura seems impressively wise, especially when compared with the uneven results of the other short films in *11'09"01*; Imamura's episode was selected to close the film, and it's easy to see why. Imamura, like Shindo Kaneto before him, has meditated deeply on what it means to represent Hiroshima in the context of Japanese national cinema. The experience of Imamura's previous explorations of Hiroshima and World War II, most notably *Kuroi ame* (*Black Rain*, 1989) and *Kanzo sensei* (*Dr. Akagi*, 1998), can be felt behind the tone of his powerful contribution to *11'09"01*. In fact, Yukichi seems like a variation on (or extension of) the similarly named Yuichi (Ishida Keisuke), a shell-shocked veteran in *Black Rain* who cannot put the war behind him.[11] But whereas *Black Rain*'s Yuichi does finally seem to recover from his traumatized state, *11'09"01*'s Yukichi does not. Instead, Yukichi exists in a completely liminal state—between human and snake, between obliviousness and awareness, between life and death. In this way, he recalls the death's head that Benjamin locates at "the heart of the allegorical way of seeing." Remember that for Benjamin, the death's head distills allegory's capacity to represent the inhuman aspects of history—"everything about history that, from the very beginning, has been untimely, sorrowful, unsuccessful"—*within* the human "face" of history as progress and redemption.[12] The death's head reveals the inhuman dimension beneath the human face, conjoining the face and the death's head in the flux of allegorical transformation.

Yukichi shocks us when he presents the horror of the inhuman snake within the human being—when he slithers around the makeshift cage his family has built to contain him, or when he eats a live rat whole. This shock arises from the recognition of the human and inhuman alongside each other, from the state of constant metamorphosis where man and snake must coexist. Indeed, the film's final image of a snake "acting" like a man (replacing the man "acting" like a snake) only confirms the impossibility of interpreting Yukichi as "acting" at all—he *is* a man, just as he *is* a snake. When the snake speaks about history, when it insists that "there is no such thing as a Holy War," there is no doubt that this statement emanates from an inhuman death's head as well as a human face, from 9/11/01 as well as 8/6/45. The statement comes, finally, from a Ground Zero of allegorical representation that understands *Jetztzeit* not only as a flash between past and present but also as an opportunity to shape the future.

NOTES

INTRODUCTION: THE ALLEGORICAL MOMENT

1. As this description suggests, my account of the allegorical moment should be read as being in dialogue with (and inspired by) recent groundbreaking work in film studies that has explored different forms of embodied spectatorship. See particularly Linda Williams, "Film Bodies: Gender, Genre, and Excess," *Film Quarterly* 44.4 (Summer 1991): 2–13; Carol J. Clover, *Men, Women, and Chain Saws: Gender in the Modern Horror Film*; Vivian Sobchack, *The Address of the Eye: A Phenomenology of Film Experience*; Steven Shaviro, *The Cinematic Body*; and the essays collected in Linda Williams, ed., *Viewing Positions: Ways of Seeing Film*.

2. For useful overviews of trauma studies, see Ruth Leys, *Trauma: A Genealogy*; Dominick LaCapra, *Writing History, Writing Trauma*; Cathy Caruth, ed., *Trauma: Explorations in Memory*; Paul Antze and Michael Lambek, eds., *Tense Past: Cultural Essays in Trauma and Memory*; Judith Herman, *Trauma and Recovery*; Linda Belau and Petar Ramadanovic, eds., *Topologies of Trauma: Essays on the Limit of Knowledge and Memory*; and E. Ann Kaplan and Ban Wang, eds., *Trauma and Cinema: Cross-Cultural Explorations*.

3. Sigmund Freud, "Remembering, Repeating and Working-Through," in *The Standard Edition of the Complete Psychological Works* 12:147–56; Sigmund Freud, "Mourning and Melancholia," in *S. E.* 14:243–58. In the brief summary of these essays that follows, I have taken the liberty of combining their central terms in order to highlight the intersections of their arguments—a move which admittedly simplifies the differences between the two essays, but that captures their typical deployment in trauma studies. See, for example, Dominick LaCapra, *Representing the Holocaust: History, Theory, Trauma*, esp. 205–23.

4. Dominick LaCapra, "Trauma, Absence, Loss," *Critical Inquiry* 25 (Summer 1999): 696–727; 714.

5. Hayden White, "Historical Emplotment and the Problem of Truth," in Saul Friedlander, ed., *Probing the Limits of Representation: Nazism and the "Final Solution,"* 37–53.

6. Jean-François Lyotard, *The Differend: Phrases in Dispute*, 13.

7. An important branch of trauma studies theory, crystallized most notably by Cathy Caruth, *Unclaimed Experience: Trauma, Narrative, and History*, and Shoshana Felman and Dori Laub, *Testimony: Crises of Witnessing in Literature, Psychoanalysis, and History*, suffers from this rigid commitment to the "unrepresentable." Dominick LaCapra accurately characterizes the weaknesses of Caruth and Felman by describing their versions of trauma theory as conflating metaphysical notions of structural "absence" with more concrete notions of "loss" tied to specific historical events. LaCapra also notes the affinities between Caruth's deconstructionist trauma theory and the neurophysiological trauma theory of Bessel A. van der Kolk and Onno van der Hart (see their "The Intrusive Past: The Flexibility of Memory and the Engraving of Trauma," in Caruth, ed., *Trauma:*

Explorations in Memory, 158–82), where very different kinds of devotion to the unrepresentable nonetheless collaborate to remove traumatic experience from the realm of representation. See LaCapra, *Writing History, Writing Trauma*, 43–85, 107n20. For an insightful analysis of the problematic implications of an alliance between deconstruction and neurophysiology in trauma studies, see Leys, *Trauma: A Genealogy*, 229–97.

8. Berel Lang, *Holocaust Representation: Art Within the Limits of History and Ethics*, 49–50; see also 51–71.

9. LaCapra, *Writing History, Writing Trauma*, 144, 157, 107, 207; see also LaCapra's chapter on *Shoah* in his *History and Memory After Auschwitz*, 95–138. Eric L. Santner's influential distinction between *Trauerarbeit* ("the work of mourning") and "narrative fetishism" should also be noted here, as it shapes and complements LaCapra's terms. See Santner's "History Beyond the Pleasure Principle: Some Thoughts on the Representation of Trauma," in Saul Friedlander, ed., *Probing the Limits of Representation: Nazism and the "Final Solution,"* 143–54; and Santner, *Stranded Objects: Mourning, Memory, and Film in Postwar Germany*.

10. Miriam Bratu Hansen, "*Schindler's List* Is Not *Shoah*: The Second Commandment, Popular Modernism, and Public Memory," *Critical Inquiry* 22 (Winter 1996): 292–312; 302. In a related essay, Hansen interrogates further the Hollywood/modernism dichotomy by arguing for classical Hollywood cinema as a form of "vernacular modernism." See Hansen, "The Mass Production of the Senses: Classical Cinema as Vernacular Modernism," in Christine Gledhill and Linda Williams, eds., *Reinventing Film Studies*, 332–50.

11. An exception is Joan Hawkins, *Cutting Edge: Art-Horror and the Horrific Avant-garde*.

12. For instance, Dudley Andrew matter-of-factly contrasts "the standard cinema of genres" against "the ambitious cinema of art" in his *Film in the Aura of Art*, 10.

13. David Bordwell, "The Art Cinema as a Mode of Film Practice," *Film Criticism* 4.1 (1979): 56–64; 56. Although the art film has early models in French Impressionist and German Expressionist cinema, I agree with Bordwell's periodization of the art film as a "distinct mode" to the post–World War II era. At this time, a number of economic and institutional factors—the decline of American audiences and production, an increase in European imports to American art house theaters, the Paramount decision, a crumbling Production Code, the founding of the Cannes Film Festival, Roberto Rossellini's *Open City* (1945) becoming the first foreign film to gross over $1 million in the United States—solidified the industrial sense of a European art cinema based on a modernist-inflected "realism" (from locations to psychology to sex) and authorial self-expression, distinct from a Hollywood cinema based on an "invisible" style and devoted to formulaic escapism, action, and entertainment. See also Peter Lev, *The Euro-American Cinema*; Steve Neale, "Art Cinema as Institution," *Screen* 22.1 (1981): 11–39; and Barbara Wilinsky, *Sure Seaters: The Emergence of Art House Cinema*.

14. Thomas Elsaesser notes how central the "topic of fascism" becomes to the European art cinema of the 1970s and 1980s, when the older art film neorealisms are "taken back" through new melodramatic aesthetics that redefine art cinema. See Elsaesser, "Subject Positions, Speaking Positions: From *Holocaust, Our Hitler*, and *Heimat* to *Shoah* and *Schindler's List*," in Vivian Sobchack, ed., *The Persistence of History: Cinema, Television, and the Modern Event*, 145–83; 153. See also Saul Friedlander, *Reflections of Nazism: An Essay on Kitsch and Death*, esp. 74–81.

15. Robin Wood, *Hitchcock's Films*, 7. See also Wood's *Hitchcock's Films Revisited*.

16. Walter Kendrick, *The Thrill of Fear: 250 Years of Scary Entertainment*, 231.

17. Wood, *Hitchcock's Films*, 9, 122, 123.

18. Leo Bersani, *The Culture of Redemption*, 1.

19. Wood, *Hitchcock's Films*, 123.

20. Bersani, *The Culture of Redemption*, 1.

21. In this sense, my project intersects more broadly with the renewed critical interest in film as a means of representing history. See, for example, Vivian Sobchack, ed., *The Persistence of History*; Robert Rosenstone, ed., *Revisioning History: Film and the Construction of a New Past*; Marcia Landy, ed., *The Historical Film: History and Memory in Media*; Marcia Landy, *Cinematic Uses of the Past*; and Anton Kaes, *From "Hitler" to "Heimat": The Return of History as Film*.

22. See, for example, William Schoell's tellingly titled *Stay Out of the Shower: 25 Years of Shocker Films Beginning with "Psycho."*

23. Rick Altman, "A Semantic/Syntactic Approach to Film Genre," in Barry Keith Grant, ed., *Film Genre Reader*, 26–40; 28. My argument below is also informed by Altman's *Film/Genre*.

24. See, for example, Adam Knee, "Generic Change in the Cinema," *Iris* 20 (1995): 31–39.

25. Tom Gunning, "'Those Drawn with a Very Fine Camel's Hair Brush': The Origins of Film Genres," *Iris* 20 (1995): 49–61; 51, 52.

26. For a valuable meditation on the "disciplinary" implications of *Psycho* for cinematic spectatorship, see Linda Williams, "Discipline and Fun: *Psycho* and Postmodern Cinema," in Gledhill and Williams, eds., *Reinventing Film Studies*, 351–78.

27. Kirby Farrell, *Post-Traumatic Culture: Injury and Interpretation in the Nineties*.

28. Mark Seltzer, "Wound Culture: Trauma in the Pathological Public Sphere," *October* 80 (Spring 1997): 3–26; 3.

29. The book's final chapter, on David Cronenberg and Canadian cinema, is framed differently than the previous chapters—it is more of a consolidation of and meditation on the preceding cases than a new case in itself.

30. Alan Williams, "Introduction," in Alan Williams, ed., *Film and Nationalism*, 1–22; 5. See also Altman, *Film/Genre*, esp. 195–206; and Mette Hjort and Scott MacKenzie, eds., *Cinema and Nation*.

31. See, for example, Richard Dyer and Ginette Vincendau, eds., *Popular European Cinema*; and the *Journal of Popular British Cinema*. For an important contribution to this literature that focuses particularly on the horror film, see Steven Jay Schneider, ed., *Fear Without Frontiers: Horror Cinema Across the Globe*.

32. Geoffrey Nowell-Smith, "Art Cinema," in Nowell-Smith, ed., *The Oxford History of World Cinema*, 567–75; 567. Nowell-Smith argues for the existence, since the 1980s, of two different forms of "international art cinema," one an "official kind, very close to the mainstream both in its cinematic values and its distribution," and the other characterized by "low-budget independent films coming from a variety of countries, including the United States, which offer a different sort of experience" (575). The films examined in this book were, for the most part, released before the 1980s.

33. David Bordwell, *Narration in the Fiction Film*, 231.

34. Indeed, the "general" sense of allegory as something that stands for something else is an exceedingly loose, protean concept with a long and varied history that often

resists "general" applications. For a literary overview of allegory, see Angus Fletcher, *Allegory: The Theory of a Symbolic Mode*. For an overview that devotes special attention to film studies, see Ismail Xavier, "Historical Allegory," in Toby Miller and Robert Stam, eds., *A Companion to Film Theory*, 333–62. One critic who has offered particularly compelling and influential accounts of modern allegory (with emphases on both literature and film) is Fredric Jameson. See especially his "Class and Allegory in Contemporary Mass Culture: *Dog Day Afternoon* as a Political Film," in *Signatures of the Visible*, 35–54.

35. Walter Benjamin, *The Origin of German Tragic Drama*, 166. Future references will be noted parenthetically by the prefix "*OD*" and the page number.

36. Walter Benjamin, "Theses on the Philosophy of History," in *Illuminations*, ed. Hannah Arendt, 253–64. Further references will be noted parenthetically by the prefix "*TH*" and the page number.

37. See Tom Gunning, "The Cinema of Attraction: Early Film, Its Spectator, and the Avant-garde," *Wide Angle* 8 (Fall 1986): 63–70.

38. Walter Benjamin, *The Arcades Project*, 462 (N2a3).

39. Ibid.

40. See Rainer Nägele, *Theater, Theory, Speculation: Walter Benjamin and the Scenes of Modernity*, 78–79.

41. See, for example, Leo Charney and Vanessa R. Schwartz, eds., *Cinema and the Invention of Modern Life*, especially the essays by Tom Gunning, Ben Singer, and Miriam Bratu Hansen.

42. For insightful studies of the philosophical implications related to this connection, see Beatrice Hanssen, *Walter Benjamin's Other History: Of Stones, Animals, Human Beings, and Angels*; and Max Pensky, *Melancholy Dialectics: Walter Benjamin and the Play of Mourning*.

43. David Cronenberg, quoted in William Beard and Piers Handling, "The Interview," in Handling, ed., *The Shape of Rage: The Films of David Cronenberg*, 159–98; 173.

1. HISTORY WITHOUT A FACE: SURREALISM, MODERNITY, AND THE HOLOCAUST IN THE CINEMA OF GEORGES FRANJU

1. André Schwarz-Bart, *The Last of the Just*, 369.

2. Jean Cocteau, *The Art of Cinema*, 121.

3. Georges Franju, quoted in Raymond Durgnat, *Franju*, 16–17.

4. Iain Sinclair, "Homeopathic Horror," *Sight and Sound* 5.4 (April 1995): 24–27; 26.

5. The release date of *Eyes Without a Face* is commonly given as 1959, but its official Paris premiere did not occur until March 2, 1960. See the extensive filmography (and bibliography) contained in Gérard Leblanc, Pierre Gaudin, and Françoise Morier, eds., *Georges Franju, Cineaste*. When the film reached the United States, its title was changed to *The Horror Chamber of Dr. Faustus*.

6. Richard Roud, *A Passion for Films: Henri Langlois and the Cinémathèque Française*, 17.

7. Franju, quoted in Durgnat, *Franju*, 28.

8. Walter Benjamin, "Surrealism: The Last Snapshot of the European Intelligentsia," in *Reflections*, ed. Peter Demetz, 177–92; 187. My readings of this essay, and of Benja-

min's work in general, are informed especially by Miriam Hansen, "Benjamin, Cinema, and Experience: 'The Blue Flower in the Land of Technology,'" *New German Critique* 40 (Winter 1987): 179–224; and Susan Buck-Morss, *The Dialectics of Seeing: Walter Benjamin and the Arcades Project*, esp. 253–86.

9. J. P. T. Bury, *France: The Insecure Peace: From Versailles to the Great Depression*, 26; cited in Sidra Stich, "Anxious Visions," in Stich, ed., *Anxious Visions: Surrealist Art*, 27.

10. See Hal Foster, "Armor Fou," *October* 56 (Spring 1991): 65–97; and Stich, "Anxious Visions," 26–27.

11. Paul Fussell locates the dominant form of ironic "modern understanding" in the "application of mind and memory to the events of the Great War." See his *The Great War and Modern Memory*, 35.

12. Benjamin, "Surrealism," 191.

13. Ibid., 187, 179. For further discussion of Benjamin's materialism in relation to Surrealism, see Margaret Cohen, *Profane Illumination: Walter Benjamin and the Paris of Surrealist Revolution*.

14. Benjamin, "Surrealism," 189–90. Benjamin's ambivalent relation to Surrealism surfaces also in his desire to bring his *Arcades Project* (*Das Passagen-Werk*, 1927–1940) "out of an all-too ostensible proximity to the Surrealist movement which could be fatal for me" (letter from Benjamin to Gershom Scholem, November 30, 1928; quoted in Buck-Morss, *The Dialectics of Seeing*, 5). On Benjamin's vexed relation to Surrealism, see also Susan Buck-Morss, *The Origin of Negative Dialectics: Theodor W. Adorno, Walter Benjamin, and the Frankfurt Institute*, 124–32; and Walter Benjamin, "Traumkitsch," in *Gesammelte Schriften*, vol. II.2, ed. Rolf Tiedemann and Herman Schweppenhaüser, 620–22; translated as "Dream Kitsch: Gloss on Surrealism," in Michael W. Jennings, Howard Eiland, and Gary Smith, eds., *Walter Benjamin: Selected Writings* 2:3–5.

15. Benjamin, "Surrealism," 188–89.

16. André Breton, "Second Manifesto of Surrealism," in *Manifestoes of Surrealism*, 185, 181.

17. This formulation risks simplifying some of the more intricate debates in Surrealist thought, as well as Benjamin's admiration for some of Breton's ideas, but the fundamental nature of the split between Breton and Bataille is what is most crucial here. This split will resurface in a somewhat different guise later in the chapter, when the different versions of "redeeming the real" presented by Siegfried Kracauer and André Bazin are examined.

18. Georges Bataille, "Eye," in *Visions of Excess: Selected Writings, 1927–1939*, ed. Allan Stoekl, 19n1. Compare Breton's equally enthusiastic but very different response to *L'Age d'or*, where the praise is based not on horror, but on "total love." See André Breton, "*L'Age d'or*: Total Love," in Ado Kyrou, *Luis Buñuel: An Introduction*, 185–86.

19. Franju, quoted in Durgnat, *Franju*, 20.

20. I am indebted to James Lastra for calling the *Documents* material to my attention, and for making it available to me. For a related discussion concerning Buñuel's *Las Hurdes: Land Without Bread* (1933), see Lastra's "Why Is This Absurd Picture Here?: Ethnology/Equivocation/Buñuel," *October* 89 (Summer 1999): 51–68. For further information on and excerpts from *Documents*, see Alastair Brotchie, ed., *Encyclopaedia Acephalica*.

21. For an examination of Painlevé's own fascinating career, see Andy Masaki Bellows, Marina McDougall, and Brigitte Berg, eds., *Science Is Fiction: The Films of Jean Painlevé*.

22. Georges Bataille, "Abattoir," *Documents* 6 (November 1929): 329; quoted in Denis Hollier, *Against Architecture: The Writings of Georges Bataille*, xiii. Hollier notes that slaughterhouses and museums are the dialectical poles in Bataille's project of "defining the sacred nucleus," and that "some strange destiny condemn[s] museums to rise up on the site of abandoned slaughterhouses." La Villette eventually became a "park of science and industry" (xiii, xiv, xv). According to Alice Yaeger Kaplan, La Villette also happens to be the birthplace of French fascist groups organized specifically by anti-Semitism, circa 1894. See her *Reproductions of Banality: Fascism, Literature, and French Intellectual Life*, xxviii.

23. In terms of a horror subtext, it is worth noting that Bataille's metaphor resonates with the famous voyage of the vampire in F. W. Murnau's *Nosferatu* (1922).

24. Franju, quoted in G. Roy Levin, ed., *Documentary Explorations*, 121.

25. Siegfried Kracauer, *Theory of Film: The Redemption of Physical Reality* (1960), 306. For an important discussion of the different versions of this often misunderstood book, and a persuasive argument that "the elided trauma that disfigures" it is "the political, philosophical, and world-historical impact of the Holocaust," see Miriam Hansen, "'With Skin and Hair': Kracauer's Theory of Film, Marseille 1940," *Critical Inquiry* 19 (Spring 1993): 437–69; 438. See also Hansen, "Introduction," in Kracauer's *Theory of Film* (1997), vii–xlv.

26. Kracauer's insistence on film's "realistic tendency" over the "formative tendency" (or "disengaged creativity") in *Theory of Film* results in a qualified denigration of much avant-garde cinema, including *Un Chien andalou* (36, 301). Yet Kracauer also privileges film as *the* medium for accessing history's very real horrors, and thus forgives "fantasy" elements in horror films where "[monsters] may be staged and manipulated so skillfully that they merge with their real-life environment and evoke the illusion of being virtually real. Is nature not capable of spawning monsters?" (87). This oblique reference to World War II returns in his praise of *Land Without Bread* (Luis Buñuel, 1933): "this terrifying documentary bared the depths of human misery, prefiguring the near future with its unspeakable horrors and sufferings" (181). Buñuel's film, like *Blood of the Beasts*, is a Surrealist documentary; so in the end, Kracauer's views on Surrealism's potential for the profane illumination of traumatic history may ultimately have more in common with Benjamin than a first glance implies. Kracauer began the *Theory of Film* project in 1940, while living in exile in Marseille. There he saw Benjamin almost daily until Benjamin's suicide in September 1940. See Hansen, "'With Skin and Hair,'" 444. For a discussion of the connections between Kracauer's film theory and Surrealism, see Ian Aitken, "Distraction and Redemption: Kracauer, Surrealism and Phenomenology," *Screen* 39.2 (Summer 1998): 124–40.

27. Benjamin, "Surrealism," 190, 181.

28. Ibid., 181, 182.

29. Hal Foster, *Compulsive Beauty*, 162. Foster discusses Benjamin at length in order to stage a bracing redefinition of Surrealism as a movement animated by the compulsion to repeat, with accompanying connections to the Freudian uncanny and death drive.

30. Buck-Morss, *The Dialectics of Seeing*, 261. My argument here is indebted to Buck-Morss's excellent chapter "Dream World of Mass Culture" (253–86).

31. Benjamin, quoted in ibid., 261.

32. Franju, quoted in Levin, ed., *Documentary Explorations*, 119, 121.

33. James Clifford, "On Ethnographic Surrealism," in *The Predicament of Culture: Twentieth-Century Ethnography, Literature, and Art*, 121–22, 121.

34. It is worth noting in this context that Franju mentions *Trépanation pour crise d'épilepsie Bravais-Jacksonnienne* as one of his favorite science films. According to Franju, the film details the surgical dismantling of a patient's brain by having the patient sit and face the audience during the entire procedure. It is only after the grueling operation that the narrator reveals that the patient could feel no pain—and then the patient stares into the camera and smiles. Franju's verdict: "It was an atrocious film, but a beautiful and poetic one, because it was so realistic . . . [the patient's] suffering and the fear of the spectator are undivided." See Durgnat, *Franju*, 28. For a sustained examination of early science films and their relation to discourses of the body, see Lisa Cartwright, *Screening the Body: Tracing Medicine's Visual Culture.*

35. Franju, quoted in Levin, ed., *Documentary Explorations*, 124.

36. My understanding of Benjaminian shock is informed especially by Susan Buck-Morss, "Aesthetics and Anaesthetics: Walter Benjamin's Artwork Essay Reconsidered," *October* 62 (Fall 1992): 3–41; Miriam Hansen, "Of Mice and Ducks: Benjamin and Adorno on Disney," *South Atlantic Quarterly* 92.1 (Winter 1993): 27–61; and Tom Gunning, "An Aesthetic of Astonishment: Early Film and the (In)credulous Spectator," in Linda Williams, ed., *Viewing Positions*, 114–33.

37. Walter Benjamin, "On Some Motifs in Baudelaire," in *Illuminations*, ed. Hannah Arendt, 155–200; 157. Benjamin's formulation of shock and experience draws on Bergson, Proust, and Freud. I will return to the influence of Freud's *Beyond the Pleasure Principle* later in the chapter.

38. Benjamin, "Baudelaire," 163.

39. Walter Benjamin, "The Work of Art in the Age of Mechanical Reproduction," in *Illuminations*, ed. Hannah Arendt, 217–52; 250n19 (emphasis added).

40. Hansen, "Of Mice and Ducks," 39.

41. Henry Rousso, *The Vichy Syndrome: History and Memory in France Since 1944*, 10. Throughout Rousso's influential study, film figures prominently. In fact, one of the major reasons that Rousso specifies 1971 as the end of the "resistancialism" era is the French reception of Marcel Ophuls's *Le Chagrin et la pitié* (*The Sorrow and the Pity*, 1970) (see ibid., 100–14).

42. Charles de Gaulle, quoted in Rousso, *Vichy Syndrome*, 16.

43. Rousso, *Vichy Syndrome*, 10 (emphasis in original).

44. The most thorough historical account of these issues is Michael R. Marrus and Robert O. Paxton, *Vichy France and the Jews.*

45. Rousso, *Vichy Syndrome*, 53.

46. Philip Watts, *Allegories of the Purge: How Literature Responded to the Postwar Trials of Writers and Intellectuals in France*, 4, 58, 8.

47. What follows below will not be an attempt to provide a systematic historical account of French cinema during the Occupation and the purge; for such an account, see Alan Williams, *Republic of Images: A History of French Filmmaking*, 245–98.

48. Jacques Doniol-Valcroze, quoted in Jim Hillier, "Introduction," in Hillier, ed., *Cahiers du Cinéma: The 1950s*, 4.

49. Of course, to speak of *Cahiers* as a "collective" masks the significant differences of opinion between many of its individual members, including the notable divergences between the views of André Bazin and those of his "disciples," the New Wave directors. However, as Doniol-Valcroze's quotation above demonstrates, it is possible to speak of *Cahiers* and the New Wave, especially during these early years, in terms of a general (but

not uncontested) consensus. For additional context, see Hillier, ed., *Cahiers du Cinéma: The 1950s*. It is also worth noting how many of the New Wave directors, decades after the Occupation, return to the subject of those years. See, for example, Truffaut's *Le Dernier Métro* (*The Last Metro*, 1980) and Chabrol's valuable newsreel compilation *The Eye of Vichy* (1993). For critical commentary on this phenomenon, see Lynn A. Higgins, *New Novel, New Wave, New Politics: Fiction and the Representation of History in Postwar France*.

50. Jean-Luc Godard, quoted in Jean Narboni and Tom Milne, eds., *Godard on Godard*, 146–47.

51. François Truffaut, "A Certain Tendency of the French Cinema," in Bill Nichols, ed., *Movies and Methods: An Anthology*, 224–37. Quotations will be noted parenthetically by the prefix "CT" followed by the page number.

52. Watts, *Allegories of the Purge*, 18.

53. Ibid., 19.

54. Robert Benayoun, "The King Is Naked," in Peter Graham, ed., *The New Wave*, 157–80; 174, 177.

55. Truffaut, quoted in Gérard Gozlan, "In Praise of André Bazin," in Graham, ed., *The New Wave*, 52–71; 69. On Drieu la Rochelle, see Kaplan, *Reproductions of Banality*, 92–107. On Brasillach, see Alice Kaplan, *The Collaborator: The Trial and Execution of Robert Brasillach*. It is important to note Brasillach's special relevance for cinema scholarship, since his work as a film critic and film historian was well-known; Brasillach is the coauthor (with fellow fascist Maurice Bardèche) of *Histoire du cinéma*, an early history of film first published in 1935, then revised in 1943, 1948, 1954, 1963, and 1964. It was translated into English as *The History of Motion Pictures* in 1938. For a careful examination of the revisions made between editions in the context of the authors' fascist and anti-Semitic views, see Kaplan, *Reproductions of Banality*, 142–60.

56. Claude Chabrol expresses a related "anti-politics" in his 1959 essay "Little Themes," in Graham, ed., *The New Wave*, 73–77. According to Alan Williams, a young Chabrol, "despite his socialist leanings," once "frequented a group of right-wing anarchists whose leader was Jean-Marie Le Pen, much later to become a notorious racist agitator" (*Republic of Images*, 344). Even Godard would not begin his overtly political cinematic phase until 1967, in reaction to the Vietnam War. See Williams, *Republic of Images*, 385.

57. John Hess, "*La Politique des auteurs*, Part One: World View as Aesthetic," *Jump Cut* 1 (May-June 1974): 19–22; 19. See also Hess, "*La Politique des auteurs*, Part Two: Truffaut's Manifesto," *Jump Cut* 2 (July-August 1974): 20–22.

58. Williams, *Republic of Images*, 312.

59. Susan Hayward, *French National Cinema*, 143–44, 234, 238, 237.

60. Dudley Andrew, "On Certain Tendencies of the French Cinema," in Denis Hollier, ed., *A New History of French Literature*, 993–1000; 997, 998.

61. Williams, *Republic of Images*, 367. Franju's personal favorite among his own documentaries is *Hôtel des invalides* (1952), a stinging indictment of the hypocrisy behind the famous Paris veterans hospital that also functions as a war museum. See Durgnat, *Franju*, 47–49.

62. François Truffaut, *The Films in My Life*, 317; see also 321. For Truffaut's interview with Franju, see François Truffaut, "Entretien avec Georges Franju," *Cahiers du cinéma* 101 (November 1959): 1–12. The same issue includes a revised version of an

essay Franju originally wrote in 1937 on Fritz Lang. See Georges Franju, "Le Style de Fritz Lang," *Cahiers du cinéma* 101 (November 1959): 16–22; translated as "The Style of Fritz Lang" in Leo Braudy and Morris Dickstein, eds., *Great Film Directors: A Critical Anthology*, 583–89. Franju's essay certainly bears the imprint of the signature *Cahiers* discourse of the *auteur*, but it also constructs a more political, sociological Lang than *Cahiers* would often present. See also Jean-André Fieschi and André-S. Labarthe, "Nouvel entretien avec Georges Franju," *Cahiers du cinéma* 149 (November 1963): 1–17.

63. Franju, quoted in Truffaut, "Entretien avec Georges Franju," 2; excerpt translated as "Interview with Georges Franju" in Truffaut, *The 400 Blows*, ed. David Denby, 208–12.

64. "Les Dix meilleurs films de l'anne," *Cahiers du cinéma* 104 (February 1960): 1–2.

65. Godard, quoted in Narboni and Milne, eds., *Godard on Godard*, 130; see also 99–101, 147–49.

66. "Les Dix meilleurs films de l'anne," *Cahiers du cinéma* 116 (February 1961): 1–2.

67. Franju, quoted in Truffaut, "Entretien avec Georges Franju," 11. Also cited in Roy Armes, *French Cinema Since 1946* 2:18.

68. Quoted in Durgnat, *Franju*, 91–92.

69. Jacques Rivette, quoted in Jean Domarchi, Jacques Doniol-Valcroze, Jean-Luc Godard, Pierre Kast, Jacques Rivette, and Eric Rohmer, "Hiroshima, notre amour," in Hillier, ed., *Cahiers du Cinéma: The 1950s*, 59–70; 69.

70. See chapter 3 for a related critique of *Hiroshima, mon amour* in the context of Japanese cinema.

71. Godard, quoted in Domarchi et. al., "Hiroshima, notre amour," 67.

72. Jean Domarchi, quoted in ibid., 68.

73. Rivette, quoted in ibid., 67–68.

74. Again, film historiography has provided several valuable accounts of the Left Bank as distinct from the New Wave—see especially Williams, *Republic of Images*, 327–78. Williams's willingness to examine a number of directors at length and juxtapose their career trajectories results in an admirably sophisticated account of not only the New Wave and Left Bank but also contemporary figures like Franju who are more difficult to classify: Louis Malle, Jean-Pierre Melville, Jacques Demy, and Jean Rouch. But even some of the best recent scholarship on French cinema has sometimes colluded with the incorporative rhetoric demonstrated above by *Cahiers*. For example, Lynn A. Higgins's illuminating *New Novel, New Wave, New Politics*, which argues that both the French New Novel and French New Wave produce political texts that are deeply haunted by the traumatic history of World War II rather than the ahistorical, apolitical texts they are often assumed to generate, fails to distinguish meaningfully between the New Wave and the Left Bank. As a result, the primary cinematic examples Higgins provides for the "New Wave" during the crucial years 1959–1964 are drawn entirely from Resnais, rather than from any of the *Cahiers* critics/directors.

75. Eric Rohmer, quoted in André Bazin, Jacques Doniol-Valcroze, Pierre Kast, Roger Leenhardt, Jacques Rivette, and Eric Rohmer, "Six Characters in Search of *auteurs*: A Discussion about the French Cinema," in Hillier, ed., *Cahiers du Cinéma: The 1950s*, 31–46; 44.

76. André Bazin, quoted in Bazin et al., "Six Characters," 44, 45.

77. André Bazin, "The Ontology of the Photographic Image," in *What Is Cinema?*, vol. 1, ed. and trans. Hugh Gray, 9–16; 15.

78. Benayoun, "The King Is Naked," 160 (emphasis in original).

79. Siegfried Kracauer, "Photography," in *The Mass Ornament: Weimar Essays*, ed. and trans. Thomas Y. Levin, 47–63; 61. See also my discussion of this essay in chapter 4.

80. Kracauer, *Theory of Film*, 306.

81. Kristin Ross, *Fast Cars, Clean Bodies: Decolonization and the Reordering of French Culture*, 10, 10.

82. Ross, *Fast Cars, Clean Bodies*, 11.

83. Ibid., 21. Ross notes that the cultural centrality of the car in France "to a large extent *precedes* the car's becoming commonplace in French life . . . although in the early 1960s the automobile could no longer be considered a luxury item, it was not yet a banality either" (27–29).

84. See Ross, *Fast Cars, Clean Bodies*, 128.

85. According to David Denby, this scene was apparently absent from the film's original cut, but Truffaut subsequently restored it. See Truffaut, *The 400 Blows*, 211n, 171.

86. Truffaut admits that this counter-discourse of prison imagery in the film functions at least partially as a direct homage to Franju himself. Truffaut told Franju that one of the most striking shots in *The 400 Blows*, an image of three small children locked in a cage at the reformatory, was composed with Franju in mind: "Frankly, I thought of you: look, here's a shot for Franju . . . " Quoted in Truffaut, "Interview with Georges Franju," 210.

87. The fact that Truffaut openly promoted *The 400 Blows* as autobiographical lends an additional redemptiveness to the conclusion—we can rest assured that "Antoine" will not spend his life in prison, but instead become a successful director. Interestingly, one of the many autobiographical incidents that Truffaut includes in the film undergoes a significant, dehistoricizing transformation—Truffaut claims that Antoine's lie about the reason for his absence from school ("my mother died") was substituted for Truffaut's own lie in 1943: "My father's been arrested by the Germans." Quoted in Michèle Manceaux, "People," in Truffaut, *The 400 Blows*, 215–23; 217.

88. Jean-Paul Sartre, "Introduction: 'A Victory,'" in Henri Alleg, *The Question*, 13–36; 14.

89. John Talbott, *The War Without a Name: France in Algeria, 1954–1962*, xiii.

90. Ross, *Fast Cars, Clean Bodies*, 124.

91. See Rousso, *Vichy Syndrome*, 75–82.

92. Sartre, "Introduction," 18.

93. Henri Alleg, *The Question*, 60.

94. See Simone de Beauvoir, *Force of Circumstance*, 367. On the dissemination of these accounts of torture, see Rita Maran, *Torture: The Role of Ideology in the French-Algerian War*, 144–46; and Talbott, *War Without a Name*, 92.

95. On the issue of censorship during the Algerian War, see Higgins, *New Novel, New Wave, New Politics*, 98–100. It is worth noting that even in this climate of censorship, many French intellectuals chose to voice their dissent in different ways. One notable document of dissent was the "Manifesto of the 121," a 1960 letter protesting the persecution of military conscriptees who refused to serve in Algeria. Truffaut and Resnais are among the 121 signatories, while Franju and Godard are absent. On the manifesto, see Higgins, *New Novel, New Wave, New Politics*, 7; the manifesto itself is reprinted in Hervé

Hamon and Patrick Rotman, *Les Porteurs de valises: La Résistance française á la guerre d'Algérie* (Paris: Albin Michel, 1979), 393–96.

96. Franju, quoted in Durgnat, *Franju*, 78.

97. André Breton, "Second Manifesto of Surrealism," in *Manifestoes of Surrealism*, 153.

98. André Breton, "Manifesto of Surrealism," in *Manifestoes of Surrealism*, 15. Breton was not alone among the Surrealists in his admiration for *The Monk*; Antonin Artaud translated the novel into French, and Ado Kyrou filmed it in 1972 from a scenario by Luis Buñuel and Jean-Claude Carrière.

99. Noël Carroll calls the eighteenth-century emergence of the horror genre "the return of the Enlightenment's repressed." See his *The Philosophy of Horror, or Paradoxes of the Heart*, 56. Carroll's formulation echoes Robin Wood, "An Introduction to the American Horror Film," in Robin Wood and Richard Lippe, eds., *The American Nightmare: Essays on the Horror Film*, 7–28. Wood's pathbreaking essay (discussed more fully in chapter 5) includes a brief mention of the "highly significant" connection between Surrealism and the horror film, as exemplified by Buñuel's admiration for (and uncredited contribution to) *The Beast with Five Fingers* (Robert Florey, 1946) and Franju's for *The Fly* (Kurt Neumann, 1958). See Wood, 13–14.

100. See William Veeder, "The Nurture of the Gothic, or How Can a Text Be Both Popular and Subversive?" in Robert K. Martin and Eric Savoy, eds., *American Gothic: New Interventions in a National Narrative*, 20–39; 23.

101. Peter Brooks, "Melodrama, Body, Revolution," in Jacky Bratton, Jim Cook, and Christine Gledhill, eds., *Melodrama: Stage Picture Screen*, 11–24; 18, 12. Brooks is also drawing on Dorinda Outram, *The Body and the French Revolution: Sex, Class, and Political Culture*.

102. Michel Foucault, *The Birth of the Clinic: An Archaeology of Medical Perception*, 196.

103. Mel Gordon, *The Grand Guignol: Theatre of Fear and Terror*, 8.

104. Gordon, *Grand Guignol*, 21.

105. Tom Gunning, "The Horror of Opacity: The Melodrama of Sensation in the Plays of André de Lorde," in Bratton, Cook, and Gledhill, eds., *Melodrama: Stage Picture Screen*, 50–61; 55.

106. Gunning, "Horror of Opacity," 59.

107. Peter Brooks's seminal text on melodrama is *The Melodramatic Imagination: Balzac, Henry James, Melodrama, and the Mode of Excess*.

108. Gunning, "Horror of Opacity," 56.

109. Robert A. Nye, *Crime, Madness, and Politics in Modern France*, 272.

110. Paul Margueritte, quoted in Nye, *Crime, Madness, and Politics*, 273–74.

111. André de Lorde, "Fear in Literature," in Gordon, *Grand Guignol*, 117.

112. Franju, in his typically derisive fashion, commented on the Edinburgh faintings by saying that "now he knew why Scotsmen wore skirts." See Durgnat, *Franju*, 79. Pauline Kael includes a brief but provocative account of an audience's reaction to the film in her *I Lost It at the Movies*, 6–7. I should add that when I saw *Eyes Without a Face* during a theatrical rerelease in Chicago in 1995, this sequence still evoked very audible groans, gasps, and nervous laughter from the spectators.

113. De Beauvoir, *Force of Circumstance*, 366–67.

114. Franju, quoted in Durgnat, *Franju*, 83.

115. Eric L. Santner, "History Beyond the Pleasure Principle: Some Thoughts on the Representation of Trauma," in Saul Friedlander, ed., *Probing the Limits of Representation: Nazism and the "Final Solution,"* 143–54; 146. See also Santner's *Stranded Objects: Mourning, Memory, and Film in Postwar Germany.*

116. Sigmund Freud, *Beyond the Pleasure Principle,* ed. and trans. James Strachey, 14. The criticism relating to the *fort/da* game and *Beyond the Pleasure Principle* is extensive. Two recent contributions of note are Leo Bersani, *The Freudian Body: Psychoanalysis and Art;* and Elisabeth Bronfen, *Over Her Dead Body: Death, Femininity, and the Aesthetic,* 15–38.

117. Kaja Silverman, *Male Subjectivity at the Margins,* 59, 58.

118. Benjamin, "Theses on the Philosophy of History," 253–64; 255. See also the introduction to the present volume.

119. Freud, *Beyond the Pleasure Principle,* 15.

120. Margaret R. Higonnet, "Women in the Forbidden Zone: War, Women, and Death," in Sarah Webster Goodwin and Elisabeth Bronfen, eds., *Death and Representation,* 195. Higonnet is referring to a World War I context, but her observations are equally relevant here.

121. Kaplan, *Reproductions of Banality,* 16. See also Watts, *Allegories of the Purge,* 29–31. Watts notes that "while calling his anti-Semitic articles 'denunciation,' the prosecution never linked Brasillach's anti-Semitic railings to acts of persecution" (26).

122. For further details on specific cases, see Maran, *Torture.*

123. Bronfen, *Over Her Dead Body,* xi, xi, x.

124. Ibid., xi, x.

125. Franju, quoted in Roud, *A Passion for Films,* 51.

126. Franju, quoted in ibid., 36.

127. Durgnat, *Franju,* 79. See Sinclair, "Homeopathic Horror," for the 1995 *Sight and Sound* feature. For more information on the reception of *Eyes Without a Face,* particularly in Britain, see David Taylor, "Masks, Masques, and the Illusion of Reality: The Films of Georges Franju," in Stefan Jaworzyn, ed., *Shock Xpress 2,* 6–16; 7–8. *Eyes Without a Face* received another limited theatrical rerelease in the United States in 2003.

128. This is not to say that *Eyes Without a Face* lacks a connection to a tradition of classic horror cinema as well. Jean Cocteau, who collaborated with Franju on the director's adaptation of *Thomas l'Imposteur* (1964), noted the horror heritage of *Eyes Without a Face:* "The film's ancestors live in Germany, the Germany of the great cinematographic era of *Nosferatu.*" See Cocteau, *The Art of Cinema,* 121. Franju himself notes his affinity with a German Expressionist tradition by commenting on his consistent use of either Marcel Fradetal (*Blood of the Beasts*) or Eugen Schüfftan (*Eyes Without a Face*) as director of photography: "I have the best understanding [with them]. . . . They come from the same school, the German school, the German Jewish school." Quoted in Armes, *French Cinema Since 1946* 2:28. As a provocative corollary to this connection, Mel Gordon claims that German Expressionist film actually owes more to the Grand Guignol stage than German Expressionist painting or theater. See Gordon, *The Grand Guignol,* 41–42.

129. See John McCarty, *Splatter Movies: Breaking the Last Taboo of the Screen,* for the unofficial coinage of "splatter." McCarty claims that "splatter movies, offshoots of the horror film genre, aim not to scare their audiences, necessarily, nor to drive them to the

edges of their seats in suspense, but to *mortify* them with scenes of explicit gore" (1). For an illuminating analysis of "gross-out" in relation to both horror and comedy, see William Paul, *Laughing Screaming: Modern Hollywood Horror and Comedy*.

2. "DIRECT EMOTIONAL REALISM": THE PEOPLE'S WAR, CLASSLESSNESS, AND MICHAEL POWELL'S *PEEPING TOM*

1. Isabel Quigly, "The Small Savages," *The Spectator* (February 5, 1960): 179–82; 182.

2. Isabel Quigly, "Filthy Pictures," *The Spectator* (April 15, 1960): 544–46; 544.

3. Ian Christie, "The Scandal of *Peeping Tom*," in Christie, ed., *Powell, Pressburger, and Others*, 53–59; 53. Christie provides a valuable overview of the film's critical reception in Britain during its original release.

4. See Dilys Powell, "Dilys Powell's Film of the Week," *Sunday Times* (London), June 19, 1994, 46. For Dilys Powell's original review, see her "Focus-Pocus and Worse," *Sunday Times* magazine, April 10, 1960, 25.

5. Ian Christie, *Arrows of Desire: The Films of Michael Powell and Emeric Pressburger*, 94.

6. In this sense, this chapter differs significantly from the many previous studies of *Peeping Tom* that have focused instead on interpreting the film psychoanalytically on the basis of its self-conscious references to psychoanalytic concepts. However, I do not wish to imply a dismissal of previous psychoanalytic studies of the film because their sensitive close readings certainly inform my claims and, in many ways, have made my own discussion possible. Of particular significance to me are those analyses of *Peeping Tom* that participate in the evolving relationship between feminist and Lacanian criticism, including Linda Williams, "When the Woman Looks," in Mary Ann Doane, Patricial Mellencamp, and Linda Williams, eds., *Re-Vision: Essays in Feminist Film Criticism*, 83–99, esp. 90–93; Kaja Silverman, *The Acoustic Mirror: The Female Voice in Psychoanalysis and Cinema*, 32–41; Carol J. Clover, *Men, Women, and Chain Saws*, 166–230; Parveen Adams, "Father, Can't You See I'm Filming?" in Joan Copjec, ed., *Supposing the Subject*, 185–200; Laura Mulvey, *Peeping Tom* laserdisc liner notes and audio commentary (Criterion Collection, Voyager, 1994); and Elisabeth Bronfen, "Killing Gazes, Killing in the Gaze: On Michael Powell's *Peeping Tom*," in Renata Salecl and Slavoj Zizek, eds., *Gaze and Voice as Love Objects*, 59–89.

7. Richard Hoggart, *The Uses of Literacy: Changing Patterns in English Mass Culture*, 279, 280, 24.

8. Harold Macmillan, quoted in Andrew Gamble, *The Conservative Nation*, 66; cited in John Hill, *Sex, Class, and Realism: British Cinema, 1956–1963*, 6.

9. J. Hill, *Sex, Class, and Realism*, 5.

10. Macmillan, quoted in Lindsay Anderson, "Get Out and Push!" in Tom Maschler, ed., *Declaration*, 154–78; 162.

11. Raymond Williams, *Culture and Society, 1780–1950*, 299–300. For a broader contextualization of Williams (as well as Hoggart) in relation to the emergence of cultural studies, see Dick Hebdige, *Subculture: The Meaning of Style*, 5–19. On their place within a British sociological tradition examining working-class culture, see Chas Critcher, "Sociology, Cultural Studies, and the Post-War Working Class," in John Clarke, Chas Critcher, and Richard Johnson, eds., *Working-Class Culture*, 13–40.

12. Indeed, Macmillan (not yet the prime minister who would declare the class war's end, but chancellor of the exchequer) helped precipitate Britain's disastrous military incursion in Egypt following Gamal Abdel Nasser's nationalization of the Suez Canal in 1956 by invoking the ghosts of Munich and "appeasement." Macmillan defended the call to arms to resolve the Suez crisis by proclaiming, "It is because I have seen it all happen before" (quoted in Arthur Marwick, *A History of the Modern British Isles, 1914–1999*, 211).

13. Robert Murphy, *British Cinema and the Second World War*, 3.

14. See Graham Dawson and Bob West, "Our Finest Hour? The Popular Memory of World War II and the Struggle Over National Identity," in Geoff Hurd, ed., *National Fictions: World War Two in British Films and Television*, 8–13. The classic historical account of the British home front during World War II is Angus Calder, *The People's War: Britain 1939–45*.

15. James Chapman, *The British at War: Cinema, State, and Propaganda, 1939–1945*, 161.

16. Antonia Lant, *Blackout: Reinventing Women for Wartime British Cinema*, 35.

17. Robert Colls and Philip Dodd, "Representing the Nation: British Documentary Film, 1930–45," *Screen* 26.1 (January-February 1985): 21–33; 25.

18. See Andrew Higson, "'Britain's Outstanding Contribution to the Film': The Documentary-Realist Tradition," in Charles Barr, ed., *All Our Yesterdays: 90 Years of British Cinema*, 72–97, esp. 84–88.

19. Murphy, *British Cinema and the Second World War*, 133.

20. Dilys Powell, *Films Since 1939*, 20, 40, 40.

21. Michael Balcon, quoted in Murphy, *British Cinema and the Second World War*, 132.

22. Julian Petley, "The Lost Continent," in Barr, ed., *All Our Yesterdays*, 98–119; 100.

23. Charles Barr, "Introduction: Amnesia and Schizophrenia," in Barr, ed., *All Our Yesterdays*, 1–30; 15.

24. Christine Gledhill, "'An Abundance of Understatement': Documentary, Melodrama, and Romance," in Christine Gledhill and Gillian Swanson, eds., *Nationalising Femininity: Culture, Sexuality and British Cinema in the Second World War*, 213–29; 214.

25. Quigly, "Filthy Pictures," 544.

26. Michael Powell, quoted in British Broadcasting Corporation, "Artists at Work: Michael Powell and Leo Marks," in David Lazar, ed., *Michael Powell: Interviews*, 18–21; 18–19.

27. Leo Marks, quoted in Chris Rodley, "Introduction: Leo Marks Interviewed by Chris Rodley," in Leo Marks, *Peeping Tom*, vii–xxvi; xiv. See also Leo Marks, *Between Silk and Cyanide: A Codemaker's War, 1941–1945*.

28. Marks, quoted in Rodley, "Introduction: Leo Marks Interviewed," xiv, xxi.

29. Michael Powell, quoted in Bertrand Tavernier, "An Interview with Michael Powell," in Lazar, ed., *Michael Powell: Interviews*, 25–43; 25.

30. Michael Powell, *Million Dollar Movie*, 391.

31. Christie, *Arrows of Desire*, 98.

32. The film *49th Parallel*, for example, was produced in harmonious cooperation with the Ministry of Information, while *Blimp* came under fire from Winston Churchill himself. See Ian Christie, "*Blimp*, Churchill, and the State," in Christie, ed., *Powell, Pressburger, and Others*, 105–20.

33. Andrew Moor, "No Place Like Home: Powell, Pressburger, Utopia," in Robert Murphy, ed., *The British Cinema Book*, 2d ed. (London: British Film Institute, 2001), 109–115; 111.

34. Lant, *Blackout*, 197.

35. M. Powell, *Million Dollar Movie*, 391.

36. Quigly, "Filthy Pictures," 546.

37. Ibid.

38. Michael Powell, *A Life in Movies: An Autobiography*, 354.

39. For an account of *Room at the Top*'s contemporary significance, see Penelope Houston, "Room at the Top?" *Sight and Sound* 28.2 (Spring 1959): 56–59.

40. Leonard Mosley, *Daily Express*, April 3, 1959; quoted in J. Hill, *Sex, Class, and Realism*, 191.

41. Isabel Quigly, "On the Make," *The Spectator* (January 30, 1959): 144–45; 144.

42. Robert Murphy, *Sixties British Cinema*, 15. As Murphy explains, *Room at the Top*'s rating initially prevented its exhibition in theaters owned by the two major distribution circuits in Britain, the Rank Organization and the Associated British Picture Corporation (ABC). Only later would Rank and ABC regularly exhibit (and produce) X features, and the resounding success of *Room at the Top* influenced such change.

43. Derek Monsey, *Sunday Express*, January 25, 1959; quoted in J. Hill, *Sex, Class, and Realism*, 191.

44. The following account of the New Wave draws on J. Hill, *Sex, Class, and Realism*, 5–34, 127–44; and Murphy, *Sixties British Cinema*, 10–33.

45. [J. D. Scott], "In the Movement," *The Spectator* (October 1, 1954): 399–400; 400. See also Blake Morrison, *The Movement: English Poetry and Fiction of the 1950s*.

46. Anderson, "Get Out and Push!" 157, 159, 159.

47. Murphy, *British Cinema and the Second World War*, 204.

48. Christine Geraghty, "Masculinity," in Hurd, ed., *National Fictions*, 63–67; 64–65. See also Geraghty's *British Cinema in the Fifties: Gender, Genre, and the 'New Look,'* 175–95.

49. Neil Rattigan, "The Last Gasp of the Middle Class: British War Films of the 1950s," in Wheeler Winston Dixon, ed., *Re-Viewing British Cinema, 1900–1992: Essays and Interviews*, 143–53; 148.

50. Anderson, "Get Out and Push!" 161, 177, 161.

51. M. Powell, quoted in Tavernier, "An Interview with Michael Powell," 43.

52. J. Hill, *Sex, Class, and Realism*, 136. The interior quotation is from Andrew Higson, "Space, Place, Spectacle: Landscape and Townscape in the 'Kitchen Sink' Film," in Higson, ed., *Dissolving Views: Key Writings on British Cinema*, 133–56; 145.

53. Quigly, "On the Make," 145.

54. Higson, "Space, Place, Spectacle," 149, 143. In Higson's essay, this quotation addresses the function of landscape in the films of the New Wave, but his observations are equally pertinent to the treatment of character. For a related discussion, see R. Barton Palmer, "What Was New in the British New Wave?: Re-Viewing *Room at the Top*," *Journal of Popular Film and Television* 14.3 (Fall 1986): 125–35.

55. In an excellent reading of the film, Carol J. Clover notes that the shot which precedes this one, the punctured bull's-eye insignia of Powell's (and formerly, Powell and Pressburger's) "Archers" production logo, also takes on special resonance in the context

of *Peeping Tom*'s fascination with both the "assaultive" and "reactive" gazes of spectatorship (Clover, *Men, Women, and Chain Saws*, 181).

56. Laura Mulvey, in her audio commentary on the laserdisc edition of *Peeping Tom*, notes the film's debt to German Expressionism. She astutely reads Mark's whistling as a possible reference to Peter Lorre's whistling killer in *M* (Fritz Lang, 1931).

57. This is an idea foregrounded by *Room at the Top*'s publicity campaign in Britain, where Joe Lampton is identified as "a modern Angry Young Man, an ex-P.O.W. who returns to a post-war Yorkshire industrial town fiercely determined to better himself" (*Room at the Top* pressbook, collection of the British Film Institute).

58. Christie, "The Scandal of *Peeping Tom*," 54.

59. Peter Hutchings, *Hammer and Beyond: The British Horror Film*, 7. Hutchings's excellent volume is read usefully in conjunction with the accounts of the British horror film provided by David Pirie, *A Heritage of Horror: The English Gothic Cinema, 1946–1972*, and Marcia Landy, *British Genres: Cinema and Society, 1930–1960*, 388–431.

60. Derek Granger, "Bring on the Ghouls," *Financial Times*, May 6, 1957, 14; cited in Hutchings, *Hammer and Beyond*, 7–8.

61. Quigly, "Filthy Pictures," 544. A number of contemporary reviews share Quigly's sense of betrayal at the association of Powell's name and artistic reputation with *Peeping Tom*. For example: "Mr. Michael Powell (who once made such outstanding films as *Black Narcissus* and *A Matter of Life and Death*) produced and directed *Peeping Tom* and I think he ought to be ashamed of himself" (Leonard Mosley, "Let's Not Peddle 'Sex' that Suits this Peeping Tom," *Daily Express*, April 18, 1960, 12); "It is made by a director of skill and sensibility. . . . The same stylist's view it is which now and then makes the torturer's stuff of the new film look like the true imaginative thing . . . instead of the vulgar squalor it really is" (D. Powell, "Focus-Pocus and Worse," 25).

62. Derek Hill, "Cheap Thrills," *Tribune*, April 29, 1960, 11.

63. Derek Hill, "The Face of Horror," *Sight and Sound* 28.1 (Winter 1958–59): 6–11; 11, 9, 10.

64. Wertham appeared in America before a Senate subcommittee hearing on the comics industry in April 1954, and by the fall of that year the Comics Magazine Association of America had imposed new codes restricting sexual and horrific content in comics. Wertham's influence in Britain can be heard in the comments of one representative attending a 1960 session of the House of Commons, who attacked current horror films for (in the synopsis of a *Times* reporter) "an exploitation of the baser, crueller, and more bestial instincts of mankind" and warned that "if modern youth was to be conditioned to violence and brutality as the Hitler Youth before the war, a crime wave was to be expected" (*The Times*, March 30, 1960, 4). On Wertham's impact on the horror genre, see David J. Skal, *The Monster Show: A Cultural History of Horror*, 233–37; and Walter Kendrick, *The Thrill of Fear*, 240–52.

65. Fredric Wertham, *Seduction of the Innocent*, 97; cited in Kendrick, *The Thrill of Fear*, 241.

66. D. Hill, "The Face of Horror," 10.

67. Ibid., 7, 9, 8.

68. Ibid., 10.

69. Ibid., 10, 10.

70. Paul Rock and Stanley Cohen, "The Teddy Boy," in Vernon Bodganor and Robert Skidelsky, eds., *The Age of Affluence, 1951–1964*, 288–320; 289, 288, 310.

71. Rock and Cohen, "The Teddy Boy," 314.

72. Murphy, *Sixties British Cinema*, 15.

73. Geraghty, *British Cinema in the Fifties*, 31.

74. J. Hill, *Sex, Class, and Realism*, 17, 17.

75. D. E. Cooper, "Looking Back on Anger," in Bogdanor and Skidelsky, eds., *The Age of Affluence 1951–1964*, 254–87; 257.

76. J. Hill, *Sex, Class, and Realism*, 163, 163.

77. Terry Lovell, "Landscapes and Stories in 1960s British Realism," in Higson, ed., *Dissolving Views*, 157–77; 174. Lovell argues for the possibility of more redemptive readings of *A Taste of Honey* than the one I have sketched here, based on the "double vision" (175) produced by the film's artificial imposition of an Hoggartian agenda on Shelagh Delaney's original play.

78. For a discussion of the vital connection between cinema's genesis in a mode of spectacle or "attractions" and the emergence of mass cultural entertainments such as amusement parks, see Gunning, "The Cinema of Attraction," 63–70.

79. Hoggart, *The Uses of Literacy*, 280, 280, 121.

80. Ibid., 45. Again, one must note that Hoggart's description of these teenage girls is tempered somewhat by observations about "why matters are not always as bad as they at first appear" (45), but the overall sense of degeneration remains.

81. Andy Boot, *Fragments of Fear: An Illustrated History of British Horror Films*, 131.

82. Hoggart, *The Uses of Literacy*, 192. Hoggart's vision of the pinup can be detected in the New Wave film *A Kind of Loving* (John Schlesinger, 1962), where a young working-class couple stumbles tragically into sex and marriage based on their naïve imitation of "false" sexuality embodied by the pinup photograph.

83. Carolyn Kay Steedman, *Landscape for a Good Woman: A Story of Two Lives*, 102.

84. Jean-Paul Török, "H-Pictures (II)," *Positif* 40 (July 1961): 41–49; 49; quoted in Petley, "The Lost Continent," 115. See also Török's "H-Pictures," *Positif* 39 (May 1961): 54–58; and "'Look at the Sea': *Peeping Tom*," in Christie, ed., *Powell, Pressburger, and Others*, 59–62.

85. Jonathan Rosenbaum, quoted in Elliott Stein, "'A Very Tender Film, a Very Nice One': Michael Powell's *Peeping Tom*," *Film Comment* 15.5 (September-October 1979): 57–59; 59.

86. Tony Rayns, "*Peeping Tom*," in John Pym, ed., *Time Out Film Guide*, 5th ed., 618.

87. M. Powell, *Million Dollar Movie*, 395.

88. Ibid., 146.

3. UNMASKING HIROSHIMA: DEMONS, HUMAN BEINGS, AND SHINDO KANETO'S *ONIBABA*

1. Shindo Kaneto, interview with the author, August 28, 2000, Montreal, Canada. Translation by Yuka Sakano, with additional transcription by Junko Yamamoto.

2. Throughout the chapter, references to "Hiroshima" should be understood to include the bombing of Nagasaki on August 9, 1945, as well. In this sense, "Hiroshima" simultaneously contains a specific reference to August 6 as well as a broader reference to the atomic event as a whole.

3. Technically, the postwar occupation of Japan was an Allied occupation, but as John W. Dower points out, "From start to finish [August 1945 to April 1952], the United States alone determined basic policy and exercised decisive command over all aspects of the occupation." See Dower, *Embracing Defeat: Japan in the Wake of World War II*, 73.

4. See Kyoko Hirano, *Mr. Smith Goes to Tokyo: Japanese Cinema Under the American Occupation, 1945–1952*, 63–65. See also Hirano, "Depiction of the Atomic Bombings in Japanese Cinema During the U.S. Occupation Period," in Mick Broderick, ed., *Hibakusha Cinema: Hiroshima, Nagasaki, and the Nuclear Image in Japanese Film*, 103–119, esp. 112–15.

5. Donald Richie, "'Mono no aware': Hiroshima in Film," in Broderick, ed., *Hibakusha Cinema*, 20–37; 23, 25.

6. A version of this documentary aired on television in Hiroshima in 1977, but Shindo refers to the project as incomplete and ongoing in my August 28, 2000, interview with him.

7. Carole Cavanaugh, "A Working Ideology for Hiroshima: Imamura Shôhei's *Black Rain*," in Dennis Washburn and Carole Cavanaugh, eds., *Word and Image in Japanese Cinema*, 250–70; 252.

8. David M. Desser, "Japan: An Ambivalent Nation, an Ambivalent Cinema," *Swords and Ploughshares* 9.3–4 (Spring-Summer 1995).

9. Richie, "'Mono no aware,'" 30. Although Richie wrote this essay in 1961, he still stands behind its claims today (Donald Richie, interview with the author, June 8, 2000, Tokyo, Japan).

10. Cavanaugh, "A Working Ideology for Hiroshima," 252. For a similar version of this argument that extends to the realms of Japanese disaster films and *anime*, see Susan J. Napier, "Panic Sites: The Japanese Imagination of Disaster from *Godzilla* to *Akira*," in John Whittier Treat, ed., *Contemporary Japan and Popular Culture*, 235–62. For accounts of *Godzilla* as something closer to a confrontation of the past than an evasion, see Chon A. Noriega, "Godzilla and the Japanese Nightmare: When *Them!* Is U.S.," in Broderick, ed., *Hibakusha Cinema*, 54–74; and Yoshikuni Igarashi, *Bodies of Memory: Narratives of War in Postwar Japanese Culture, 1945–1970*, 114–22.

11. Richie, "'Mono no aware,'" 35.

12. I will unravel these issues in further detail below, but for a useful introduction to this terrain, see Michael J. Hogan, ed., *Hiroshima in History and Memory*.

13. See Hansen, "*Schindler's List* Is Not *Shoah*."

14. Benjamin, "Theses on the Philosophy of History," 262, 255. This is not to say that *Onibaba* is absolutely unique for its era, even as a postwar Japanese film that engages Hiroshima allegorically—a number of important films in addition to *Godzilla*, including Kurosawa's *Ikimono no kiroku* (*Record of a Living Being*, 1955—discussed later in this chapter), Teshigahara Hiroshi's *Suna no onna* (*Woman in the Dunes*, 1963) and *Tanin no kao* (*The Face of Another*, 1966), Kobayashi Masaki's *Kwaidan* (1964), Shindo's own *Kuroneko* (1968), and even Mizoguchi Kenji's *Ugetsu monogatari* (*Ugetsu*, 1953) immediately come to mind—but *Onibaba*'s particular cross-pollination of the horror film, historical trauma, and national identity provides the specific "moment of danger" at the heart of this study. For a fascinating account of *Ugetsu* and *Kwaidan* in terms of "structures of emulsion in post-atomic Japanese cinema," see Akira Mizuta Lippit, "Antigraphy: Notes on Atomic Writing and Postwar Japanese Cinema," *Review of Japanese Culture and Society* 10 (December 1998): 56–65; 59.

15. Lisa Yoneyama, *Hiroshima Traces: Time, Space, and the Dialectics of Memory*, 38.

16. See Yoneyama, *Hiroshima Traces*, 201–202; and Maya Morioka Todeschini, "'Death and the Maiden': Female *Hibakusha* as Cultural Heroines and the Politics of A-bomb Memory," in Broderick, ed., *Hibakusha Cinema*, 222–52.

17. Yoneyama, *Hiroshima Traces*, 210.

18. Shindo Kaneto, interview with the author, August 28, 2000.

19. I am grateful to Keiko McDonald for this translation.

20. James J. Orr, *The Victim as Hero: Ideologies of Peace and National Identity in Postwar Japan*, 6.

21. Orr, *The Victim as Hero*, 10, 10, 137.

22. Yoneyama, *Hiroshima Traces*, 11.

23. Indeed, the film's cinematic and thematic emphases on humans behaving as animals, even to the point of merging the human and the animal, underscores this difficulty of distinction. For a provocative meditation on the human/animal divide in relation to Hiroshima, see Georges Bataille, "Concerning the Accounts Given by the Residents of Hiroshima," in Caruth, ed., *Trauma: Explorations in Memory*, 221–35.

24. Conrad Totman, *A History of Japan*, 161–63.

25. Dower, *Embracing Defeat*, 27–28.

26. See Dower, *Embracing Defeat*, 302–18.

27. Laura Hein and Mark Selden, "Commemoration and Silence: Fifty Years of Remembering the Bomb in America and Japan," in Hein and Selden, eds., *Living with the Bomb: American and Japanese Cultural Conflicts in the Nuclear Age*, 3–34; 4.

28. John Whittier Treat, *Writing Ground Zero: Japanese Literature and the Atomic Bomb*, ix.

29. Todeschini, "'Death and the Maiden,'" 222–52.

30. Keiko I. McDonald, *Japanese Classical Theater in Films*, 335n2.

31. Tadao Sato, *Currents in Japanese Cinema*, 78. See also David Desser's explanation and expansion of Sato's claims in *Eros Plus Massacre: An Introduction to the Japanese New Wave Cinema*, 108–144.

32. Sato, *Currents in Japanese Cinema*, 81, 81.

33. Hiroyuki Agawa, *Devil's Heritage*, 222; quoted in James Goodwin, "Akira Kurosawa and the Atomic Age," in Broderick, ed., *Hibakusha Cinema*, 178–202; 194.

34. Keiko McDonald, "Introduction," *Post Script* 20.1 (Fall 2000): 3–6; 3. This volume, edited by McDonald, is a special issue devoted to Kurosawa's films.

35. Mitsuhiro Yoshimoto, *Kurosawa: Film Studies and Japanese Cinema*, 1.

36. Akira Kurosawa, *Something Like an Autobiography*, 187.

37. Sato, *Currents in Japanese Cinema*, 199; Donald Richie, *The Films of Akira Kurosawa*, 112; Stephen Prince, *The Warrior's Camera: The Cinema of Akira Kurosawa*, 160. All three of these critics register significant admiration for *Record* while describing its confusions. For accounts that tend to interpret these confusions as productive in their own right, see Goodwin, "Akira Kurosawa and the Atomic Age," 186; and Yoshimoto, *Kurosawa*, 248.

38. Kurosawa, quoted in Richie, *The Films of Akira Kurosawa*, 109, 112, 109.

39. Eric Cazdyn, *The Flash of Capital: Film and Geopolitics in Japan*, 5, 6–7; see also 54.

40. Michael Raine, "Contemporary Japan as Punishment Room in Kon Ichikawa's *Shokei no heya*," in James Quandt, ed., *Kon Ichikawa*, 175–89; 183. In my analysis that

follows, I have taken the liberty of extending Raine's specific sense of "sun tribe" youth to the more general, symbolic figure of an infant child in *Record*.

41. Raine, "Contemporary Japan as Punishment Room," 188n16.

42. Richie, *The Films of Akira Kurosawa*, 112.

43. Kurosawa, quoted in Richie, *The Films of Akira Kurosawa*, 112.

44. Yoshimoto, *Kurosawa*, 248.

45. Shindo, quoted in Joan Mellen, *Voices from the Japanese Cinema*, 81.

46. See McDonald, *Japanese Classical Theater in Films*, 125–44.

47. Ibid., 130, 131.

48. Ibid., 125. As McDonald notes, there is also the possibility of additional characters in Noh who function as subordinate "physical extensions" of the protagonist or deuteragonist (126).

49. Kurosawa, quoted in Richie, *The Films of Akira Kurosawa*, 117.

50. Kurosawa, *Something Like an Autobiography*, 193.

51. See Yoshinobu Inoura and Toshio Kawatake, *The Traditional Theater of Japan*, 113–15.

52. See Kunio Komparu, *The Noh Theater: Principles and Perspectives*, 49–51.

53. On *Kurozuka*, see Komparu, *The Noh Theater*, 68–69; and McDonald, *Japanese Classical Theater in Films*, 129–31. McDonald cites *Kurozuka* as a source (along with Shakespeare's *Macbeth*) for Kurosawa's *Throne of Blood*.

54. Komparu, *The Noh Theater*, 69.

55. Desser, *Eros Plus Massacre*, 4.

56. Desser, *Eros Plus Massacre*, 67, 11, 118.

57. Cazdyn, *The Flash of Capital*, 53.

58. Nagisa Oshima, "In Protest Against the Massacre of *Night and Fog in Japan*," in Oshima, *Cinema, Censorship, and the State: The Writings of Nagisa Oshima, 1956–1978*, ed. Annette Michelson, 54–58; 56–57.

59. Nagisa Oshima, "Is It a Breakthrough? (The Modernists of Japanese Film)," in Oshima, *Cinema, Censorship, and the State*, 26–35; 31.

60. Oshima, "Is It a Breakthrough?" 28–29.

61. Ibid., 27, 31, 31.

62. Raine, "Contemporary Japan as Punishment Room," 187.

63. Although Oshima does not discuss Shindo explicitly in "Is it a Breakthrough?" his comments elsewhere suggest that his general opinion of Shindo's work may be (at times) even lower than his opinion of either the realists or the modernists. For example, he dismisses Shindo's drama *Hadaka no shima* (*The Island*, 1960) as lacking any interest "at all" (quoted in Mellen, *Voices from the Japanese Cinema*, 76) and disparages Shindo's horror film *Kuroneko* (1968) as "an example of a Hollywood movie" that "has nothing to do with anything serious" (quoted in Mellen, *Voices from the Japanese Cinema*, 266). Yet in a 1967 essay that characterizes the current status of the older generation of Japanese directors (Oshima is twenty years younger than Shindo) as "the silence of the masters," Oshima speaks about how "the greatness of Shindo Kaneto, which enables him to continue his creative work furiously in the midst of this . . . shines through because of the creative flame that burns brightly inside him" (Nagisa Oshima, "On the Attitude of Film Theorists," in Oshima, *Cinema, Censorship, and the State*, 133–43; 136, 137). For his own part, Shindo mentions Oshima among those Japanese directors one generation younger

than himself that have crafted important, socially conscious films (see Mellen, *Voices from the Japanese Cinema*, 93).

64. Desser, *Eros Plus Massacre*, 25.

65. For more detailed accounts, see Desser, *Eros Plus Massacre*, 31–36; Igarashi, *Bodies of Memory*, 132–43; and George R. Packard, III, *Protest in Tokyo: The Security Treaty Crisis of 1960*.

66. Igarashi, *Bodies of Memory*, 132.

67. Desser, *Eros Plus Massacre*, 30.

68. Desser supports his interpretation of the minimal connection between the two films by asserting that *Night and Fog* did not receive its commercial premiere in Japan until October 1963, long after the production of Oshima's film (although he admits that Oshima would certainly have heard and read about Resnais's film before then). I would argue that this sort of interpretation depends on a rather limiting form of intentionality that my own account seeks to complicate. See Desser, *Eros Plus Massacre*, 30.

69. Maureen Turim, *The Films of Oshima Nagisa: Images of a Japanese Iconoclast*, 53.

70. Igarashi, *Bodies of Memory*, 142.

71. Packard, *Protest in Tokyo*, 336.

72. Ibid., 61.

73. Oshima, quoted in Noël Burch, *To the Distant Observer: Form and Meaning in the Japanese Cinema*, 326.

74. Dower, *Embracing Defeat*, 506.

75. Benjamin, *The Origin of German Tragic Drama*, 178, 179.

76. In this sense, *Night and Fog* might well be a more important contribution to Japan's efforts to represent Hiroshima than Resnais's subsequent *Hiroshima, mon amour*. Shindo's own opinion of *Hiroshima, mon amour* in relation to the Japanese context: "[*Hiroshima, mon amour*] did not aim to describe Hiroshima and its devastation by the atomic bomb. Hiroshima is used only as a place where the love story is set . . . I dare say that this is a very unsatisfying film for the Japanese, who experienced the catastrophe of the atomic bomb." Shindo Kaneto, e-mail communication with the author, July 24, 2002 (translation by Yuka Sakano).

4. "ONLY A MOVIE": SPECTERS OF VIETNAM IN WES CRAVEN'S *LAST HOUSE ON THE LEFT*

1. In fact, *Last House*'s advertising campaign was so effective, and so widely imitated, that the film quickly gained a reputation as "the original 'it's only a movie' movie." Although this reputation is somewhat misleading, since ads for the earlier horror film *Color Me Blood Red* (Herschell Gordon Lewis, 1965) used a very similar phrase, the tagline remains attached to *Last House* to this day. For a thorough, informative account of the influence of *Last House*'s advertising campaign, see David A. Szulkin, *Wes Craven's "Last House on the Left": The Making of a Cult Classic*, 163–81.

2. Michael Rogin, *Ronald Reagan, the Movie and Other Episodes in Political Demonology*, xiii, xvi.

3. Kracauer, "Photography," 47–63; 61.

4. Wes Craven, quoted in Maitland McDonagh, *Filmmaking on the Fringe*, 182.

5. Milton J. Bates, *The Wars We Took to Vietnam: Cultural Conflict and Storytelling*, 175. Bates's insightful account of the intersection of the Vietnam War and the "generation war" (174–213) informs my discussion below.

6. I am grateful to Isabel Pinedo, who supported my claims of a connection between *Last House* and Kent State during a conference presentation of an early version of this chapter by drawing my attention to the resemblance between these two images.

7. Mary Vecchio's presence in the photograph made her the (sometimes unwilling) subject of mass-media attention from the moment of Kent State up until the present. For a journalistic account of Vecchio's curious "celebrity" story, see Linda White, "Two Photographs That Changed America: The Pulitzer Images of Eddie Adams and John Filo," master's thesis, Ohio University (1995), 103–20.

8. James Miller, *"Democracy Is in the Streets": From Port Huron to the Siege of Chicago*, 311; cited in Bates, *The Wars We Took to Vietnam*, 175.

9. David Whitten, quoted in Szulkin, *Wes Craven's "Last House on the Left,"* 125. Richard Meyers claims that Hallmark borrowed the title "Last House on the Left" from Stanley Kubrick's *A Clockwork Orange* (1971) (Richard Meyers, *For One Week Only: The World of Exploitation Films*, 95). Although there is no explicit mention of the phrase "last house on the left" in either Kubrick's film or Anthony Burgess's 1962 source novel, in Kubrick's version the home of Mr. Alexander (Patrick Magee) is indeed the last house on the left side of a remote road. It is in this house (named "HOME") that Alex (Malcolm McDowell) and his gang commit a brutal rape and battery, and to which Alex, in a plot twist strongly reminiscent of *The Virgin Spring*, later returns to be tortured himself. Craven nods to *A Clockwork Orange* in *Last House* by having Sadie (Jeramie Rain) sing a few notes of "Singin' in the Rain" while in a bathtub, just as Alex does in Kubrick's film.

10. Todd Gitlin, *The Sixties: Years of Hope, Days of Rage*, 414; cited in Bates, *The Wars We Took to Vietnam*, 175. Gitlin, like James Miller in *"Democracy Is in the Streets,"* traces the end of the New Left to Kent State, but adds that "the movement collaborated in its own demise" (415). I will return to this admittedly broad sketch of a complex historical moment later in the chapter, but those wishing to examine Kent State in greater historical detail should consult Scott L. Bills, ed., *Kent State/May 4: Echoes Through a Decade*, which includes an extensive annotated bibliography.

11. For an account of the Vietnam War's impact as a perceived attack on American masculinity that provokes "remasculinizing" representations in fiction and film, see Susan Jeffords, *The Remasculinization of America: Gender and the Vietnam War*.

12. James A. Michener, *Kent State: What Happened and Why*, 7, 7.

13. Michener, *Kent State*, 546, 550, 546.

14. Albert Auster and Leonard Quart, *How the War Was Remembered: Hollywood and Vietnam*, 48.

15. The graphic quality of these violent acts varies from version to version of the film, since *Last House*'s "true" running time is a matter of great confusion. For a thorough comparison of the existing versions in circulation, see Szulkin, *Wes Craven's "Last House on the Left,"* 152–62, 206–207.

16. *Joe* foregrounds the socioeconomic disparity between the working-class Joe Curran and Melissa's father, the upper-class Bill Compton (Dennis Patrick), but then squelches any serious interrogation of class issues by stressing their united front against the counterculture rather than their class-based differences.

17. For an account of *Last House* that recognizes the film's ability to engage the notion that "certain youth culture movements vociferously condemning the Vietnam War cathartically reveled in a violent America," see Tony Williams, *Hearths of Darkness: The Family in the American Horror Film*, 137–41; 137.

18. For illuminating discussions of this phenomenon, see Robin Wood, *Hollywood from Vietnam to Reagan*, 70–94; Vivian Sobchack, "Bringing It All Back Home: Family Economy and Generic Exchange," in Gregory A. Waller, ed., *American Horrors: Essays on the Modern American Horror Film*, 175–94; and Williams, *Hearths of Darkness*.

19. See Szulkin, *Wes Craven's "Last House on the Left,"* 15–16. During the three years following *Last House*'s release, Craven struggled in vain to "attract funding for scripts outside of the horror and exploitation genres," including an unproduced biographical film about an American colonel "court-martialed for reporting American atrocities in Vietnam" (Szulkin, 147).

20. Wes Craven, "MPAA: The Horror in My Life," *Films in Review* 47.5–6 (September-October 1996): 34–39; 36.

21. *Joe* (review), *Variety*, July 15, 1970.

22. Bates, *The Wars We Took to Vietnam*, 86–88; 88. See also Tom Wells, *The War Within: America's Battle Over Vietnam*, 426.

23. See Szulkin, *Wes Craven's "Last House on the Left,"* 16, 204.

24. Roland Barthes, *Camera Lucida: Reflections on Photography*, 26, 26, 26, 55. For further critical discussion of Barthes's profound book (as well as his earlier work on the image), see Jean-Michel Rabaté, ed., *Writing the Image After Roland Barthes*.

25. Kracauer, "Photography," 52.

26. Wells, *The War Within*, 426.

27. Miller, *"Democracy Is in the Streets,"* 310–11.

28. Gitlin, *The Sixties*, 410.

29. Vicki Goldberg, *The Power of Photography: How Photographs Changed Our Lives*, 239.

30. Michener, *Kent State*, 7, 544.

31. "The Kent State Four," *National Review* (May 18, 1971): 514–16; 514. The defense attorney at the trial of the Ohio National Guardsmen (none of whom were convicted) "used Filo's photograph to buttress his claim that outside agitators had sparked the Kent State conflict" (Goldberg, *The Power of Photography*, 240).

32. "An American Tragedy," *60 Minutes*, CBS-TV, January 9, 1977; cited in White, "Two Photographs That Changed America," 112–13.

33. See, for example, the May 5, 1970, issues of the *New York Times*, *Washington Post*, *Chicago Tribune*, and *Chicago Sun-Times*. The *Newsweek* cover story appears in the May 18, 1970, issue.

34. Lauren Berlant, "The Face of America and the State of Emergency," in *The Queen of America Goes to Washington City: Essays on Sex and Citizenship*, 175–220; 187, 220.

35. Gitlin, *The Sixties*, 411.

36. Milton Viorst, *Fire in the Streets: America in the 1960s*, 543.

37. Gitlin, *The Sixties*, 414.

38. Lesley Wischmann, "Dying on the Front Page: Kent State and the Pulitzer Prize," *Journal of Mass Media Ethics* 2.2 (Spring-Summer 1987): 67–74; 69.

39. Rogin, *Ronald Reagan, the Movie*, xiii.

40. Gilles Deleuze and Félix Guattari, *A Thousand Plateaus: Capitalism and Schizophrenia*, 177.

41. Walter Benjamin, "A Short History of Photography" (1931), *Screen* 13.1 (Spring 1972): 5–26; 25.

42. Benjamin, "Theses on the Philosophy of History," 255.

43. Roger Ebert's review (discussed later in this chapter) mentions that "the story is also based on a true incident, we're told at the beginning of the movie, but I have my doubts; I think the producers may simply be trying one of those 'only the names have been changed' capers." Roger Ebert, *"Last House on the Left," Chicago Sun-Times*, October 26, 1972, 58.

44. Eric Schaefer, "Resisting Refinement: The Exploitation Film and Self-Censorship," *Film History* 6 (1994): 293–313. See also Schaefer's *"Bold! Daring! Shocking! True!": A History of Exploitation Films, 1919–1959*.

45. Christian Metz, "Photography and Fetish," *October* 34 (Fall 1985): 81–90; 81–82, 82, 81.

46. For discussions of news photography as an analgesic, see John Berger, "Photographs of Agony," in *About Looking*, 37–40; and Susan Sontag, *On Photography*, esp. 16–21. For a study that argues against the analgesic view, see John Taylor, *Body Horror: Photojournalism, Catastrophe, and War*.

47. Garrett Stewart, "Photo-gravure: Death, Photography, and Film Narrative," *Wide Angle* 9.1 (1987): 11–31; 22.

48. Daniel C. Hallin, *The "Uncensored War": The Media and Vietnam*, 10, 11, 129–30, 148. For an account of the broader spectrum of 1960s American television in its social context, see Lynn Spigel and Michael Curtin, eds., *The Revolution Wasn't Televised: Sixties Television and Social Conflict*.

49. Margie Burns, *"Easy Rider* and *Deliverance*, or, the Death of the Sixties," *University of Hartford Studies in Literature* 22.2–3 (1990): 44–58; 44.

50. Richard Slotkin, *Regeneration Through Violence: The Mythology of the American Frontier, 1600–1860*, 5.

51. For a fascinating account of this trend, see J. Hoberman, *The Dream Life: Movies, Media, and the Mythology of the Sixties*, esp. 163–246, 296–315.

52. John Hellmann, *American Myth and the Legacy of Vietnam*, x.

53. See David Cook, *Lost Illusions: American Cinema in the Shadow of Watergate and Vietnam, 1970–1979*, 193–97.

54. Robert Bly, "The Collapse of James Dickey," *The Sixties* 9 (Spring 1967): 70–79. Bly's critique of Dickey's *Buckdancer's Choice* (1965) resonates with the anti-Southern imagery of some Vietnam-era American films by conflating Dickey's Southernness with a pro-war political stance. Bly concludes by accusing Dickey of "pulling out Southern language in long strings, like taffy" and being "a toady of the government, supporting all movements toward Empire, a sort of Georgia cracker Kipling" (79).

55. Anthony Thwaite, "Out of Bondage," *New Statesman* (September 11, 1970): 310–11; 311. See also Richard J. Calhoun and Robert W. Hill, *James Dickey*, 110.

56. Although James Dickey receives sole credit for the *Deliverance* screenplay, this line appears in neither his novel nor the published version of his screenplay (James Dickey, *Deliverance* [1982]). In his afterword to the screenplay, Dickey offers qualified praise for the film but concludes that "it is not the film as I would have it" (156). The author, who spent time on the film's set and appears in the small role of Sheriff Bullard,

speaks disparagingly of what he witnessed of the script-to-film process: "Details are changed, whole sequences are changed, dialogue is altered or improvised until . . . nothing but the bones are left" (155). In short, attempts to trace Dickey's "individual" vision from the novel to the film are, not surprisingly, more difficult than the screenwriting credit reveals.

57. Bates, *The Wars We Took to Vietnam*, 30. For an illuminating companion discussion of "the centrality of Indian dispossession in pre–Civil War America" in terms of forming the "American political core," see Michael Rogin, "Liberal Society and the Indian Question," in *Ronald Reagan, the Movie*, 134–68; 140.

58. Michener, *Kent State*, 49.

59. On the class and race dynamics of the film, see John Hartigan, "Reading Trash: *Deliverance* and the Poetics of White Trash," *Visual Anthropology Review* 8.2 (Fall 1992): 8–15; esp. 9.

60. Kathleen Stewart, *A Space on the Side of the Road: Cultural Poetics in an "Other" America*, 6, 123.

61. Clover, *Men, Women, and Chain Saws*, 134, 131.

62. Ibid., 165.

63. For a useful discussion of *Deliverance* as a film about "mis-remembering" identity and identification, see Linda Ruth Williams, "Blood Brothers," *Sight and Sound* 4.9 (September 1994): 16–19; 19.

64. A number of roughly contemporaneous horror films bear this out, often through a literal return of the dead. Especially worthy of mention here are *Night of the Living Dead* (George A. Romero, 1968) and *Deathdream* (Bob Clark, 1972), discussed in chapter 5 and in the introduction to this volume, respectively. See also Sumiko Higashi, "*Night of the Living Dead*: A Horror Film about the Horrors of the Vietnam Era," in Linda Dittmar and Gene Michaud, eds., *From Hanoi to Hollywood: The Vietnam War in American Film*, 175–88; and Wood, *Hollywood from Vietnam to Reagan*, 114–21, 133–34.

65. The peace sign icon makes a striking reappearance near the end of the film in a shot depicting the dead body of Krug's son, Junior, who wears the same peace sign necklace given to him by Mari that was given to her by her father. In this way, the state of "peace" as empty promise applies to both the Stillos and the Collingwoods.

66. Joseph Conrad, "Heart of Darkness," in *"Heart of Darkness" and Other Tales*, ed. Cedric Watts, 249.

67. Gitlin, *The Sixties*, 410. A similar incident had occurred in 1968 at a small college in Orangeburg, South Carolina, when three black student participants in a civil rights demonstration were killed by police; again, the national press reaction was muted.

68. Bill Warren, "Introduction," in Warren, ed., *The Middle of the Country: The Events of May 4th as Seen by Students and Faculty at Kent State University*, 21.

69. Wood, *Hollywood from Vietnam to Reagan*, 124, 124, 124–25. Wood's reading of *Last House* originally appeared in his "Neglected Nightmares," *Film Comment* 16.2 (March-April 1980): 24–32. See also his *Ingmar Bergman*, esp. 100–105.

70. In this regard, Wood attacks Roger Ebert's "characteristic critic-as-superstar complacency" (123), which manifests itself in Ebert's designation of *Last House* not as a serious artistic achievement but as a "guilty pleasure" (see Ebert's "Guilty Pleasures," *Film Comment* 14.4 [July-August 1978]: 49–51). Wood astutely notes the inaccuracies in Ebert's account of the film's plot, but he does not acknowledge Ebert's courageous

championing of *Last House* during its original release. See Wood, *Hollywood from Vietnam to Reagan*, 121–24.

71. Wood, *Hollywood from Vietnam to Reagan*, 124.

72. Although the debt to Bergman is uncredited, Craven confirms that *The Virgin Spring* influenced him consciously during the writing of *Last House* and was not just a fabrication constructed by Hallmark's publicity division after the fact. See Szulkin, *Wes Craven's "Last House on the Left,"* 35. For more on comparisons between the two films, see Michael Brashinsky, "The Spring, Defiled: Ingmar Bergman's *Virgin Spring* and Wes Craven's *Last House on the Left*," in Andrew Horton and Stuart Y. McDougal, eds., *Play it Again, Sam: Retakes on Remakes*, 162–71.

73. Bosley Crowther, review of *The Virgin Spring*, *New York Times*, November 15, 1960.

74. The rape scene also caused considerable controversy in Bergman's native Sweden; the Swedish censorship board passed the film without cuts, but rumors abounded that Bergman had threatened to remove the film from consideration if cuts were proposed. A public request that the Swedish attorney general inspect the rape sequence was made, but not pursued. See Birgitta Steene, *Ingmar Bergman: A Guide to References and Resources*, 101–103.

75. Test-marketed titles were *Krug and Company*, *Sex Crime of the Century*, and *The Men's Room*; the shooting title was *Night of Vengeance*. For an invaluable, exhaustive record of the film's production, distribution, and reception (to which my own account that follows is indebted), see Szulkin, *Wes Craven's "Last House on the Left,"* esp. 119–51.

76. "Film Ratings' Clarity Fogged by Murky Meaning," *Hartford Courant*, September 3, 1972, 2B. This editorial does not mention either *Last House* or the Paris Cinema by name, but Hallmark publicist David Whitten provides some of the missing details: "During the first week of the engagement, the Paris [Cinema] manager called up Hallmark's Boston office in a state of panic. The man was extremely upset; he said, 'I've got people picketing, I've got people calling up the theater on the phone, I've got people calling me at home . . . I want to pull this film!' Hallmark sent me over to run the theater until things calmed down" (quoted in Szulkin, *Wes Craven's "Last House on the Left,"* 129). Whitten wrote the "open letter" response that appeared in the *Courant* several days later.

Ironically, one of the editorial's complaints against the film, that it should have had an X rating (or, in today's terms, an NC-17) rather than an R, was somewhat well-founded. According to Craven, *Last House* producer Sean Cunningham had grown so frustrated with the MPAA's demands to trim the film for an R that he spliced an official "This Film Rated R" banner onto their original uncut version and then sent it out for release. See Craven, "MPAA," 36. In Chicago, *Last House* played as an eighteen and over "adults only" film; in New York, it was rated R.

77. [David Whitten], "An Open Letter to the Critics of *The Last House on the Left*," *Hartford Courant*, September 7, 1972, 74.

78. Wes Craven substantiates the need to mollify these mainstream, middle-class viewers through his personal experiences following the film's opening: "A lot of people really hated us vociferously for [making *Last House*] . . . especially among the culture we lived in, middle-class people with kids. When they saw that film, people literally wouldn't leave their children alone with me. . . . They would get up and walk away from

the table when I went out to dinner" (quoted in Szulkin, *Wes Craven's "Last House on the Left,"* 136).

79. Ebert, *"Last House on the Left,"* 58.

80. Gene Siskel, "Present Shock," *Chicago Tribune,* October 31, 1972, 4.

81. Howard Thompson, *"Last House on the Left,"* *New York Times,* December 22, 1972, 21. For the New York marketing campaign, Hallmark placed newspaper advertisements which featured both the disclaimer and quotes from Ebert.

82. Chas. Balun, *The Connoisseur's Guide to the Contemporary Horror Film*; an expanded version published by Fantaco (Albany, N.Y.) in 1992 includes the same review of *Last House.*

83. Pierre Bourdieu, *Distinction: A Social Critique of the Judgement of Taste,* 488, 489.

84. Bourdieu, *Distinction,* 6.

85. Chas. Balun, "I Spit in Your Face: Films That Bite," in Paul M. Sammon, ed., *Splatterpunks: Extreme Horror,* 167–83; 169, 169.

86. Bourdieu, *Distinction,* 7.

87. Ibid., 56.

88. Ibid., 56–57, 489.

89. See, for example, Peter Biskind, *Easy Riders, Raging Bulls: How the Sex-Drugs-and-Rock 'n' Roll Generation Saved Hollywood*; Cook, *Lost Illusions,* esp. 67–157; and Wood, *Hollywood from Vietnam to Reagan.*

90. See, for example, Geoff King, *New Hollywood Cinema: An Introduction,* 36–48.

91. See Cook, *Lost Illusions,* 68–69. For the broader history and theory of *auteurism,* see John Caughie, ed., *Theories of Authorship.*

92. Stephen Prince, "Graphic Violence in the Cinema: Origins, Aesthetic Design, and Social Effects," in Prince, ed., *Screening Violence,* 1–44; 6–13.

5. TRAUMA AND NATION MADE FLESH: DAVID CRONENBERG AND THE FOUNDATIONS OF THE ALLEGORICAL MOMENT

1. David Cronenberg, quoted in Beard and Handling, "The Interview," in Handling, ed., *The Shape of Rage,* 173.

2. *The Dead Zone* and *M. Butterfly* are also unusual in the Cronenberg canon because they are his only films to date (with the additional exception of *Spider* [2002]) with screenplays neither written nor cowritten by the director himself. This is not to say that certain Cronenberg films cannot be read productively as allegorical texts in relation to historical events. *Shivers* (1975) and *Rabid* (1977), for instance, bear investigation in light of Quebec's Quiet Revolution and the October Crisis of 1970, and many critics have noted how a number of Cronenberg's films seem to address the AIDS epidemic. For an excellent consideration of Cronenberg's cinema in connection with AIDS, see Andrew Parker, "Grafting David Cronenberg: Monstrosity, AIDS Media, National/Sexual Difference," in Marjorie Garber, Jann Matlock, and Rebecca L. Walkowitz, eds., *Media Spectacles,* 209–31.

3. Benjamin, *The Origin of German Tragic Drama,* 166.

4. Ibid., 217.

5. See, for example, Herman, *Trauma and Recovery.*

6. Here I am distilling research on nationalism and national identity by a number of scholars. See especially Benedict Anderson, *Imagined Communities: Reflections on the Origin and Spread of Nationalism*; Lauren Berlant, *The Anatomy of National Fantasy: Hawthorne, Utopia, and Everyday Life*; and Wolfgang Schivelbusch, *The Culture of Defeat: On National Trauma, Mourning, and Recovery*.

7. Marshall Delaney [Robert Fulford], "You Should Know How Bad This Film Is. After All, You Paid For It," *Saturday Night* (September 1975): 83–85; 83, 83, 84.

8. Delaney, "You Should Know How Bad This Film Is," 85.

9. For an account of the genesis of the CFDC, see Michael Dorland, *So Close to the State/s: The Emergence of Canadian Feature Film Policy*, 110–14.

10. Margaret Atwood, *Survival: A Thematic Guide to Canadian Literature*, 33, 33.

11. Robert Fothergill, "Coward, Bully, or Clown: The Dream-Life of a Younger Brother," in Seth Feldman and Joyce Nelson, eds., *Canadian Film Reader*, 234–50; 242–43. Geoff Pevere argues for the continuing relevance of Fothergill's observations in his "Images of Men," *Canadian Forum* (February 1985): 24–28.

12. Anderson, *Imagined Communities*, 6.

13. Michael Dorland, "Theses on Canadian Nationalism: In Memoriam George P. Grant," *CineAction* 16 (Spring 1989): 3–5; 4. Dorland's brief but valuable essay evokes the insights of George Grant, one of Canada's most important critical thinkers on the question of nationalism. See especially Grant's *Lament for a Nation: The Defeat of Canadian Nationalism* (1965). For an excellent introduction to Grant that also contextualizes him in relation to two other key figures in Canadian thought, see Arthur Kroker, *Technology and the Canadian Mind: Innis/McLuhan/Grant*.

14. Tony Wilden, *The Imaginary Canadian*, 1.

15. Berlant, *The Anatomy of National Fantasy*, 24.

16. Cronenberg, quoted in Chris Rodley, ed., *Cronenberg on Cronenberg*, 25.

17. Cronenberg, quoted in Beard and Handling, "The Interview," 174.

18. For Cronenberg's biography, see Peter Morris, *David Cronenberg: A Delicate Balance*.

19. Cronenberg, quoted in Rodley, ed., *Cronenberg on Cronenberg*, 36.

20. Homi K. Bhabha, "Introduction: Narrating the Nation," in Bhabha, ed., *Nation and Narration*, 1–7; 4.

21. Andrew Higson, "The Concept of National Cinema," *Screen* 30.4 (Autumn 1989): 36–46; 37. See also Higson's more recent revisiting of these issues in his "The Limiting Imagination of National Cinema," in Hjort and MacKenzie, eds., *Cinema and Nation*, 63–74.

22. For the often neglected "prehistory" of Canadian cinema, see Peter Morris, *Embattled Shadows: A History of Canadian Cinema*.

23. Gary Evans, *In the National Interest: A Chronicle of the National Film Board of Canada from 1949 to 1989*, 318. See also Evans's *John Grierson and the National Film Board: The Politics of Wartime Propaganda*.

24. Michael Dorland, "The Shadow of Canadian Cinema: Bruce Elder's Immodest Proposal," in Douglas Fetherling, ed., *Documents in Canadian Film*, 316–22; 319–20.

25. Peter Morris, "Backwards to the Future: John Grierson's Film Policy for Canada," in Gene Walz, ed., *Flashback: People and Institutions in Canadian Film History*, 17–35; 31, 18. See also John Grierson, "A Film Policy for Canada," in Fetherling, ed., *Documents in Canadian Film*, 51–67. For an extended revisionist account of Grierson, see Joyce Nelson, *The Colonized Eye: Rethinking the Grierson Legend*.

26. For accounts of the tortured bureaucratic machinations of the Canadian Co-operation Project, see Pierre Berton, *Hollywood's Canada: The Americanization of Our National Image*, 167–91; and Dorland, *So Close to the State/s*, 77–80.

27. Morris, "Backwards to the Future," 31.

28. Cronenberg, quoted in Rodley, ed., *Cronenberg on Cronenberg*, 35, 39.

29. Jay Scott, "Burnout in the Great White North," in Seth Feldman, ed., *Take Two*, 29–35; 31. Scott distinguishes between the promise of an "old new wave" located in the late 1960s and early 1970s that includes *Goin' Down the Road*, and the disappointment of a "new new wave" traced to the mid-1970s that includes Cronenberg, a man "very busy imitating American movies to commercial, if not aesthetic, advantage" (32).

30. See Christine Ramsay, "Canadian Narrative Cinema from the Margins: 'The Nation' and Masculinity in *Goin' Down the Road*," *Canadian Journal of Film Studies* 2.2–3 (1993): 27–49; and Ramsay's liner notes for the *Goin' Down the Road* DVD (Seville Pictures, 2002).

31. Christopher E. Gittings, *Canadian National Cinema*, 158.

32. Cronenberg, quoted in Rodley, ed., *Cronenberg on Cronenberg*, 36.

33. Manjunath Pendakur, *Canadian Dreams and American Control: The Political Economy of the Canadian Film Industry*, 29–30.

34. Even the CFDC's financially successful afterlife as Telefilm Canada, especially in the 1990s, has been critiqued for its abandonment of cultural development in favor of industrial development. See Dorland, *So Close to the State/s*, 145.

35. Geoff Pevere, "Middle of Nowhere: Ontario Movies After 1980," *Post Script* 15.1 (Fall 1995): 9–22; 11.

36. Jim Leach, "The Body Snatchers: Genre and Canadian Cinema," in Barry Keith Grant, ed., *Film Genre Reader*, 357–69; 366.

37. Barry Keith Grant, "Introduction," *Post Script* 15.1 (Fall 1995): 3–5; 3. See also Peter Harcourt, *Movies and Mythologies: Towards a National Cinema*.

38. William Beard, "The Canadianness of David Cronenberg," *Mosaic* 27.2 (June 1994): 113–33; 131, 129, 129, 130, 130, 130, 131–32. My disagreement with Beard on this point does not diminish my admiration for his sensitive and thorough close readings of Cronenberg's films. See his *The Artist as Monster: The Cinema of David Cronenberg*.

39. Gaile McGregor, "Grounding the Countertext: David Cronenberg and the Ethno-specificity of Horror," *Canadian Journal of Film Studies* 2.1 (1993): 43–62; 57, 48.

40. Bart Testa, "Technology's Body: Cronenberg, Genre, and the Canadian Ethos," *Post Script* 15.1 (Fall 1995): 38–56; 51.

41. Jim Leach, "North of Pittsburgh: Genre and National Cinema from a Canadian Perspective," in Barry Keith Grant, ed., *Film Genre Reader II*, 474–93; 482.

42. Cronenberg, quoted in Gavin Smith, "Cronenberg: Mind Over Matter," *Film Comment* 33.2 (March-April 1997): 14–29; 17.

43. Cronenberg, quoted in Rodley, ed., *Cronenberg on Cronenberg*, 60.

44. *Night of the Living Dead* (review), *Variety*, October 16, 1968.

45. Delaney, "You Should Know How Bad This Film Is," 85.

46. Elliot Stein, "*The Night of the Living Dead*," *Sight and Sound* 39.2 (Spring 1970): 105.

47. Joseph Lewis, quoted in R. H. W. Dillard, "*Night of the Living Dead*: It's Not Like Just a Wind That's Passing Through," in Waller, ed., *American Horrors*, 16.

48. See Piers Handling, "A Canadian Cronenberg," in Handling, ed., *The Shape of Rage*, 98–114; 98. This is not to say that Fulford's review went completely unchallenged in Canada. See, for example, Maurice Yacowar, "You Shiver Because It's Good," *Cinema Canada* 34–35 (February 1977): 54–55. However, even post-*Videodrome* critical evaluations of Canadian cinema sometimes minimize or dismiss Cronenberg's work within that context. For example, see Gittings, *Canadian National Cinema*, a thoroughly researched volume which points out that "there is probably more scholarly and journalistic work published on Cronenberg than on any other Canadian film-maker" (278), but then devotes less than three pages to his films—and these three pages offer only a largely disparaging reading of *Dead Ringers* (1988), widely regarded as one of Cronenberg's most ambitious, complex, and effective films (278–80). See also R. Bruce Elder, *Image and Identity: Reflections on Canadian Film and Culture*, an expansive study that refers to Cronenberg only in a footnoted rejection of *Shivers* as a "*schlock* commercial vehicle . . . constructed on the model of the American B-Movie" (420*n*). Elder's dismissal of Cronenberg echoes the implications of an earlier controversial essay, "The Cinema We Need" (1985), in which Elder designates narrative film itself as a component of the "closed system of thought" that threatens to reduce Canada to nothing more than "a geographic landmass within the empire of technology" belonging to the United States. See Bruce Elder, "The Cinema We Need," in Fetherling, ed., *Documents in Canadian Film*, 260–71; 262, 271. Fetherling's volume also includes a number of instructive critical responses to Elder's essay.

49. Wood, "An Introduction to the American Horror Film," 23, 23, 24. Wood's equation of "apocalyptic" and "progressive" horror simplifies the conservative aspects of apocalyptic discourse. For a discussion of these conservative aspects in a cinematic context, see Christopher Sharrett, "The American Apocalypse: Scorsese's *Taxi Driver*," in Sharrett, ed., *Crisis Cinema: The Apocalyptic Idea in Postmodern Narrative Film*, 221–35.

50. Robin Wood, "Cronenberg: A Dissenting View," in Handling, ed., *The Shape of Rage*, 115–35; 130, 130. See also Wood's *Hollywood from Vietnam to Reagan*, 114–21. For Cronenberg's defense of *Shivers* in response to Wood, see Beard and Handling, "The Interview," 176–79; 192. For more recent critical engagements with Wood's analysis of Cronenberg, see Murray Smith, "A(moral) Monstrosity," in Michael Grant, ed., *The Modern Fantastic: The Films of David Cronenberg*, 69–83; and Lianne McLarty, "'Beyond the Veil of the Flesh': Cronenberg and the Disembodiment of Horror," in Barry Keith Grant, ed., *The Dread of Difference: Gender and the Horror Film*, 231–52.

51. Again, a notable exception is Yacowar's "You Shiver Because It's Good," which notes that the film "dramatizes the horror of what we often take to be one of the happiest triumphs of our time, the new sexual permissiveness" (54) and that it is shocking because "Cronenberg's zombies are what we want to be" (55).

52. Wood, "An Introduction to the American Horror Film," 24.

53. John D'Emilio and Estelle B. Freedman, *Intimate Matters: A History of Sexuality in America*, 304, 304, 305. Throughout this section, I will draw on *Intimate Matters* as applicable to both American and Canadian contexts; unfortunately, I have not found a comparable Canadian study. I do not wish to imply that the impact of the sexual revolution was identical in both countries, but I believe there is enough evidence to warrant general cross-referencing in this case. Gallup polls conducted in the late 1960s and early 1970s show a comparable liberal shift in sexual values in both countries during this period, with Canadians slightly more liberal than their American

counterparts (Seymour Martin Lipset, *Continental Divide: The Values and Institutions of the United States and Canada*, 87). In *Sexual Behaviour in Canada: Patterns and Problems* (1977), a social science anthology roughly contemporaneous with *Shivers*, editor Benjamin Schlesinger reports that although the sexual revolution "has had a tremendous impact upon individuals and families in Canadian society," he "was not surprised to find very little research and only a handful of published articles dealing with human sexuality in Canada. We had relied almost entirely on the American output of books, booklets, and research" (ix, x). On a droll but pertinent note, Maurice Yacowar adds, "Who but a comic would ever postulate a Canadian Academy for Erotic Enquiry? Cronenberg did, in *Stereo* [1969]. The idea of such an institute, of course, is comic only in Canada (pity)" ("The Comedy of Cronenberg," in Handling, ed., *The Shape of Rage*, 80–86; 80).

54. Wood, "An Introduction to the American Horror Film," 24.

55. Cronenberg's presentation of Starliner Towers as a collective "being," foregrounded throughout the film by provocative intercutting between apartments, mirrors J. G. Ballard's novel *High-Rise* (also published in 1975). Of course, Cronenberg would later adapt Ballard's *Crash* (1973).

56. D'Emilio and Freedman, *Intimate Matters*, 302, 306. Of course, the sexual revolution cannot be simplified entirely in this manner. D'Emilio and Freedman recognize second-wave feminism and gay liberation as vital components of the sexual revolution "effective enough to challenge the hegemony of mid-twentieth-century orthodoxy," but conclude that "neither movement had the strength in the short run to remake thoroughly the mores of the nation" (325).

57. The extremity of this imagery might tempt one to read *Shivers* (as well as *Rabid*) as a thinly disguised metaphor for the herpes epidemic that would come to be seen as the "seamy underside of the sexual liberation of the 1960s and 1970s," but this interpretation of herpes would not really circulate widely until the early 1980s (Allan M. Brandt, *No Magic Bullet: A Social History of Venereal Disease in the United States Since 1880*, 179–181; 179). Both of these early Cronenberg films have been read as "prophetic" (or, in the case of *The Fly* [1986], contemporary) AIDS allegories; Andrew Parker points out that a more productive way of thinking about this coincidence is to realize that the "mainstream media press response to AIDS has taken its representational bearings from preexisting, culturally pervasive" scripts that structure news reports as well as horror films ("Grafting David Cronenberg," 217).

58. Wood, "Cronenberg: A Dissenting View," 128.

59. D'Emilio and Freedman, *Intimate Matters*, 327.

60. Michel Foucault, *The History of Sexuality*, vol. 1, *An Introduction*, 94.

61. David Sanjek notes the connotations of the sexual revolution in this scene: "The aquatic context puts one in mind of the effort in psychological and social transformation carried out at such places as California's Esalen Institute in the 1960s and 1970s" ("Dr. Hobbes's Parasites: Victims, Victimization, and Gender in David Cronenberg's *Shivers*," *Cinema Journal* 36.1 [Fall 1996]: 55–74; 67).

62. Carole Pateman, *The Sexual Contract*, 44.

63. Although some critics have likened *Night* to *Invasion of the Body Snatchers* (Don Siegel, 1956), *Night* owes its most considerable debt to another landmark film in the sci-fi/horror "disaster" and "revenge of nature" cycles—Alfred Hitchcock's *The Birds* (1963). But as William Paul observes, *Night* departs markedly from Hitchcock's film

as well: "For all the uncertainty and bleakness of its conclusion, *The Birds* nonetheless manages to move toward the formation of a more tightly knit group in a newly constituted family. . . . By the end of [*Night*], all the members of the defending group are either dead or living dead, so there is not even the possibility of redemption, . . . There is a literal sickness at the core of both the family and society" (Paul, *Laughing Screaming*, 260). Romero states that he was inspired by Richard Matheson's science fiction novel *I Am Legend* (1954) (George A. Romero, "Preface," in John Russo, *Night of the Living Dead*, 5–14; 11); Matheson's novel was filmed twice in its own right, as *The Last Man on Earth* (Sidney Salkow, 1964) and *The Omega Man* (Boris Sagal, 1971).

64. Presumably, this attack is violent rather than sexual because the maintenance man is protecting the parasite and the parasitic cause of preventing escape or rescue from the building before total infection of the population is achieved. Similar acts of "infected" violence in the film, such as the murder of Rollo Linsky and the car crashing into St. Luc and Forsythe, would support this reading.

65. Even Ben's most "unsympathetic" moment, his shooting of Harry Cooper, is thoroughly motivated by Harry's near-fatal betrayal of Ben during an escape attempt and tacitly endorsed by Helen Cooper's silent refusal to plead for her despicable husband's life.

66. J. Hoberman and Jonathan Rosenbaum, *Midnight Movies*, 112–13.

67. Romero, "Preface," *Night of the Living Dead*, 11. See also Paul R. Gagne, *The Zombies That Ate Pittsburgh: The Films of George A. Romero*, 36–38.

68. Indeed, Richard Dyer has read the film intriguingly by emphasizing its representation of race, calling the film's horror "the horror of whiteness" (Richard Dyer, "White," *Screen* 29.4 [Autumn 1988]: 44–64; 62). Dyer's reading becomes more persuasive in conjunction with Romero's sequels *Dawn of the Dead* (1979) and *Day of the Dead* (1985), where issues of race are developed in increasingly sophisticated ways amid less and less "hopeful" prospects for humanity's survival.

69. Higashi, "*Night of the Living Dead*," 180.

70. Barry Keith Grant, "Taking Back the *Night of the Living Dead*: George Romero, Feminism, and the Horror Film," in Barry Keith Grant, ed., *The Dread of Difference*, 200–212; 204, 205. Grant focuses on "feminist" revisions in Romero's "Dead" films after the original *Night*, focusing especially on the 1990 remake of *Night of the Living Dead*, written by Romero and directed by Tom Savini.

71. Again, Romero's sequels to *Night* will paint a much less "hopeful" picture about controlling the zombie epidemic.

72. Paul, *Laughing Screaming*, 262, 263.

73. Cronenberg, quoted in Beard and Handling, "The Interview," 176.

74. Martin Scorsese, "Internal Metaphors, External Horror," in Wayne Drew, ed., *David Cronenberg*, 54.

75. Martin Scorsese, quoted in Rodley, ed., *Cronenberg on Cronenberg*, xxiv. See also Beard and Handling, "The Interview," 181.

76. Patricia Pearson, "Crash, Bam, Thank You, Ma'am," *Saturday Night* (October 1996): 119–22; 119, 119. I am grateful to Rachel Lindheim for calling this article to my attention.

77. Pearson, "Crash, Bam, Thank You, Ma'am," 122.

78. Dudley Andrew, "The Unauthorized Auteur Today," in Jim Collins, Hilary Radner, and Ava Preacher Collins, eds., *Film Theory Goes to the Movies*, 77–85; 80, 85.

79. Tom Gunning, *The Films of Fritz Lang: Allegories of Vision and Modernity*, 4–5, 5.

80. Bordwell, "The Art Cinema as a Mode of Film Practice," 59.

81. *Crash* also matches a lesser-known preoccupation in Cronenberg's films with automobiles and motorcycles; see especially *The Italian Machine* (1976) and *Fast Company* (1979). Cronenberg is an auto enthusiast who collects and races vintage cars.

82. For a comprehensive account of *Crash's* tortured British reception, see Mark Kermode and Julian Petley, "Road Rage," *Sight and Sound* 7.6 (June 1997): 16–18; and Martin Barker, Jane Arthurs, and Ramaswami Harindranath, *The Crash Controversy: Censorship Campaigns and Film Reception*.

83. See "Guardian Angels," *New Yorker* (November 25, 1996): 47–48.

84. For example, Bart Testa blasted Cronenberg for his "amazing failure to stage any good car crashes" and condemned the film's sex scenes for having "none of porn's sexual energy and instead exhibit[ing] the director's boyish pride in their putative outrageousness" (Bart Testa, review of *Crash*, *Film Studies Association of Canada Newsletter* 21.1 [Fall 1996]: 15–17; 15).

85. Anthony Lane, "Off the Road," *New Yorker* (March 31, 1997): 106–107; 107.

86. Murray Pomerance, review of *Crash*, *Film Studies Association of Canada Newsletter* 21.1 (Fall 1996): 20.

87. Cronenberg, quoted in Rodley, ed., *Cronenberg on Cronenberg*, 194.

88. J. G. Ballard, "Introduction to the French Edition," *Crash* (1974); reprinted in V. Vale and Andrea Juno, eds., *J. G. Ballard*, 96–98; 98.

89. Jean Baudrillard, "*Crash*," in *Simulacra and Simulation*, 111–19; 118–19.

90. Fred Botting and Scott Wilson, "Automatic Lover," *Screen* 39.2 (Summer 1998): 186–92; 186.

91. J. G. Ballard's *Crash* concludes with a similarly ambivalent but possibly transcendent image of flight: "The aircraft rise from the runways of the airport, carrying the remnants of Vaughan's semen to the instrument panels and radiator grilles of a thousand crashing cars, the leg stances of a million passengers" (224).

92. Cronenberg, quoted in Gavin Smith, "Cronenberg: Mind Over Matter," 17.

93. Walter Benjamin, "The Storyteller," in *Illuminations*, ed. Hannah Arendt, 83–110; 101.

94. Benjamin, "The Storyteller," 84.

95. Jim Leach, review of *Crash*, *Film Studies Association of Canada Newsletter* 21.1 (Fall 1996): 19.

96. See Bordwell, "Art Cinema as a Mode of Film Practice," 57.

97. Seltzer, "Wound Culture," 3, 3, 5.

98. Michael Warner, "The Mass Public and the Mass Subject," in Bruce Robbins, ed., *The Phantom Public Sphere*, 234–56; 250, 251.

99. Hal Foster, "Death in America," *October* 75 (Winter 1996): 37–59; 58.

100. Barbara Creed, "Anal Wounds, Metallic Kisses," *Screen* 39.2 (Summer 1998): 175–79; 178, 179.

101. Kenneth Anger, *Hollywood Babylon*, 401. Anger's famous chronicle of Hollywood scandal has a concluding chapter on the death of Old Hollywood that includes photographs of Mansfield's wrecked car and dead dog—both of these images return in *Crash*, the former reproduced exactly as part of Vaughan's file of clippings.

102. Cronenberg, quoted in Gavin Smith, "Cronenberg: Mind Over Matter," 20.

103. David Bordwell, Janet Staiger, and Kristin Thompson, *The Classical Hollywood Cinema: Film Style and Mode of Production to 1960*, 14.

104. This work is indebted heavily to the scholarship of Richard Dyer. See his *Stars* and *Heavenly Bodies: Film Stars and Society*.

105. Miriam Hansen, *Babel and Babylon: Spectatorship in American Silent Film*, 246–47, 294, 294.

106. The "Canadian" context provided by Cronenberg's work might also shed new light on other Canadian (or at least Canadian-financed) horror films that have received only the slightest critical attention. These include Bob Clark's *Deathdream* (1972) and *Black Christmas* (1975) and the prolific genre work of William Fruet (including *Death Weekend* [1976], *Funeral Home* [1982], and *Spasms* [1983]), whose early credits include writing *Goin' Down the Road*.

AFTERWORD: 9/11/01, 8/6/45, GROUND ZERO

1. Jonathan Mandell, "History Is Impatient to Embrace Sept. 11," *New York Times*, November 18, 2001, AR1, 38.

2. Michiko Kakutani, "The Age of Irony Isn't Over After All," *New York Times*, October 9, 2001, E1, E5; E1.

3. See, for example, Andy Seiler, "Hollywood Goes to War Sooner Than Expected," *USA Today*, November 28, 2001 (*see* www.usatoday.com).

4. This incident, like so many others in the film, is taken directly from the source text. See Lt. Gen. Harold G. Moore and Joseph L. Galloway, *We Were Soldiers Once . . . and Young: Ia Drang, the Battle That Changed the War in Vietnam*, 190–91. In this context, it is worth noting that Randall Wallace is also the screenwriter of *Pearl Harbor* (Michael Bay, 2001).

5. For a fascinating, related discussion of these terms in another context, see Berlant, "The Face of America and the State of Emergency."

6. See, for example, Benjamin, "The Work of Art in the Age of Mechanical Reproduction," 234–35.

7. The durability of this connection could be glimpsed during the August 6, 2002, televised press conference held by New York City mayor Michael Bloomberg and New York State governor George Pataki. While announcing the plans to mark the one-year anniversary of 9/11, Pataki claimed that 9/11 is a date that "will live in hearts and minds" just as December 7, 1941, does.

8. The episode of director Ken Loach (representing the United Kingdom) comes closest to Imamura's in terms of placing the past and present in allegorical dialogue, but Loach relies upon more familiar documentary techniques that allow him to cut explicitly (rather than allegorically) between past and present. In addition to Loach and Imamura, the directors of *11'09"01* are Samira Makhmalbaf (Iran), Claude Lelouch (France), Youssef Chahine (Egypt), Danis Tanovic (Bosnia-Herzegovina), Idrissa Ouedraogo (Burkina Faso), Alejandro González Iñárritu (Mexico), Amos Gitai (Israel), Mira Nair (India), and Sean Penn (United States).

9. Benjamin, "Theses on the Philosophy of History," 255.

10. Imamura Shohei, quoted in "Interview with Shohei Imamura About the *11'09"01—September 11* Project" (*see* www.artificial-eye.com/dvd/ART240dvd/inter11.html).

11. Imamura's *Black Rain* is based on Ibuse Masuji's 1965 novel of the same name, but Imamura imports the character of Yuichi from Ibuse's 1950 short story "Yōhai taichō" ("Lieutenant Lookeast").

12. Benjamin, *The Origin of German Tragic Drama,* 166, 166.

Adams, Parveen. "Father, Can't You See I'm Filming?" In Joan Copjec, ed., *Supposing the Subject*, 185–200. London: Verso, 1994.

Agawa, Hiroyuki. *Devil's Heritage*. Trans. John M. Maki. Tokyo: Hokuseido Press, 1957.

Aitken, Ian. "Distraction and Redemption: Kracauer, Surrealism and Phenomenology." *Screen* 39.2 (Summer 1998): 124–40.

Alleg, Henri. *The Question*. New York: George Braziller, 1958.

Altman, Rick. *Film/Genre*. London: British Film Institute, 1999.

——. "A Semantic/Syntactic Approach to Film Genre." In Barry Keith Grant, ed., *Film Genre Reader*, 26–40.

"An American Tragedy." *60 Minutes*, CBS-TV, January 9, 1977.

Anderson, Benedict. *Imagined Communities: Reflections on the Origin and Spread of Nationalism* (1983). Rev. ed. London: Verso, 1994.

Anderson, Lindsay. "Get Out and Push!" In Tom Maschler, ed., *Declaration*, 154–78. London: MacGibbon and Kee, 1957.

Andrew, Dudley. "On Certain Tendencies of the French Cinema." In Denis Hollier, ed., *A New History of French Literature*, 993–1000. Cambridge: Harvard University Press, 1989.

——. *Film in the Aura of Art*. Princeton: Princeton University Press, 1984.

——. "The Unauthorized Auteur Today." In Jim Collins, Hilary Radner, and Ava Preacher Collins, eds., *Film Theory Goes to the Movies*, 77–85. New York: Routledge, 1993.

Anger, Kenneth. *Hollywood Babylon*. New York: Dell, 1975.

Antze, Paul and Michael Lambek, eds. *Tense Past: Cultural Essays in Trauma and Memory*. New York: Routledge, 1996.

Armes, Roy. *French Cinema Since 1946*. Vol. 2. London: A. Zwemmer, 1970.

Atwood, Margaret. *Survival: A Thematic Guide to Canadian Literature*. Toronto: House of Anansi Press, 1972.

Auster, Albert and Leonard Quart. *How the War Was Remembered: Hollywood and Vietnam*. New York: Praeger, 1988.

Ballard, J. G. *Crash* (1973). New York: Noonday Press, 1994.

——. "Introduction to the French Edition." *Crash* by J. G. Ballard (Paris: Calmann-Lévy, 1974). Reprinted in V. Vale and Andrea Juno, eds., *J. G. Ballard*, 96–98. San Francisco: Re/Search, 1988.

Balun, Chas. *The Connoisseur's Guide to the Contemporary Horror Film*. Westminster, Calif.: privately printed, 1983; rpt., Albany: Fantaco, 1992.

——. "I Spit in Your Face: Films That Bite." In Paul M. Sammon, ed., *Splatterpunks: Extreme Horror*, 167–83. New York: St. Martin's, 1990.

Barker, Martin, Jane Arthurs, and Ramaswami Harindranath. *The Crash Controversy: Censorship Campaigns and Film Reception*. London: Wallflower Press, 2001.

Barr, Charles. "Introduction: Amnesia and Schizophrenia." In Barr, ed., *All Our Yesterdays*, 1–30.

Barr, Charles, ed. *All Our Yesterdays: 90 Years of British Cinema*. London: British Film Institute, 1986.

Barthes, Roland. *Camera Lucida: Reflections on Photography* (1980). Trans. Richard Howard. New York: Hill and Wang, 1996.

Bataille, Georges. "Abattoir." *Documents* 6 (November 1929): 329

——. "Concerning the Accounts Given by the Residents of Hiroshima" (trans. Alan Keenan). In Caruth, ed., *Trauma: Explorations in Memory*, 221–35.

——. "Eye." In Georges Bataille, *Visions of Excess: Selected Writings, 1927–1939*, 17–19. Ed. Allan Stoekl. Trans. Allan Stoekl, Carl R. Lovitt, and Donald M. Leslie, Jr. Minneapolis: University of Minnesota Press, 1993.

Bates, Milton J. *The Wars We Took to Vietnam: Cultural Conflict and Storytelling*. Berkeley: University of California Press, 1996.

Baudrillard, Jean. "Crash." In *Simulacra and Simulation*, 111–19. Trans. Sheila Faria Glaser. Ann Arbor: University of Michigan Press, 1994.

Bazin, André. "The Ontology of the Photographic Image." In Bazin, *What Is Cinema?* Vol. 1:9–16. Ed. and trans. Hugh Gray. Berkeley: University of California Press, 1967.

Bazin, André, Jacques Doniol-Valcroze, Pierre Kast, Roger Leenhardt, Jacques Rivette, and Eric Rohmer. "Six Characters in Search of *auteurs*: A Discussion about the French Cinema" (trans. Liz Heron). In Hillier, ed., *Cahiers du Cinéma: The 1950s*, 31–46.

Beard, William. *The Artist as Monster: The Cinema of David Cronenberg*. Toronto: University of Toronto Press, 2001.

——. "The Canadianness of David Cronenberg." *Mosaic* 27.2 (June 1994): 113–33.

Beard, William and Piers Handling. "The Interview" (with David Cronenberg). In Handling, ed., *The Shape of Rage*, 159–98.

Belau, Linda and Petar Ramadanovic, eds. *Topologies of Trauma: Essays on the Limit of Knowledge and Memory*. New York: Other Press, 2002.

Bellows, Andy Masaki, Marina McDougall, and Brigitte Berg, eds. *Science Is Fiction: The Films of Jean Painlevé*. Cambridge: MIT Press, 2000.

Benayoun, Robert. "The King Is Naked." In Peter Graham, ed., *The New Wave*, 157–80. Garden City, N.Y.: Doubleday, 1968.

Benjamin, Walter. *The Arcades Project* (1927–1940). Trans. Howard Eiland and Kevin McLaughlin. Cambridge: Harvard University Press, 1999.

——. *The Origin of German Tragic Drama* (1928). Trans. John Osborne. London: Verso, 1996.

——. "A Short History of Photography" (1931). Trans. Stanley Mitchell. *Screen* 13.1 (Spring 1972): 5–26.

——. "On Some Motifs in Baudelaire" (1939). In Walter Benjamin, *Illuminations*, 155–200. Ed. Hannah Arendt. Trans. Harry Zohn. New York: Schocken, 1969.

——. "The Storyteller" (1936). In Walter Benjamin, *Illuminations*, 83–110. Ed. Hannah Arendt. Trans. Harry Zohn. New York: Schocken, 1969.

——. "Surrealism: The Last Snapshot of the European Intelligentsia" (1929). In Walter Benjamin, *Reflections*, 177–92. Ed. Peter Demetz. Trans. Edmund Jephcott. New York: Schocken, 1986.

——. "Theses on the Philosophy of History" (1940). In Walter Benjamin, *Illuminations*, 253–64. Ed. Hannah Arendt. Trans. Harry Zohn. New York: Schocken, 1969.

——. "Traumkitsch" (1927). In *Gesammelte Schriften*, Vol. II.2, Ed. Rolf Tiedemann and Herman Schweppenhäuser (Frankfurt: Suhrkamp, 1974), 620–22. Translated as "Dream Kitsch: Gloss on Surrealism," in *Walter Benjamin: Selected Writings*, vol. 2, ed. Michael W. Jennings, Howard Eiland, and Gary Smith, trans. Howard Eiland (Cambridge: Harvard University Press, 1999), 3–5.

——. "The Work of Art in the Age of Mechanical Reproduction" (1936). In Walter Benjamin, *Illuminations*, 217–52. Ed. Hannah Arendt. Trans. Harry Zohn. New York: Schocken, 1969.

Berger, John. "Photographs of Agony." In *About Looking*, 37–40. New York: Pantheon, 1980.

Berlant, Lauren. *The Anatomy of National Fantasy: Hawthorne, Utopia, and Everyday Life*. Chicago: University of Chicago Press, 1991.

——. "The Face of America and the State of Emergency." In *The Queen of America Goes to Washington City: Essays on Sex and Citizenship*, 175–220. Durham: Duke University Press, 1997.

Bersani, Leo. *The Culture of Redemption*. Cambridge: Harvard University Press, 1990.

——. *The Freudian Body: Psychoanalysis and Art*. New York: Columbia University Press, 1986.

Berton, Pierre. *Hollywood's Canada: The Americanization of Our National Image*. Toronto: McClelland and Stewart, 1975.

Bhabha, Homi K. "Introduction: Narrating the Nation." In Bhabha, ed., *Nation and Narration*, 1–7. London: Routledge, 1990.

Bills, Scott L., ed. *Kent State/May 4: Echoes Through a Decade*. Kent, Ohio: Kent State University Press, 1990.

Biskind, Peter. *Easy Riders, Raging Bulls: How the Sex-Drugs-and-Rock 'n' Roll Generation Saved Hollywood*. New York: Simon and Schuster, 1998.

Bly, Robert. "The Collapse of James Dickey." *The Sixties* 9 (Spring 1967): 70–79.

Boot, Andy. *Fragments of Fear: An Illustrated History of British Horror Films*. London: Creation Books, 1996.

Bordwell, David. "The Art Cinema as a Mode of Film Practice." *Film Criticism* 4.1 (1979): 56–64.

——. *Narration in the Fiction Film*. Madison: University of Wisconsin Press, 1985.

Bordwell, David, Janet Staiger, and Kristin Thompson. *The Classical Hollywood Cinema: Film Style and Mode of Production to 1960*. New York: Columbia University Press, 1985.

Botting, Fred and Scott Wilson. "Automatic Lover." *Screen* 39.2 (Summer 1998): 186–92.

Bourdieu, Pierre. *Distinction: A Social Critique of the Judgment of Taste* (1979). Trans. Richard Nice. Cambridge: Harvard University Press, 1994.

Brandt, Allan M. *No Magic Bullet: A Social History of Venereal Disease in the United States Since 1880*. New York: Oxford University Press, 1985.

Brashinsky, Michael. "The Spring, Defiled: Ingmar Bergman's *Virgin Spring* and Wes Craven's *Last House on the Left*." In Andrew Horton and Stuart Y. McDougal, eds., *Play it Again, Sam: Retakes on Remakes*, 162–71. Berkeley: University of California Press, 1998.

Breton, André. "*L'Age d'or*: Total Love." In Ado Kyrou, *Luis Buñuel: An Introduction*, 185–86. Trans. Adrienne Foulke. New York: Simon and Schuster, 1963.

———. "Manifesto of Surrealism." In *Manifestoes of Surrealism*, 1–47. Trans. Richard Seaver and Helen R. Lane. Ann Arbor: University of Michigan Press, 1994.

———. "Second Manifesto of Surrealism." In *Manifestoes of Surrealism*, 117–94. Trans. Richard Seaver and Helen R. Lane. Ann Arbor: University of Michigan Press, 1994.

British Broadcasting Corporation (BBC). "Artists at Work: Michael Powell and Leo Marks" (interview). In David Lazar, ed., *Michael Powell: Interviews*, 18–21. Jackson: University Press of Mississippi, 2003.

Broderick, Mick, ed. *Hibakusha Cinema: Hiroshima, Nagasaki, and the Nuclear Image in Japanese Film*. London: Kegan Paul International, 1996.

Bronfen, Elisabeth. "Killing Gazes, Killing in the Gaze: On Michael Powell's *Peeping Tom*." In Renata Salecl and Slavoj Zizek, eds., *Gaze and Voice as Love Objects*, 59–89. Durham: Duke University Press, 1996.

———. *Over Her Dead Body: Death, Femininity, and the Aesthetic*. New York: Routledge, 1992.

Brooks, Peter. "Melodrama, Body, Revolution." In Jacky Bratton, Jim Cook, and Christine Gledhill, eds., *Melodrama: Stage Picture Screen*, 11–24. London: British Film Institute, 1994.

———. *The Melodramatic Imagination: Balzac, Henry James, Melodrama, and the Mode of Excess*. New Haven: Yale University Press, 1976.

Brotchie, Alastair, ed. *Encyclopaedia Acephalica*. London: Atlas Press, 1995.

Buck-Morss, Susan. "Aesthetics and Anaesthetics: Walter Benjamin's Artwork Essay Reconsidered." *October* 62 (Fall 1992): 3–41.

———. *The Dialectics of Seeing: Walter Benjamin and the Arcades Project*. Cambridge: MIT Press, 1990.

———. *The Origin of Negative Dialectics: Theodor W. Adorno, Walter Benjamin, and the Frankfurt Institute*. New York: Free Press, 1977.

Burch, Noël. *To the Distant Observer: Form and Meaning in the Japanese Cinema*. Berkeley: University of California Press, 1979.

Burns, Margie. "*Easy Rider* and *Deliverance*, or, the Death of the Sixties." *University of Hartford Studies in Literature* 22.2–3 (1990): 44–58.

Bury, J. P. T. *France: The Insecure Peace: From Versailles to the Great Depression*. London: Macdonald, 1972.

Calder, Angus. *The People's War: Britain, 1939–45*. London: Jonathan Cape, 1969.

Calhoun, Richard J. and Robert W. Hill. *James Dickey*. Boston: Twayne, 1983.

Carroll, Noël. *The Philosophy of Horror, or Paradoxes of the Heart*. New York: Routledge, 1990.

Cartwright, Lisa. *Screening the Body: Tracing Medicine's Visual Culture*. Minneapolis: University of Minnesota Press, 1995.

Caruth, Cathy. *Unclaimed Experience: Trauma, Narrative, and History*. Baltimore: Johns Hopkins University Press, 1996.

Caruth, Cathy, ed. *Trauma: Explorations in Memory*. Baltimore: Johns Hopkins University Press, 1995.

Caughie, John, ed. *Theories of Authorship*. London: Routledge, 1993.

Cavanaugh, Carole. "A Working Ideology for Hiroshima: Imamura Shôhei's *Black Rain*." In Dennis Washburn and Carole Cavanaugh, eds., *Word and Image in Japanese Cinema*, 250–70. Cambridge: Cambridge University Press, 2001.

Cazdyn, Eric. *The Flash of Capital: Film and Geopolitics in Japan*. Durham: Duke University Press, 2002.

Chabrol, Claude. "Little Themes." In Peter Graham, ed., *The New Wave*, 73–77. Garden City, N.Y.: Doubleday, 1968.

Chapman, James. *The British at War: Cinema, State, and Propaganda, 1939–1945*. London: Tauris, 1998.

Charney, Leo and Vanessa R. Schwartz, eds. *Cinema and the Invention of Modern Life*. Berkeley: University of California Press, 1995.

Christie, Ian. *Arrows of Desire: The Films of Michael Powell and Emeric Pressburger*. London: Faber and Faber, 1994.

——. "*Blimp*, Churchill, and the State." In Christie, ed., *Powell, Pressburger, and Others*, 105–20.

——. "The Scandal of *Peeping Tom*." In Christie, ed., *Powell, Pressburger, and Others*, 53–59.

Christie, Ian, ed. *Powell, Pressburger, and Others*. London: British Film Institute, 1978.

Clifford, James. "On Ethnographic Surrealism." In *The Predicament of Culture: Twentieth-Century Ethnography, Literature, and Art*, 117–51. Cambridge: Harvard University Press, 1988.

Clover, Carol J. *Men, Women, and Chain Saws: Gender in the Modern Horror Film*. Princeton: Princeton University Press, 1992.

Cocteau, Jean. *The Art of Cinema*. Ed. André Bernard and Claude Gauteur. Trans. Robin Buss. London: Marion Boyars, 1992.

Cohen, Margaret. *Profane Illumination: Walter Benjamin and the Paris of Surrealist Revolution*. Berkeley: University of California Press, 1993.

Colls, Robert and Philip Dodd. "Representing the Nation: British Documentary Film, 1930–45." *Screen* 26.1 (January-February 1985): 21–33.

Conrad, Joseph. *Heart of Darkness* (1899). In *"Heart of Darkness" and Other Tales*, ed. Cedric Watts, 135–252. New York: Oxford University Press, 1992.

Cook, David. *Lost Illusions: American Cinema in the Shadow of Watergate and Vietnam, 1970–1979*. New York: Scribner's, 2000.

Cooper, D. E. "Looking Back on Anger." In Vernon Bogdanor and Robert Skidelsky, eds., *The Age of Affluence, 1951–1964*, 254–87. London: Macmillan, 1970.

Craven, Wes. "MPAA: The Horror in My Life." *Films in Review* 47.5—6 (September-October 1996): 34–39.

Creed, Barbara. "Anal Wounds, Metallic Kisses." *Screen* 39.2 (Summer 1998): 175–79.

Critcher, Chas. "Sociology, Cultural Studies, and the Post-War Working Class." In John Clarke, Chas Critcher, and Richard Johnson, eds., *Working-Class Culture*, 13–40. New York: St. Martin's, 1979.

Cronenberg, David. (Interviewed.) *See* William Beard and Piers Handling, "The Interview."

——. (Interviewed). *See* Gavin Smith, "Cronenberg, Mind Over Matter."

Crowther, Bosley. Review of *The Virgin Spring*, directed by Ingmar Bergman. *New York Times*, November 15, 1960.

Dawson, Graham and Bob West. "Our Finest Hour? The Popular Memory of World War II and the Struggle Over National Identity." In Geoff Hurd, ed., *National Fictions: World War Two in British Films and Television*, 8–13. London: British Film Institute, 1984.

de Beauvoir, Simone. *Force of Circumstance*. Trans. Richard Howard. New York: Putnam, 1965.

Delaney, Marshall [Robert Fulford]. "You Should Know How Bad This Film Is. After All, You Paid For It." *Saturday Night* (September 1975): 83–85.

Deleuze, Gilles and Félix Guattari. *A Thousand Plateaus: Capitalism and Schizophrenia* (1980). Trans. Brian Massumi. Minneapolis: University of Minnesota Press, 1987.

de Lorde, André. "Fear in Literature" (1927) (trans. Daniel Gerould). In Mel Gordon, *The Grand Guignol: Theatre of Fear and Terror*, 112–17.

D'Emilio, John and Estelle B. Freedman. *Intimate Matters: A History of Sexuality in America*. New York: Harper and Row, 1989.

Desser, David. *Eros Plus Massacre: An Introduction to the Japanese New Wave Cinema*. Bloomington: Indiana University Press, 1988.

——. "Japan: An Ambivalent Nation, an Ambivalent Cinema." *Swords and Ploughshares* 9.3–4 (Spring-Summer 1995) (*see* www.acdis.uiuc.edu/homepage_docs/pubs_docs/ S%26P_docs/S&P_Sp-Su_1995_docs/desser.html).

Dickey, James. *Deliverance* (screenplay). Carbondale: Southern Illinois University Press, 1982.

Dillard, R. H. W. "*Night of the Living Dead*: It's Not Like Just a Wind That's Passing Through." In Waller, ed., *American Horrors*, 14–29.

Domarchi, Jean, Jacques Doniol-Valcroze, Jean-Luc Godard, Pierre Kast, Jacques Rivette, and Eric Rohmer. "Hiroshima, notre amour" (trans. Liz Heron). In Hillier, ed., *Cahiers du Cinéma: The 1950s*, 59–70.

Dorland, Michael. "The Shadow of Canadian Cinema: Bruce Elder's Immodest Proposal." In Fetherling, ed., *Documents in Canadian Film*, 316–22.

——. *So Close to the State/s: The Emergence of Canadian Feature Film Policy*. Toronto: University of Toronto Press, 1998.

——. "Theses on Canadian Nationalism: In Memoriam George P. Grant." *CineAction* 16 (Spring 1989): 3–5.

Dower, John W. *Embracing Defeat: Japan in the Wake of World War II*. New York: Norton, 1999.

Durgnat, Raymond. *Franju*. Berkeley: University of California Press, 1968.

Dyer, Richard. *Heavenly Bodies: Film Stars and Society*. New York: St. Martin's, 1986.

——. *Stars*. London: British Film Institute, 1979.

——. "White." *Screen* 29.4 (Autumn 1988): 44–64.

Dyer, Richard and Ginette Vincendau, eds. *Popular European Cinema*. London: Routledge, 1992.

Ebert, Roger. "Guilty Pleasures." *Film Comment* 14.4 (July-August 1978): 49–51.

——. Review of *Last House on the Left*, directed by Wes Craven. *Chicago Sun-Times*, October 26, 1972, 58.

Elder, R. Bruce. "The Cinema We Need." In Fetherling, ed., *Documents in Canadian Film*, 260–71.

——. *Image and Identity: Reflections on Canadian Film and Culture*. Waterloo: Wilfrid Laurier University Press, 1989.

Elsaesser, Thomas. "Subject Positions, Speaking Positions: From *Holocaust, Our Hitler,* and *Heimat* to *Shoah* and *Schindler's List*." In Sobchack, ed., *The Persistence of History*, 145–83.

Evans, Gary. *In the National Interest: A Chronicle of the National Film Board of Canada from 1949 to 1989*. Toronto: University of Toronto Press, 1991.

——. *John Grierson and the National Film Board: The Politics of Wartime Propaganda*. Toronto: University of Toronto Press, 1984.

Farrell, Kirby. *Post-Traumatic Culture: Injury and Interpretation in the Nineties*. Baltimore: Johns Hopkins University Press, 1998.

Felman, Shoshana and Dori Laub. *Testimony: Crises of Witnessing in Literature, Psychoanalysis, and History*. New York: Routledge, 1992.

Fetherling, Douglas, ed. *Documents in Canadian Film*. Peterborough: Broadview Press, 1988.

Fieschi, Jean-André and André-S. Labarthe. "Nouvel entretien avec Georges Franju" (interview). *Cahiers du cinéma* 149 (November 1963): 1–17.

"Film Ratings' Clarity Fogged by Murky Meaning." *Hartford Courant*, September 3, 1972, 2B.

Fletcher, Angus. *Allegory: The Theory of a Symbolic Mode*. Ithaca: Cornell University Press, 1964.

Foster, Hal. "Armor Fou." *October* 56 (Spring 1991): 65–97.

——. *Compulsive Beauty*. Cambridge: MIT Press, 1995.

——. "Death in America." *October* 75 (Winter 1996): 37–59.

Fothergill, Robert. "Coward, Bully, or Clown: The Dream-Life of a Younger Brother." In Seth Feldman and Joyce Nelson, eds., *Canadian Film Reader*, 234–50. Toronto: Peter Martin, 1977.

Foucault, Michel. *The Birth of the Clinic: An Archaeology of Medical Perception*. Trans. A. M. Sheridan Smith. New York: Vintage, 1994.

——. *The History of Sexuality*. Vol. 1, *An Introduction* (1976). Trans. Robert Hurley. New York: Vintage, 1990.

Franju, Georges. (Interviewed.) *See* Fieschi, Jean-André and André-S. Labarthe.

——. (Interviewed). *See* Truffaut, François, "Entretien avec Georges Franju."

——. "Le Style de Fritz Lang." *Cahiers du cinéma* 101 (November 1959): 16–22. Translated as "The Style of Fritz Lang" (trans. Sallie Iannotti) in Leo Braudy and Morris Dickstein, eds., *Great Film Directors: A Critical Anthology*, 583–89 (New York: Oxford University Press, 1978).

Freud, Sigmund. *Beyond the Pleasure Principle* (1920). Ed. and trans. James Strachey. New York: Norton, 1989.

——. "Mourning and Melancholia" (1917). In *The Standard Edition of the Complete Psychological Works of Sigmund Freud* 14:243–58. Ed. and trans. James Strachey. London: Hogarth, 1957.

——. "Remembering, Repeating and Working-Through" (1914). In *The Standard Edition of the Complete Psychological Works of Sigmund Freud* 12:147–56. Ed. and trans. James Strachey. London: Hogarth, 1958.

Friedlander, Saul. *Reflections of Nazism: An Essay on Kitsch and Death* (1982). Trans. Thomas Weyr. Bloomington: Indiana University Press, 1993.

Friedlander, Saul, ed. *Probing the Limits of Representation: Nazism and the "Final Solution."* Cambridge: Harvard University Press, 1992.

Fussell, Paul. *The Great War and Modern Memory*. London: Oxford University Press, 1977.

Gamble, Andrew. *The Conservative Nation*. London: Routledge and Kegan Paul, 1974.

Gagne, Paul R. *The Zombies That Ate Pittsburgh: The Films of George A. Romero*. New York: Dodd, Mead, 1987.

Geraghty, Christine. *British Cinema in the Fifties: Gender, Genre, and the 'New Look.'* London: Routledge, 2000.

———. "Masculinity." In Geoff Hurd, ed., *National Fictions: World War Two in British Films and Television*, 63–67. London: British Film Institute, 1984.

Gitlin, Todd. *The Sixties: Years of Hope, Days of Rage*. New York: Bantam, 1987.

Gittings, Christopher E. *Canadian National Cinema*. London: Routledge, 2002.

Gledhill, Christine. "'An Abundance of Understatement': Documentary, Melodrama, and Romance." In Christine Gledhill and Gillian Swanson, eds., *Nationalising Femininity: Culture, Sexuality, and British Cinema in the Second World War*, 213–29. Manchester: Manchester University Press, 1996.

Goldberg, Vicki. *The Power of Photography: How Photographs Changed Our Lives*. New York: Abbeville Press, 1991.

Goodwin, James. "Akira Kurosawa and the Atomic Age." In Broderick, ed., *Hibakusha Cinema*, 178–202.

Gordon, Mel. *The Grand Guignol: Theatre of Fear and Terror*. New York: Amok Press, 1988.

Gozlan, Gérard. "In Praise of André Bazin." In Peter Graham, ed., *The New Wave*, 52–71. Garden City, N.Y.: Doubleday, 1968.

Granger, Derek. "Bring on the Ghouls." *Financial Times* (London), May 6, 1957, 14.

Grant, Barry Keith. "Introduction." Special Issue on Canadian Cinema. *Post Script* 15.1 (Fall 1995): 3–5.

———. "Taking Back the *Night of the Living Dead*: George Romero, Feminism, and the Horror Film." In Barry Keith Grant, ed., *The Dread of Difference*, 200–212.

Grant, Barry Keith, ed. *The Dread of Difference: Gender and the Horror Film*. Austin: University of Texas Press, 1996.

———. *Film Genre Reader*. Austin: University of Texas Press, 1986.

———. *Planks of Reason: Essays on the Horror Film*. Metuchen, N.J.: Scarecrow Press, 1984.

Grant, George. *Lament for a Nation: The Defeat of Canadian Nationalism* (1965). Ottawa: Carleton University Press, 1994.

Grierson, John. "A Film Policy for Canada" (1944). In Fetherling, ed., *Documents in Canadian Film*, 51–67.

"Guardian Angels." *New Yorker* (November 25, 1996): 47–48.

Gunning, Tom. "An Aesthetic of Astonishment: Early Film and the (In)credulous Spectator." In Linda Williams, ed., *Viewing Positions*, 114–33.

———. "The Cinema of Attraction: Early Film, Its Spectator, and the Avant-garde." *Wide Angle* 8 (Fall 1986): 63–70.

———. *The Films of Fritz Lang: Allegories of Vision and Modernity*. London: British Film Institute, 2000.

———. "The Horror of Opacity: The Melodrama of Sensation in the Plays of André de Lorde." In Jacky Bratton, Jim Cook, and Christine Gledhill, eds., *Melodrama: Stage Picture Screen*, 50–61. London: British Film Institute, 1994.

———. "'Those Drawn with a Very Fine Camel's Hair Brush': The Origins of Film Genres." *Iris* 20 (1995): 49–61.

Hallin, Daniel C. *The "Uncensored War": The Media and Vietnam.* New York: Oxford University Press, 1986.

Hammond, Paul. "Available Light." In Hammond, ed., *The Shadow and Its Shadow: Surrealist Writing on the Cinema*, 1–48. Edinburgh: Polygon, 1991.

Hamon, Hervé, and Patrick Rotman. *Les Porteurs de valises: La Résistance française á la guerre d'Algérie.* Paris: Albin Michel, 1979.

Handling, Piers. "A Canadian Cronenberg." In Handling, ed., *The Shape of Rage*, 98–114.

Handling, Piers, ed. *The Shape of Rage: The Films of David Cronenberg.* Toronto: General Publishing, 1983.

Hansen, Miriam. *Babel and Babylon: Spectatorship in American Silent Film.* Cambridge: Harvard University Press, 1991.

——. "Benjamin, Cinema, and Experience: 'The Blue Flower in the Land of Technology.'" *New German Critique* 40 (Winter 1987): 179–224.

——. "Introduction." In Kracauer, *Theory of Film: The Redemption of Physical Reality* (1960), vii–xlv. Princeton: Princeton University Press, 1997.

——. "The Mass Production of the Senses: Classical Cinema as Vernacular Modernism." In Christine Gledhill and Linda Williams, eds., *Reinventing Film Studies*, 332–50. New York: Oxford University Press, 2000.

——. "Of Mice and Ducks: Benjamin and Adorno on Disney." *South Atlantic Quarterly* 92.1 (Winter 1993): 27–61.

——. "*Schindler's List* Is Not *Shoah*: The Second Commandment, Popular Modernism, and Public Memory." *Critical Inquiry* 22 (Winter 1996): 292–312.

——. " 'With Skin and Hair': Kracauer's Theory of Film, Marseille 1940." *Critical Inquiry* 19 (Spring 1993): 437–69.

Hanssen, Beatrice. *Walter Benjamin's Other History: Of Stones, Animals, Human Beings, and Angels.* Berkeley: University of California Press, 2000.

Harcourt, Peter. *Movies and Mythologies: Towards a National Cinema.* Toronto: Canadian Broadcasting Corporation, 1977.

Hartigan, John. "Reading Trash: *Deliverance* and the Poetics of White Trash." *Visual Anthropology Review* 8.2 (Fall 1992): 8–15.

Hawkins, Joan. *Cutting Edge: Art-Horror and the Horrific Avant-garde.* Minneapolis: University of Minnesota Press, 2000.

Hayward, Susan. *French National Cinema.* London: Routledge, 1993.

Hebdige, Dick. *Subculture: The Meaning of Style.* London: Methuen, 1979.

Hein, Laura and Mark Selden. "Commemoration and Silence: Fifty Years of Remembering the Bomb in America and Japan." In Hein and Selden, eds., *Living with the Bomb: American and Japanese Cultural Conflicts in the Nuclear Age*, 3–34. Armonk, N.Y.: M. E. Sharpe, 1997.

Hellmann, John. *American Myth and the Legacy of Vietnam.* New York: Columbia University Press, 1986.

Herman, Judith. *Trauma and Recovery* (1992). New York: Basic Books, 1997.

Hess, John. "*La Politique des auteurs*, Part One: World View as Aesthetic." *Jump Cut* 1 (May-June 1974): 19–22.

——. "*La Politique des auteurs*, Part Two: Truffaut's Manifesto," *Jump Cut* 2 (July-August 1974): 20–22.

Higashi, Sumiko. "*Night of the Living Dead*: A Horror Film about the Horrors of the Vietnam Era." In Linda Dittmar and Gene Michaud, eds., *From Hanoi to Hollywood: The Vietnam War in American Film*, 175–88. New Brunswick: Rutgers University Press, 1990.

Higgins, Lynn A. *New Novel, New Wave, New Politics: Fiction and the Representation of History in Postwar France*. Lincoln: University of Nebraska Press, 1996.

Higonnet, Margaret R. "Women in the Forbidden Zone: War, Women, and Death." In Sarah Webster Goodwin and Elisabeth Bronfen, eds., *Death and Representation*, 192–212. Baltimore: Johns Hopkins University Press, 1993.

Higson, Andrew. "'Britain's Outstanding Contribution to the Film': The Documentary-Realist Tradition." In Barr, ed., *All Our Yesterdays*, 72–97.

——. "The Concept of National Cinema." *Screen* 30.4 (Autumn 1989): 36–46.

——. "The Limiting Imagination of National Cinema." In Hjort and MacKenzie, eds., *Cinema and Nation*, 63–74.

——. "Space, Place, Spectacle: Landscape and Townscape in the 'Kitchen Sink' Film." In Higson, ed., *Dissolving Views: Key Writings on British Cinema*, 133–56. London: Cassell, 1996.

Hill, Derek. "Cheap Thrills." *Tribune* (London), April 29, 1960, 11.

——. "The Face of Horror." *Sight and Sound* 28.1 (Winter 1958–59): 6–11.

Hill, John. *Sex, Class, and Realism: British Cinema, 1956–1963*. London: British Film Institute, 1986.

Hillier, Jim. "Introduction." In Hillier, ed., *Cahiers du Cinéma: The 1950s*, 1–17.

Hillier, Jim, ed. *Cahiers du Cinéma: The 1950s*. Cambridge: Harvard University Press, 1985.

Hirano, Kyoko. "Depiction of the Atomic Bombings in Japanese Cinema During the U.S. Occupation Period." In Broderick, ed., *Hibakusha Cinema*, 103–119.

——. *Mr. Smith Goes to Tokyo: Japanese Cinema Under the American Occupation, 1945–1952*. Washington, D.C.: Smithsonian Institution Press, 1992.

Hjort, Mette and Scott MacKenzie, eds. *Cinema and Nation*. London: Routledge, 2000.

Hoberman, J. *The Dream Life: Movies, Media, and the Mythology of the Sixties*. New York: New Press, 2003.

Hoberman, J. and Jonathan Rosenbaum. *Midnight Movies*. New York: Harper and Row, 1983.

Hogan, Michael J., ed. *Hiroshima in History and Memory*. Cambridge: Cambridge University Press, 1996.

Hoggart, Richard. *The Uses of Literacy: Changing Patterns in English Mass Culture*. Fair Lawn, N.J.: Essential Books, 1957.

Hollier, Denis. *Against Architecture: The Writings of Georges Bataille*. Trans. Betsy Wing. Cambridge: MIT Press, 1995.

Houston, Penelope. "Room at the Top?" *Sight and Sound* 28.2 (Spring 1959): 56–59.

Hutchings, Peter. *Hammer and Beyond: The British Horror Film*. Manchester: Manchester University Press, 1993.

Igarashi, Yoshikuni. *Bodies of Memory: Narratives of War in Postwar Japanese Culture, 1945–1970*. Princeton: Princeton University Press, 2000.

Imamura, Shohei. "Interview with Shohei Imamura About the *11'09"01—September 11* Project" (*see* www.artificial-eye.com/dvd/ART240dvd/inter11.html).

Inoura, Yoshinobu and Toshio Kawatake. *The Traditional Theater of Japan*. New York: Weatherhill, 1981.

Jameson, Fredric. "Class and Allegory in Contemporary Mass Culture: *Dog Day Afternoon* as a Political Film." In *Signatures of the Visible*, 35–54. New York: Routledge, 1990.

Jeffords, Susan. *The Remasculinization of America: Gender and the Vietnam War*. Bloomington: Indiana University Press, 1989.

Joe (review), directed by John G. Avildsen. *Variety*, July 15, 1970.

Kael, Pauline. *I Lost It at the Movies*. New York: Bantam Books, 1966.

Kaes, Anton. *From "Hitler" to "Heimat": The Return of History as Film*. Cambridge: Harvard University Press, 1992.

Kakutani, Michiko. "The Age of Irony Isn't Over After All." *New York Times*, October 9, 2001, E1, E5.

Kaplan, Alice. *The Collaborator: The Trial and Execution of Robert Brasillach*. Chicago: University of Chicago Press, 2000.

Kaplan, Alice Yaeger. *Reproductions of Banality: Fascism, Literature, and French Intellectual Life*. Minneapolis: University of Minnesota Press, 1986.

Kaplan, E. Ann and Ban Wang, eds. *Trauma and Cinema: Cross-Cultural Explorations*. Hong Kong: Hong Kong University Press, 2004.

Kendrick, Walter. *The Thrill of Fear: 250 Years of Scary Entertainment*. New York: Grove Weidenfeld, 1991.

"The Kent State Four." *National Review* (May 18, 1971): 514–16.

Kermode, Mark and Julian Petley. "Road Rage." *Sight and Sound* 7.6 (June 1997): 16–18.

King, Geoff. *New Hollywood Cinema: An Introduction*. London: Tauris, 2002.

Knee, Adam. "Generic Change in the Cinema." *Iris* 20 (1995): 31–39.

Komparu, Kunio. *The Noh Theater: Principles and Perspectives*. Trans. Jane Corddry. New York: Weatherhill, 1983.

Kracauer, Siegfried. "Photography" (1927). In Kracauer, *The Mass Ornament: Weimar Essays*, 47–63. Ed. and trans. Thomas Y. Levin. Cambridge: Harvard University Press, 1995.

——. *Theory of Film: The Redemption of Physical Reality*. New York: Oxford University Press, 1960.

Kroker, Arthur. *Technology and the Canadian Mind: Innis/McLuhan/Grant*. New York: St. Martin's, 1984.

Kurosawa, Akira. *Something Like an Autobiography* (1982). Trans. Audie E. Bock. New York: Vintage, 1983.

LaCapra, Dominick. *History and Memory After Auschwitz*. Ithaca: Cornell University Press, 1998.

——. *Representing the Holocaust: History, Theory, Trauma*. Ithaca: Cornell University Press, 1994.

——. "Trauma, Absence, Loss." *Critical Inquiry* 25 (Summer 1999): 696–727.

——. *Writing History, Writing Trauma*. Baltimore: Johns Hopkins University Press, 2001.

Landy, Marcia. *British Genres: Cinema and Society, 1930–1960*. Princeton: Princeton University Press, 1991.

——. *Cinematic Uses of the Past.* Minneapolis: University of Minnesota Press, 1996.

Landy, Marcia, ed. *The Historical Film: History and Memory in Media.* New Brunswick: Rutgers University Press, 2001.

Lane, Anthony. "Off the Road." *New Yorker* (March 31, 1997): 106–107.

Lang, Berel. *Holocaust Representation: Art Within the Limits of History and Ethics.* Baltimore: Johns Hopkins University Press, 2000.

Lant, Antonia. *Blackout: Reinventing Women for Wartime British Cinema.* Princeton: Princeton University Press, 1991.

Lastra, James. "Why Is This Absurd Picture Here?: Ethnology/Equivocation/Buñuel." *October* 89 (Summer 1999): 51–68.

Leach, Jim. "The Body Snatchers: Genre and Canadian Cinema." In Barry Keith Grant, ed., *Film Genre Reader*, 357–69.

——. "North of Pittsburgh: Genre and National Cinema from a Canadian Perspective." In Barry Keith Grant, ed., *Film Genre Reader II*, 474–93. Austin: University of Texas Press, 1995.

——. Review of *Crash*, directed by David Cronenberg. *Film Studies Association of Canada Newsletter* 21.1 (Fall 1996): 19.

Leblanc, Gérard, Pierre Gaudin, and Françoise Morier, eds. *Georges Franju, Cineaste.* Paris: Maison de la Villette, 1992.

"Les Dix meilleurs films de l'anne." *Cahiers du cinéma* 104 (February 1960): 1–2

"Les Dix meilleurs films de l'anne." *Cahiers du cinéma* 116 (February 1961): 1–2.

Lev, Peter. *The Euro-American Cinema.* Austin: University of Texas Press, 1993.

Levin, G. Roy, ed. *Documentary Explorations.* Garden City, N.Y.: Doubleday, 1971.

Leys, Ruth. *Trauma: A Genealogy.* Chicago: University of Chicago Press, 2000.

Lippit, Akira Mizuta. "Antigraphy: Notes on Atomic Writing and Postwar Japanese Cinema." *Review of Japanese Culture and Society* 10 (December 1998): 56–65.

Lipset, Seymour Martin. *Continental Divide: The Values and Institutions of the United States and Canada.* New York: Routledge, 1990.

Lovell, Terry. "Landscapes and Stories in 1960s British Realism." In Andrew Higson, ed., *Dissolving Views: Key Writings on British Cinema*, 157–77. London: Cassell, 1996.

Lyotard, Jean-François. *The Differend: Phrases in Dispute* (1983). Trans. Georges Van Den Abbeele. Minneapolis: University of Minnesota Press, 1988.

Manceaux, Michèle. "People." In Truffaut, *The 400 Blows*, 215–23. New York: Grove Press, 1969.

Mandell, Jonathan. "History Is Impatient to Embrace Sept. 11." *New York Times*, November 18, 2001, AR1, 38.

Maran, Rita. *Torture: The Role of Ideology in the French-Algerian War.* New York: Praeger, 1989.

Marks, Leo. *Between Silk and Cyanide: A Codemaker's War, 1941–1945.* New York: Touchstone, 2000.

——. (Interviewed.) *See* Chris Rodley, "Introduction."

——. *Peeping Tom* (screenplay). London: Faber and Faber, 1998.

Marrus, Michael R. and Robert O. Paxton. *Vichy France and the Jews* (1981). Stanford: Stanford University Press, 1995.

Marwick, Arthur. *A History of the Modern British Isles, 1914–1999.* Oxford: Blackwell, 2000.

McCarty, John. *Splatter Movies: Breaking the Last Taboo of the Screen*. New York: St. Martin's, 1984.

McDonagh, Maitland. *Filmmaking on the Fringe*. New York: Citadel, 1995.

McDonald, Keiko. "Introduction." Special Issue on Kurosawa Akira. *Post Script* 20.1 (Fall 2000): 3–6.

——. *Japanese Classical Theater in Films*. Rutherford: Fairleigh Dickinson University Press, 1994.

McGregor, Gaile. "Grounding the Countertext: David Cronenberg and the Ethnospecificity of Horror." *Canadian Journal of Film Studies* 2.1 (1993): 43–62.

McLarty, Lianne. "'Beyond the Veil of the Flesh': Cronenberg and the Disembodiment of Horror." In Barry Keith Grant, ed., *The Dread of Difference*, 231–52.

Mellen, Joan. *Voices from the Japanese Cinema*. New York: Liveright, 1975.

Metz, Christian. "Photography and Fetish." *October* 34 (Fall 1985): 81–90.

Meyers, Richard. *For One Week Only: The World of Exploitation Films*. Piscataway, N.J.: New Century, 1983.

Michener, James A. *Kent State: What Happened and Why*. New York: Random House, 1971.

Miller, James. *"Democracy Is in the Streets": From Port Huron to the Siege of Chicago*. New York: Simon and Schuster, 1987.

Moor, Andrew. "No Place Like Home: Powell, Pressburger, Utopia." In Robert Murphy, ed., *The British Cinema Book*, 109–15. 2d ed. London: British Film Institute, 2001.

Moore, Lt. Gen. Harold G.. and Joseph L. Galloway. *We Were Soldiers Once . . . and Young: Ia Drang, the Battle That Changed the War in Vietnam*. New York: HarperCollins, 1993.

Morris, Peter. "Backwards to the Future: John Grierson's Film Policy for Canada." In Gene Walz, ed., *Flashback: People and Institutions in Canadian Film History*, 17–35. Montreal: Mediatexte, 1986.

——. *David Cronenberg: A Delicate Balance*. Toronto: ECW Press, 1994.

——. *Embattled Shadows: A History of Canadian Cinema*. Montreal: McGill-Queen's University Press, 1978.

Morrison, Blake. *The Movement: English Poetry and Fiction of the 1950s*. Oxford: Oxford University Press, 1980.

Mosley, Leonard. "Let's Not Peddle 'Sex' that Suits this Peeping Tom." *Daily Express* (London), April 18, 1960, 12.

Mulvey, Laura. Liner notes and audio commentary. *Peeping Tom*, directed by Michael Powell. Criterion Collection, Voyager, 1994. Laserdisc.

Murphy, Robert. *British Cinema and the Second World War*. London: Continuum, 2000.

——. *Sixties British Cinema*. London: British Film Institute, 1992.

Nägele, Rainer. *Theater, Theory, Speculation: Walter Benjamin and the Scenes of Modernity*. Baltimore: Johns Hopkins University Press, 1991.

Napier, Susan J. "Panic Sites: The Japanese Imagination of Disaster from *Godzilla* to *Akira*." In John Whittier Treat, ed., *Contemporary Japan and Popular Culture*, 235–62. Honolulu: University of Hawai'i Press, 1996.

Narboni, Jean and Tom Milne, eds. *Godard on Godard*. Trans. Tom Milne. New York: Da Capo Press, 1986.

Neale, Steve. "Art Cinema as Institution." *Screen* 22.1 (1981): 11–39.

Nelson, Joyce. *The Colonized Eye: Rethinking the Grierson Legend*. Toronto: Between the Lines, 1988.

Night of the Living Dead (review), directed by George A. Romero. *Variety*, October 16, 1968.

Noriega, Chon A. "Godzilla and the Japanese Nightmare: When *Them!* Is U.S." In Broderick, ed., *Hibakusha Cinema*, 54–74.

Nowell-Smith, Geoffrey. "Art Cinema." In Nowell-Smith, ed., *The Oxford History of World Cinema*, 567–75. New York: Oxford University Press, 1996.

Nye, Robert A. *Crime, Madness, and Politics in Modern France: The Medical Concept of National Decline*. Princeton: Princeton University Press, 1984.

Orr, James J. *The Victim as Hero: Ideologies of Peace and National Identity in Postwar Japan*. Honolulu: University of Hawai'i Press, 2001.

Oshima, Nagisa. "In Protest Against the Massacre of *Night and Fog in Japan*." In Nagisa Oshima, *Cinema, Censorship, and the State: The Writings of Nagisa Oshima, 1956–1978*. Ed. Annette Michelson, trans. Dawn Lawson, 54–58. Cambridge: MIT Press, 1992.

——. "Is It a Breakthrough? (The Modernists of Japanese Film)." In Nagisa Oshima, *Cinema, Censorship, and the State: The Writings of Nagisa Oshima, 1956–1978*. Ed. Annette Michelson, trans. Dawn Lawson, 26–35. Cambridge: MIT Press, 1992.

——. "On the Attitude of Film Theorists." In Nagisa Oshima, *Cinema, Censorship, and the State: The Writings of Nagisa Oshima, 1956–1978*. Ed. Annette Michelson, trans. Dawn Lawson, 133–43. Cambridge: MIT Press, 1992.

Outram, Dorinda. *The Body and the French Revolution: Sex, Class, and Political Culture*. New Haven: Yale University Press, 1989.

Packard, George R., III. *Protest in Tokyo: The Security Treaty Crisis of 1960*. Princeton: Princeton University Press, 1966.

Palmer, R. Barton. "What Was New in the British New Wave?: Re-Viewing *Room at the Top*." *Journal of Popular Film and Television* 14.3 (Fall 1986): 125–35.

Parker, Andrew. "Grafting David Cronenberg: Monstrosity, AIDS Media, National/Sexual Difference." In Marjorie Garber, Jann Matlock, and Rebecca L. Walkowitz, eds., *Media Spectacles*, 209–31. London: Routledge, 1993.

Pateman, Carole. *The Sexual Contract*. Stanford: Stanford University Press, 1988.

Paul, William. *Laughing Screaming: Modern Hollywood Horror and Comedy*. New York: Columbia University Press, 1994.

Pearson, Patricia. "Crash, Bam, Thank You, Ma'am." *Saturday Night* (October 1996): 119–22.

Pendakur, Manjunath. *Canadian Dreams and American Control: The Political Economy of the Canadian Film Industry*. Detroit: Wayne State University Press, 1990.

Pensky, Max. *Melancholy Dialectics: Walter Benjamin and the Play of Mourning* (1993). Amherst: University of Massachusetts Press, 2001.

Petley, Julian. "The Lost Continent." In Barr, ed., *All Our Yesterdays*, 98–119.

Pevere, Geoff. "Images of Men." *Canadian Forum* (February 1985): 24–28.

——. "Middle of Nowhere: Ontario Movies After 1980." *Post Script* 15.1 (Fall 1995): 9–22.

Pirie, David. *A Heritage of Horror: The English Gothic Cinema, 1946–1972*. New York: Avon, 1973.

Pomerance, Murray. Review of *Crash*, directed by David Cronenberg. *Film Studies Association of Canada Newsletter* 21.1 (Fall 1996): 20.

Powell, Dilys. "Dilys Powell's Film of the Week." *Sunday Times* (London), June 19, 1994, 46.

——. *Films Since 1939*. London: Longmans, Green, 1947.

——. "Focus-Pocus and Worse." *Sunday Times* (London) magazine (April 10, 1960): 25.

Powell, Michael. (Interviewed.) *See* British Broadcasting Corporation, "Artists at Work."

——. (Interviewed.) *See* Bertrand Tavernier, "An Interview with Michael Powell."

——. *A Life in Movies: An Autobiography*. London: Heinemann, 1986.

——. *Million Dollar Movie*. New York: Random House, 1992.

Prince, Stephen. "Graphic Violence in the Cinema: Origins, Aesthetic Design, and Social Effects." In Prince, ed., *Screening Violence*, 1–44. New Brunswick: Rutgers University Press, 2000.

——. *The Warrior's Camera: The Cinema of Akira Kurosawa*. Rev. ed. Princeton: Princeton University Press, 1999.

Quigly, Isabel. "Filthy Pictures." *The Spectator* (April 15, 1960): 544–46.

——. "On the Make." *The Spectator* (January 30, 1959): 144–45.

——. "The Small Savages." *The Spectator* (February 5, 1960): 179–82.

Rabaté, Jean-Michel, ed. *Writing the Image After Roland Barthes*. Philadelphia: University of Pennsylvania Press, 1997.

Raine, Michael. "Contemporary Japan as Punishment Room in Kon Ichikawa's *Shokei no heya*." In James Quandt, ed., *Kon Ichikawa*, 175–89. Toronto: Cinematheque Ontario, 2001.

Ramsay, Christine. "Canadian Narrative Cinema from the Margins: 'The Nation' and Masculinity in *Goin' Down the Road*." *Canadian Journal of Film Studies* 2.2–3 (1993): 27–49.

——. Liner notes. *Goin' Down the Road*, directed by Don Shebib. Seville Pictures, 2002. DVD.

Rattigan, Neil. "The Last Gasp of the Middle Class: British War Films of the 1950s." In Wheeler Winston Dixon, ed., *Re-Viewing British Cinema, 1900–1992: Essays and Interviews*, 143–53. Albany: State University of New York Press, 1994.

Rayns, Tony. "*Peeping Tom*" (review). In John Pym, ed., *Time Out Film Guide*, 618. 5th ed. Harmondsworth: Penguin, 1996.

Richie, Donald. *The Films of Akira Kurosawa*. 3d ed. Berkeley: University of California Press, 1996.

——. "'Mono no aware': Hiroshima in Film." In Broderick, ed., *Hibakusha Cinema*, 20–37.

——. Interview with the author. June 8, 2000, Tokyo, Japan.

Rock, Paul and Stanley Cohen. "The Teddy Boy." In Vernon Bogdanor and Robert Skidelsky, eds., *The Age of Affluence, 1951–1964*, 288–320. London: Macmillan, 1970.

Rodley, Chris. "Introduction: Leo Marks Interviewed by Chris Rodley." In Marks, *Peeping Tom*, vii–xxvi.

Rodley, Chris, ed. *Cronenberg on Cronenberg*. London: Faber and Faber, 1997.

Rogin, Michael. "Liberal Society and the Indian Question." In Rogin, *Ronald Reagan, the Movie*, 134–68.

——. *Ronald Reagan, the Movie and Other Episodes in Political Demonology*. Berkeley: University of California Press, 1988.

Romero, George A. "Preface." In John Russo, *Night of the Living Dead* (novelization) (1974), 5–14. New York: Pocket Books, 1981.

Room at the Top pressbook, collection of the British Film Institute.

Rosenbaum, Jonathan. "Real Horror Shows." *Chicago Reader*, November 24, 1995, 43.

Rosenstone, Robert, ed. *Revisioning History: Film and the Construction of a New Past.* Princeton: Princeton Univsersity Press, 1995.

Ross, Kristin. *Fast Cars, Clean Bodies: Decolonization and the Reordering of French Culture.* Cambridge: MIT Press, 1995.

Roud, Richard. *A Passion for Films: Henri Langlois and the Cinémathèque Française.* New York: Viking Press, 1983.

Rousso, Henry. *The Vichy Syndrome: History and Memory in France Since 1944.* Trans. Arthur Goldhammer. Cambridge: Harvard University Press, 1991.

Sanjek, David. "Dr. Hobbes's Parasites: Victims, Victimization, and Gender in David Cronenberg's *Shivers*." *Cinema Journal* 36.1 (Fall 1996): 55–74.

Santner, Eric L. "History Beyond the Pleasure Principle: Some Thoughts on the Representation of Trauma." In Friedlander, ed., *Probing the Limits of Representation*, 143–54.

——. *Stranded Objects: Mourning, Memory, and Film in Postwar Germany.* Ithaca: Cornell University Press, 1990.

Sartre, Jean-Paul. "Introduction: 'A Victory.'" In Henri Alleg, *The Question*, 13–36.

Sato, Tadao. *Currents in Japanese Cinema.* Trans. Gregory Barrett. Tokyo: Kodansha International, 1982.

Schaefer, Eric. *"Bold! Daring! Shocking! True!": A History of Exploitation Films, 1919–1959.* Durham: Duke University Press, 1999.

——. "Resisting Refinement: The Exploitation Film and Self-Censorship." *Film History* 6 (1994): 293–313.

Schivelbusch, Wolfgang. *The Culture of Defeat: On National Trauma, Mourning, and Recovery.* Trans. Jefferson Chase. New York: Metropolitan Books, 2003.

Schlesinger, Benjamin, ed. *Sexual Behaviour in Canada: Patterns and Problems.* Toronto: University of Toronto Press, 1977.

Schneider, Steven Jay, ed. *Fear Without Frontiers: Horror Cinema Across the Globe.* Godalming, Eng.: FAB Press, 2003.

Schoell, William. *Stay Out of the Shower: 25 Years of Shocker Films Beginning with "Psycho."* New York: Dembner Books, 1985.

Schwarz-Bart, André. *The Last of the Just* (1959). Trans. Stephen Becker. New York: Atheneum, 1961.

Scorsese, Martin. "Internal Metaphors, External Horror." In Wayne Drew, ed., *David Cronenberg*, 54. London: British Film Institute, 1984.

[Scott, J. D.]. "In the Movement." *The Spectator* (October 1, 1954): 399–400.

Scott, Jay. "Burnout in the Great White North." In Seth Feldman, ed., *Take Two*, 29–35. Toronto: Irwin, 1984.

Seiler, Andy. "Hollywood Goes to War Sooner Than Expected." *USA Today*, November 28, 2001 (*see* www.usatoday.com).

Seltzer, Mark. "Wound Culture: Trauma in the Pathological Public Sphere." *October* 80 (Spring 1997): 3–26.

Sharrett, Christopher. "The American Apocalypse: Scorsese's *Taxi Driver*." In Sharrett, ed., *Crisis Cinema: The Apocalyptic Idea in Postmodern Narrative Film*, 221–35. Washington, D.C.: Maisonneuve Press, 1993.

Shaviro, Steven. *The Cinematic Body*. Minneapolis: University of Minnesota Press, 1993.

Shindo, Kaneto. Interview with the author, August 28, 2000, Montreal, Canada. Trans. Yuka Sakano, with additional transcription by JunkoYamamoto.

——. E-mail communication with the author, July 24, 2002. Trans. Yuka Sakano.

Silverman, Kaja. *The Acoustic Mirror: The Female Voice in Psychoanalysis and Cinema*. Bloomington: Indiana University Press, 1988.

——. *Male Subjectivity at the Margins*. New York: Routledge, 1992.

Sinclair, Iain. "Homeopathic Horror." *Sight and Sound* 5.4 (April 1995): 24–27.

Siskel, Gene. "Present Shock." *Chicago Tribune*, October 31, 1972, 4.

Skal, David J. *The Monster Show: A Cultural History of Horror*. New York: Penguin, 1993.

Slotkin, Richard. *Regeneration Through Violence: The Mythology of the American Frontier, 1600–1860*. Middletown, Conn.: Wesleyan University Press, 1973.

Smith, Gavin. "Cronenberg: Mind Over Matter." *Film Comment* 33.2 (March-April 1997): 14–29.

Smith, Murray. "A(moral) Monstrosity." In Michael Grant, ed., *The Modern Fantastic: The Films of David Cronenberg*, 69–83. Westport, Conn.: Praeger, 2000.

Sobchack, Vivian. *The Address of the Eye: A Phenomenology of Film Experience*. Princeton: Princeton University Press, 1992.

——. "Bringing It All Back Home: Family Economy and Generic Exchange." In Waller, ed., *American Horrors*, 175–94.

Sobchack, Vivian, ed. *The Persistence of History: Cinema, Television, and the Modern Event*. New York: Routledge, 1996.

Sontag, Susan. *On Photography*. New York: Farrar, Straus, and Giroux, 1977.

Spigel, Lynn and Michael Curtin, eds. *The Revolution Wasn't Televised: Sixties Television and Social Conflict*. New York: Routledge, 1997.

Steedman, Carolyn Kay. *Landscape for a Good Woman: A Story of Two Lives*. New Brunswick: Rutgers University Press, 1994.

Steene, Birgitta. *Ingmar Bergman: A Guide to References and Resources*. Boston: G. K. Hall, 1987.

Stein, Elliott. Review of *Night of the Living Dead*, directed by George A. Romero. *Sight and Sound* 39.2 (Spring 1970): 105.

——. "'A Very Tender Film, a Very Nice One': Michael Powell's *Peeping Tom*." *Film Comment* 15.5 (September-October 1979): 57–59.

Stern, Lesley. *The Scorsese Connection*. Bloomington: Indiana University Press, 1995.

Stewart, Garrett. "Photo-gravure: Death, Photography, and Film Narrative." *Wide Angle* 9.1 (1987): 11–31.

Stewart, Kathleen. *A Space on the Side of the Road: Cultural Poetics in an "Other" America*. Princeton: Princeton University Press, 1996.

Stich, Sidra. "Anxious Visions." In Stich, ed., *Anxious Visions: Surrealist Art*, 11–175. Berkeley: University Art Museum, 1990.

Sturken, Marita. *Tangled Memories: The Vietnam War, the AIDS Epidemic, and the Politics of Remembering*. Berkeley: University of California Press, 1997.

Szulkin, David A. *Wes Craven's "Last House on the Left": The Making of a Cult Classic*. Guildford, Eng.: FAB Press, 1997.

Talbott, John. *The War Without a Name: France in Algeria, 1954–1962.* New York: Knopf, 1980.

Taylor, David. "Masks, Masques, and the Illusion of Reality: The Films of Georges Franju." In Stefan Jaworzyn, ed., *Shock Xpress 2*, 6–16. London: Titan Books, 1994.

Tavernier, Bertrand. "An Interview with Michael Powell." Trans. Gina Honigford. In David Lazar, ed., *Michael Powell: Interviews*, 25–43. Jackson: University Press of Mississippi, 2003.

Taylor, John. *Body Horror: Photojournalism, Catastrophe, and War.* Manchester: Manchester University Press, 1998.

Testa, Bart. Review of *Crash*, directed by David Cronenberg. *Film Studies Association of Canada Newsletter* 21.1 (Fall 1996): 15–17.

——. "Technology's Body: Cronenberg, Genre, and the Canadian Ethos." *Post Script* 15.1 (Fall 1995): 38–56.

Thompson, Howard. Review of *Last House on the Left*, directed by Wes Craven. *New York Times*, December 22, 1972, 21.

Thwaite, Anthony. "Out of Bondage." *New Statesman* (September 11, 1970): 310–11.

Todeschini, Maya Morioka. "'Death and the Maiden': Female *Hibakusha* as Cultural Heroines and the Politics of A-bomb Memory." In Broderick, ed., *Hibakusha Cinema*, 222–52.

Török, Jean-Paul. "H-Pictures." *Positif* 39 (May 1961): 54–58.

——. "H-Pictures (II)." *Positif* 40 (July 1961): 41–49.

——. "'Look at the Sea': *Peeping Tom*" (trans. Tom Milne). In Christie, ed., *Powell, Pressburger, and Others*, 59–62.

Totman, Conrad. *A History of Japan.* Oxford: Blackwell, 2000.

Treat, John Whittier. *Writing Ground Zero: Japanese Literature and the Atomic Bomb.* Chicago: University of Chicago Press, 1995.

Truffaut, François. "A Certain Tendency of the French Cinema" (1954). In Bill Nichols, ed., *Movies and Methods*, 224–37. Berkeley: University of California Press, 1976.

——. "Entretien avec Georges Franju" (interview). *Cahiers du cinéma* 101 (November 1959): 1–12. Excerpt translated as "Interview with Georges Franju," in Truffaut, *The 400 Blows*, 208–212.

——. *The Films in My Life.* Trans. Leonard Mayhew. New York: Simon and Schuster, 1978.

——. *The 400 Blows* (screenplay). Ed. David Denby. New York: Grove Press, 1969.

Turim, Maureen. *The Films of Oshima Nagisa: Images of a Japanese Iconoclast.* Berkeley: University of California Press, 1998.

van der Kolk, Bessel A. and Onno van der Hart. "The Intrusive Past: The Flexibility of Memory and the Engraving of Trauma." In Caruth, ed., *Trauma: Explorations in Memory*, 158–82.

Veeder, William. "The Nurture of the Gothic, or How Can a Text Be Both Popular and Subversive?." In Robert K. Martin and Eric Savoy, eds., *American Gothic: New Interventions in a National Narrative*, 20–39. Iowa City: University of Iowa Press, 1998.

Viorst, Milton. *Fire in the Streets: America in the 1960s.* New York: Simon and Schuster, 1979.

Waller, Gregory A., ed. *American Horrors: Essays on the Modern American Horror Film.* Urbana: University of Illinois Press, 1987.

Warner, Michael. "The Mass Public and the Mass Subject." In Bruce Robbins, ed., *The Phantom Public Sphere*, 234–56. Minneapolis: University of Minnesota Press, 1993.

Warren, Bill, ed. *The Middle of the Country: The Events of May 4th as Seen by Students and Faculty at Kent State University*. New York: Avon, 1970.

Watts, Philip. *Allegories of the Purge: How Literature Responded to the Postwar Trials of Writers and Intellectuals in France*. Stanford: Stanford University Press, 1998.

Wells, Tom. *The War Within: America's Battle Over Vietnam*. Berkeley: University of California Press, 1994.

Wertham, Fredric. *Seduction of the Innocent*. New York: Rinehart, 1954.

White, Hayden. "Historical Emplotment and the Problem of Truth." In Friedlander, ed., *Probing the Limits of Representation*, 37–53.

White, Linda. "Two Photographs That Changed America: The Pulitzer Images of Eddie Adams and John Filo." Master's thesis, Ohio University, 1995.

Whitebait, William. "Hold the Nose." *New Statesman* (April 9, 1960): 520.

[Whitten, David]. "An Open Letter to the Critics of *The Last House on the Left*." *Hartford Courant*, September 7, 1972, 74.

Wilden, Tony. *The Imaginary Canadian*. Vancouver: Pulp Press, 1980.

Wilinsky, Barbara. *Sure Seaters: The Emergence of Art House Cinema*. Minneapolis: University of Minnesota Press, 2001.

Williams, Alan. "Introduction." In Alan Williams, ed., *Film and Nationalism*, 1–22. New Brunswick: Rutgers University Press, 2002.

——. *Republic of Images: A History of French Filmmaking*. Cambridge: Harvard University Press, 1992.

Williams, Linda. "Discipline and Fun: *Psycho* and Postmodern Cinema." In Christine Gledhill and Linda Williams, eds., *Reinventing Film Studies*, 351–78. New York: Oxford University Press, 2000.

——. "Film Bodies: Gender, Genre, and Excess." *Film Quarterly* 44.4 (Summer 1991): 2–13.

——. "When the Woman Looks." In Mary Ann Doane, Patricia Mellencamp, and Linda Williams, eds., *Re-Vision: Essays in Feminist Film Criticism*, 83–99. Frederick, Md.: University Publications of America, 1984.

Williams, Linda, ed. *Viewing Positions: Ways of Seeing Film*. New Brunswick: Rutgers University Press, 1995.

Williams, Linda Ruth. "Blood Brothers." *Sight and Sound* 4.9 (September 1994): 16–19.

Williams, Raymond. *Culture and Society, 1780–1950* (1958). New York: Columbia University Press, 1983.

Williams, Tony. *Hearths of Darkness: The Family in the American Horror Film*. Madison: Fairleigh Dickinson University Press, 1996.

Wischmann, Lesley. "Dying on the Front Page: Kent State and the Pulitzer Prize." *Journal of Mass Media Ethics* 2.2 (Spring-Summer 1987): 67–74.

Wollen, Peter. "Dying for Art." *Sight and Sound* 4.12 (December 1994): 19–21.

Wood, Robin. "Cronenberg: A Dissenting View." In Handling, ed., *The Shape of Rage*, 115–35.

——. *Hitchcock's Films* (1965). New York: A. S. Barnes, 1969.

——. *Hitchcock's Films Revisited*. New York: Columbia University Press, 1989.

——. *Hollywood from Vietnam to Reagan*. New York: Columbia University Press, 1986.

——. *Ingmar Bergman.* New York: Praeger, 1969.

——. "An Introduction to the American Horror Film." In Wood and Lippe, eds., *The American Nightmare: Essays on the Horror Film,* 7–28.

——. "Neglected Nightmares." *Film Comment* 16.2 (March-April 1980): 24–32.

Wood, Robin and Richard Lippe, eds. *The American Nightmare: Essays on the Horror Film.* Toronto: Festival of Festivals, 1979.

Xavier, Ismail. "Historical Allegory." In Toby Miller and Robert Stam, eds., *A Companion to Film Theory,* 333–62. Oxford: Blackwell, 1999.

Yacowar, Maurice. "The Comedy of Cronenberg." In Handling, ed., *The Shape of Rage,* 80–86.

——. "You Shiver Because It's Good." *Cinema Canada* 34–35 (February 1977): 54–55.

Yoneyama, Lisa. *Hiroshima Traces: Time, Space, and the Dialectics of Memory.* Berkeley: University of California Press, 1999.

Yoshimoto, Mitsuhiro. *Kurosawa: Film Studies and Japanese Cinema.* Durham: Duke University Press, 2000.

INDEX

A-bomb maidens, 86, 93

Acting-out versus working-through, 4, 6

AIDS epidemic, and Cronenberg's cinema, 211n2, 215n57

Algerian War: censorship during, 44; echoes in *Eyes Without a Face*, 43; receding via mediation of everyday life, 38; torture, 51

Allegorical moments: as challenge to fundamental conceptions of self and nation, 147, 177; challenging standard views of horror film, 9–10; as collision of past and present, as memory in moment of danger, 9, 12, 14–15, 50, 86, 127, 202n14; conjoining taste and tastelessness, 142; conjuncture of Ground Zeroes of 1945 and 2001, 181; definition of, 2–3; disrupting realism/modernism dichotomy, 6, 15; as flash of unexpected recognition, 14, 15; image's betweenness, 13; as *Jetztzeit*, 13–14, 91, 184; as means of understanding national and cultural contexts, 10; need for constant surprise, 14–15; as process of embodiment, 2–3; as productive tension between binary oppositions, 3–4, 6, 81, 100, 102, 109, 126, 143; recognition and acknowledgment of "them" as "us," 81; redemptive potential and risk of incapacitation, 50; representing meaning as image, 13; as shift from compensation to confrontation of historical trauma, 8; "splatter" effects not precluding effectiveness, 53; study of, as genre criticism, 9; viewers distanced and isolated from, in *Record of a Living Being*, 100; with violence of dialectic movement, 15; as vulnerable to appropriation, 14. *See also* Allegory; Benjamin, Walter

Allegory: alignment with image of death and cinema, 16; communicating trauma, 15–16; as concept resisting general applications, 187–88n34; corpse as emblematic property, 16; death's head as "everything untimely, sorrowful, unsuccessful," 12, 15, 146, 183; definition of, 4; insisting on literalizing horror, 13; as meaning between individual interiority and historical exteriority, 146; *Onibaba* questioning construction of continuum of history, 94; reinvesting with complexity, 85–86; resisting teleological history, 15; as ruins and decay, 108. *See also* Allegorical moments; Benjamin, Walter

Altman, Rick, 9, 10

America: 9/11 (terrorist attacks of September 11, 2001), 177. *See also* Vietnam War

American cinema: *The Birds*, 215–16n63; *Deathdream* (aka *Dead of Night*), 2, 3f, 3; *Easy Rider*, 129–30; Hollywood productions, 142–43, 150, 152, 173, 186n10, 186n13; *Psycho*, 7, 8, 9, 10; *Schindler's List*, 6; *We Were Soldiers*, 178–80. *See also Deliverance*; *Joe*; *Last House on the Left*; *Night of the Living Dead*

American New Wave. *See* Hollywood Renaissance

American Occupation of Japan, 84, 90–91, 202n3

Amusement parks and fairgrounds imagery, 15, 77, 78–79, 201n78

An Andalusian Dog. See Un Chien andalou, 18, 20

Anderson, Benedict, 149

Anderson, Lindsay, 65–66

Andrew, Dudley, 32, 165

Lightning Source UK Ltd.
Milton Keynes UK
UKHW04f1014120918
328749UK00001B/1/P